FEW ARE CHOSEN

PROBLEMS IN PRESIDENTIAL SELECTION

FEW ARE CHOSEN

PROBLEMS IN PRESIDENTIAL SELECTION

Robert E. DiClerico

West Virginia University

Eric M. Uslaner

University of Maryland

McGRAW-HILL BOOK COMPANY

New York St. Louis San Francisco Auckland Bogotá
Hamburg Johannesburg London Madrid Mexico Montreal New Delhi
Panama Paris São Paulo Singapore Sydney Tokyo Toronto

This book was set in Times Roman by University Graphics, Inc.
The editors were Phillip A. Butcher and Christina Mediate;
the production supervisor was Charles Hess.
Project supervision was done by The Total Book.
The cover was designed by Janice Noto.
The cover photograph was taken by Wide World Photos.
R. R. Donnelley & Sons Company was printer and binder.

FEW ARE CHOSEN
Problems in Presidential Selection

1 2 3 4 5 6 7 8 9 0   DOC DOC   8 9 8 7 6 5 4 3

ISBN 0-07-016805-9

Library of Congress Cataloging in Publication Data

DiClerico, Robert E.
    Few are chosen.

    Includes bibliographical references and index.
        1. Presidents—United States—Nomination.
I. Uslaner, Eric M.   II. Title.
JK521.D52 1984   324.5′0973   83-11353
ISBN 0-07-016805-9 (pbk.)

For Debbie and Devon

CONTENTS

PREFACE

This book stems from our belief that there are many key problems asssociated with nominating and electing our Presidents which are in fact subject to manipulation in the best sense of that term. We believe that there is something we can do about the nominating system, the role of the media, the effect of money, our system for electing the President, the decreasing turnout in national elections, and the relations between the President and Congress. Each of these topics is dicussed in the following chapters, along with a general reform proposal that will no doubt be controversial. While we don't expect all our readers to agree with this proposal—indeed, the two of us are not in anything close to complete agreement on it—we think it is important to focus on aspects of the selection process that are amenable to change.

Although this has been a joint endeavor, Robert DiClerico had primary responsibility for drafting the introduction and the first three chapters while Eric Uslaner drafted Chapters 4 through 6 and the epilogue.We would like to express our deep appreciation to several individuals for their wise and penetrating reviews of the manuscript: Donald Gross, University of Kentucky; Paul Light, University of Virginia; Lawrence Longley, Lawrence University; Dennis M. Simon, University of Minnesota; Harold Stanley, University of Rochester; and Robert Weissberg, University of Illinois.

Others also made significant contributions. Robert DiClerico wishes to thank Allan Hammock for the release time necessary to complete this project. In addition, a very special thank you is due Cheryl Flagg whose typing talents enabled her to produce nearly flawless drafts, often on very short notice.

Eric Uslaner is particularly grateful to John Gates for his help on the research tasks large and small, from the large intellectual problems to the more numerous routine tasks involved in preparation of a book such as this, and particularly for the detailed comments that he gave on each chapter. Other colleagues, M. Margaret Conway and Michael Mumper, also provided support and helpful critiques of various ideas and drafts. Judy Staples expertly typed the numerous drafts more cheerfully than Uslaner rewrote them. And Uslaner is especially indebted to his wife Debbie for a more profound form of sustenance.

Finally, we would both like to acknowledge the valuable assistance provided to us by project supervisor Annette Bodzin. Her prodigious efforts at the editorial stage were instrumental in allowing us to meet a tight deadline.

Robert E. DiClerico
Eric M. Uslaner

FEW ARE CHOSEN

PROBLEMS IN PRESIDENTIAL SELECTION

INTRODUCTION

The Presidency has evolved into the focal point and energizing force in the American political system. This development is not altogether surprising, for among the three branches of government it possesses the greatest capacity to provide sustained national leadership. Clearly, the Supreme Court is not well suited to such a role, since the judges may speak only when spoken to and what they say must be confined to the case immediately before them. Although Congress is free to focus its attention on any issue, both size and multiplicity of interests virtually assure that it will speak with many voices. The President alone has the ability to speak with one voice on any matter he chooses.

As an instrument of national leadership, the Presidency is, of course, only as effective as the individual who wields it. Some have done so with considerable success. They knew where they wanted to take the nation and possessed the necessary political skills to get it there. Others, lacking the requisite sense of direction and political skill, were not shapers of events as much as they were shaped by them.

A scanning of just the last fifty years reveals that Presidents can affect our national life and the world in significant ways. In marked contrast with his predecessor, Franklin Roosevelt took office believing that government had an obligation to help those unable to help themselves. This conviction gave birth to an unparalleled number of federal programs which brought hope and relief to a population laboring under the greatest economic crisis in our history. Harry Truman's decision to grant massive economic assistance to Europe after

1

World War II not only proved instrumental in its revitalization but also forged an enduring bond between the two continents. The effort to reach some kind of accommodation with the Soviet Union, begun by Eisenhower and accelerated under Nixon, Ford, and Carter, created an international environment less precarious than it would have been otherwise. Civil rights for blacks would no doubt have come later rather than sooner had John Kennedy not placed the issue more prominently on the national agenda and had Lyndon Johnson not been committed to seeing this goal through to fruition. Still more recently, and in a less positive vein, it is all too clear that the events of Vietnam and Watergate spawned a public cynicism about government from which we have not yet fully recovered. Presidents can indeed make a difference.

If Presidents are of great consequence in the scheme of things, so too must be the way we go about choosing them. It is to this matter that we turn in this book. Our purpose is not to describe the intricacies of the Presidential selection process from start to finish. Rather, we shall focus on those aspects of the process that some have characterized as vulnerabilities. In examining these "problem areas" we shall consider why they are viewed as such, assess the validity of these concerns, and where appropriate suggest what corrective measures might be taken.

Efforts to democratize the nominating process, the subject of Chapter 1, have generated a robust debate for more than a decade. Some have welcomed these changes on the grounds that they have rendered the nominating process more accessible to voters and potential candidates. On the other hand, there is also a considerable body of opinion which maintains that these reforms have substantially increased the burdens of seeking the Presidency, fostered a premature resolution of the contest, eliminated an important element of quality control over candidates, and not necessarily led to outcomes that are more reflective of popular preferences.

In Chapter 2 we turn our attention to the media as actors in the Presidential selection process. Concern voiced over the role of media is at once old and new. Ever since the debut of television campaign commercials in the 1952 Presidential election, we have repeatedly been warned that they represent an unhealthy development in American electoral politics. These advertisements, it is argued, are designed more to manipulate than inform and thus they impede the rational assessment of Presidential candidates. More recently, the reporting function of the media has also captured the attention of political observers. Changes in the nominating process, along with television's expanded commitment to news, have combined to elevate the importance of the media's campaign coverage. Which candidates become the focus of their attention, what they tell us about them, and how they interpret the race can influence the selection process in ways that are significant and not always beneficial.

Although money may not be viewed as the root of *all* evil in electoral politics, many have long felt that it accounts for much of what is wrong with the way we choose our Presidents. This crucially important resource has been accused of exercising an undue influence on who can run, who wins, and what kinds of policy decisions the winner makes in office. While these concerns have prompted legislative action from time to time, not until the 1970s did Congress make a serious effort to regulate the flow of private money into Presidential campaigns. Interestingly enough, however, this landmark legislation has generated as much controversy as the problems it was attempting to correct. In Chapter 3 we consider the role of money in Presidential selection prior and subsequent to the recent campaign finance reforms.

Earlier we noted that Presidents can make a difference. This being the case, one might reasonably expect voters to take advantage of the opportunity to register their preference for President. In fact, however, analysts have recorded a steady decline in voter turnout since 1960, with only slightly more than half the eligible voters journeying to the polls in the 1980 election. Moreover, this decline has occurred despite an increasingly educated public and the elimination of many legal barriers to voting. What factors have been responsible for this trend, and should these factors themselves be a source for concern? Would the results of recent Presidential elections have been different had more people gone to the polls? What implications does low turnout have for a President's mandate to govern? These questions will constitute the focus of our attention in Chapter 4.

Over the course of the last century nearly all facets of the Presidential selection process have been altered in one way or another. The major exception is the Electoral College, which has remained essentially unchanged since 1804. For many, this is precisely the problem. Arguing that the Electoral College is replete with real and potential inequities, some critics insist that it must be redesigned, while others call for abolishing it altogether. Defenders, on the other hand, claim that the electorate, the states, our major parties, and the President have all been well served by the Founding Fathers' creation. We should, therefore, leave well enough alone. In Chapter 5 we examine the issues central to this debate.

The interface of Presidential selection and Presidential leadership, although treated at various points in the book, is addressed more comprehensively in Chapter 6. Running for President and being President are not two discrete enterprises, each unrelated to the other. On the contrary, the criteria by which candidates are judged and the alliances they must forge to win have a great deal to do with the quality of leadership we can expect from them as President. Many feel the reforms of the nominating process have served to divorce Presidential selection from Presidential governance. More precisely, the personal qualifications necessary to win bear little relationship to those required to lead. Nor is a candidate compelled to gain the confidence of those with whom he must ultimately share power once in office. Although we concur with this assessment, we shall argue that the old system suffered from these same problems, though to a lesser degree. Accordingly, in this final chapter we propose a more fundamental change in the Presidential nominating process—one which, we believe, holds out greater promise of yielding nominees who have the qualifications and support necessary to lead the nation.

DEMOCRATIZING THE NOMINATING PROCESS

At various points throughout out political history, the Presidential nomination process has been subject to changes designed to render it more open to popular participation. The most recent, and perhaps also the most sustained, effort in this regard was undertaken during most of the decade of the seventies. Initiated primarily by the Democratic party, the first round of changes came in 1971, only to be followed by a second wave in 1974, and still a third wave in 1978. Each round brought with it an evergrowing number of critics, including scholars, public officials, and journalists alike, all charging that the political system had not been well served by several of these reforms. The following provides just a sampling of the disenchantment:

> The danger of democracy is not that democracy is dangerous, but that we somehow bring ourselves to believe that the democracy of the town hall can be extended to nationwide decisions. The danger of democracy thus becomes a danger that we will lose democracy in our attempt to gain more of it. We do not expect to decide national energy policy by referendum, voting on eight or ten proposals put forward by eight or ten groups. . . . Yet we expect to pick our president, a far more complex determination and infinitely more important than an energy policy, by participatory disorder that knows no equal in American society.[1]

> Terry Sanford, former Governor of North Carolina

> In the present nominating system, the determinants of success are the size of the candidate's ambitions, the extent of his lesiure time and the tolerance of his family,

his budget and his job for almost unlimited travel. Those characteristics have almost nothing to do with the qualities that make an effective president—as the results show. It is a recklessly haphazard way to choose the candidates for that demanding office.[2]

David Broder, Washington columnist

There is no peer review—that is, there is no process by which other party and government leaders can personally screen the records and characters of the various aspirants and effectively eliminate those they find lacking in the experience and skills needed to be good candidates and effective presidents.[3]

Austin Ranney, political scientist

That the concern reflected in these statements was widely shared is evidenced by the fact that as of March 1982 no fewer than seventeen commissions, committees, panels, and study groups were engaged in a comprehensive reassessment of the Presidential nominating process.[4]

The purposes of this chapter are to outline the major reforms of the 1969–1978 period, along with their rationale; identify and assess the persuasiveness of the criticisms directed at the reforms; evaluate how the Democratic party responded to these criticisms in their 1982 rules changes; and, finally, consider what further changes in the nominating process may seem appropriate. Before turning to these matters, however, it is first necessary to provide some historical perspective on the nominating process.

THE PRESIDENTIAL NOMINATING PROCESS: A HISTORICAL OVERVIEW

Among the democracies of the world, the United States stands alone in according its citizens a significant role in determining who their choices shall be for the highest office in the land. The American electorate had not always been accorded this role, however. On the contrary, from 1800–1824, Presidential nominees were chosen by Congressional caucus; that is, the Congressional membership in each party met and decided on a candidate to carry its banner in the general election. That this practice proved to be short-lived was due to a combination of factors. For one thing, it drew heavy criticism from such notables as Andrew Jackson, Henry Clay, John Quincy Adams, and John C. Calhoun, all of whom were rejected for the Republican nomination in 1824. The caucus instead chose William Crawford who went on to lose badly in the general election. In addition, a growing number of state and local party leaders voiced their opposition to the Congressional caucus because it denied them any role whatsoever in the selection process. Third, the limited number of participants in this system was perceived as inappropriate once Jacksonian democracy had taken hold in the country.[5] Accordingly, after a brief transition period during which Presidential candidates were nominated by state legislatures or local conventions, the political parties instituted a new system, namely, national conventions. First employed in 1831, these conventions were composed of delegates chosen by each state's political party. The methods for selecting these delegates varied; in some instances the governor was allowed to pick them; in others a party's state committee made the selection. The most common practice adopted by the state parties, however, was the caucus-convention. Under this system, party members caucused at the precinct or township level and selected delegates to go on to a county caucus, which in turn elected delegates to a state convention. The state convention then picked a group of delegates to attend the party's national convention. By the turn of the century, however, many had become disillusioned with this method of nominating Presidents as well. More specifically, the process provided little opportunity for public participation; it was perceived as subject to near total manipulation by the party bosses; few regulations existed on convention procedures and even those were honored more in the breach; presiding officers at the conventions ruled with a heavy hand; strong-arm tactics were used to prevent certain delegates from entering the conventions and to intimidate others once they got there; and many of the delegates chosen by the party apparatus proved to be unsavory characters more than willing to sell their votes to the highest bidder.[6] This state of affairs gave rise to a reform movement spearheaded by the Progressives, the purpose of which was to involve the voters directly in the nominating process. As a means of achieving this goal, the reformers called for the establishment of Presidential primaries. Administered by the states rather than the parties, this mechanism would allow the voters themselves to elect their state's delegates to the national convention. In 1904 the Florida state legislature became the first to adopt a statute permitting parties to choose some or all of its delegates by primary. A year later Wisconsin, home of the Progressive movement, went one step further and passed legislation requiring that all its delegates to the Republican and Democratic national conventions be chosen by Presidential primary. Moreover, in order that the elected delegates might be provided some guidance concerning voter preferences, the legislation specified that the primary ballot also list the Presidential candidates themselves. Other states soon followed the lead of Florida and Wisconsin and by the year 1916 twenty-six states had adopted a primary of one kind or another.[7] The initial enthusiasm for primaries gradually waned, however, not only because party leaders opposed them but also because of cost, disappointing turnouts, and the refusal of many Presidential contenders to enter them. Thus, by 1935 eight states had abandoned this method of selecting delegates and returned to the caucus-convention or appointment system.[8] In subsequent years some states returned to the primary and others repealed it until "by 1968 the number appeared to have stablized at sixteen states plus the District of Columbia."[9]

In summary, by the time of the 1968 Presidential election the nominating process had evolved into a system whereby national convention delegates could be selected in one of three distinct ways: (1) the caucus-convention, which, incidentally, was the method most widely employed by the states; (2) appointment by either the governor or or state party committee; (3) and, finally, the primary. It should also be pointed out that some states actually made use of all three methods to select a certain portion of their delegation.

THE NEW REFORM ERA, 1971–1978

By 1968 a substantial number of Americans had grown frustrated with the nation's involvement in the Vietnam war. This conflict had already imposed heavy human, economic, and social costs on our society and yet showed no signs of moving toward a successful conclusion. Moreover, the sense of frustration became all the greater as many rank-and-file Democrats found themselves with no alternative to the candidacy of Lyndon Johnson, a President who remained steadfastly committed to seeing the war through to victory. All at once Eugene McCarthy, a little known Senator from the state of Minnesota, stepped forward and offered himself as an antiwar candidate for the Presidency. In the first real test of his candidacy McCarthy entered the New Hampshire primary and managed to garner 42.4 percent of the vote, while Johnson received 49.5 percent. Although he lost, McCarthy's showing was widely interpreted as a victory since he was, after all, running against an incumbent President in a state known for its patriotic fervor. Robert Kennedy had read the results the same way and decided to declare his candidacy four days after the New Hampshire primary. The popularity of both Kennedy and McCarthy convinced President Johnson that his own renomination was by no means a certainty. This belief, combined with his desire to avoid making Vietnam a political football in the campaign, caused him to withdraw from the race on March 31, 1968. Nearly one month later Vice President Hubert Humphrey threw his hat into the ring with the blessing and support of the White House. A campaign already characterized by the unexpected took yet another dramatic turn on June 1st when Robert Kennedy was assassinated just minutes after his big win in the California primary. Thus, the field was narrowed to Humphrey and McCarthy. This did not prove to be much of a contest, however. Although the Vice President had entered the race late and declined to enter a single primary, nevertheless, when the convention balloting was completed, he had received 1,760 delegate votes and McCarthy only 601. That Humphrey managed to win so decisively was attributable mainly to two factors: first, in 1968 a majority of the Democratic delegates were selected not in the primaries but rather by the caucus-convention and appointment methods; second, these methods were firmly controlled by the party leaders, most of whom had aligned themselves solidly behind Humphrey.

Not surpisingly, many McCarthy and Kennedy supporters came away from the nomination campaign bitter and disillusioned. The Democratic National

Convention had in the final analysis selected a nominee whose views on Vietnam were not measurably different from those of Lyndon Johnson. More important, this individual, unlike their own candidates, had declined to take his case to the people in the primaries. On top of all this, during the course of the nominating process McCarthy supporters repeatedly found themselves victimized by arbitrary rules and procedures employed in connection with the selection of delegates. In fact, an informal group calling itself the Commission on Democratic Selection of Presidential Nominees met for several weeks prior to the convention and detailed the structural and procedural inadequacies associated with the delegate selection process. Their findings, which were presented to the convention's Rules and Credentials Committees and circulated among the delegates, led to the proposal of two resolutions which together required that state parties provide "all Democratic voters . . . a full, meaningful, and timely opportunity to participate in the selection of delegates" to the 1972 convention.[10] Both resolutions passed easily, although it is far from clear that most delegates, absorbed as they were in convention hoopla, fully appreciated the implications of what they had done. The delegates also voted to establish a commission which was charged with recommending ways to implement these resolutions.

The First Round, 1971

In keeping with the decisions made at the 1968 convention the chairman of the Democratic National Committee in 1969 constituted the Commission on Party Structure and Delegate Selection under the chairmanship of Senator George McGovern (Congressman Donald Fraser took over the chairmanship in 1971 when McGovern decided to seek the Presidential nomination). We shall now consider the major deficiencies in delegate selection identified by the Commission as well as the remedies it proposed.

Party Rules   Virtually any game is difficult to play if one does not know the rules. To the considerable amazement of the Commission, it discovered that eight states had absolutely no rules dealing with the selection of delegates; in several others the rules were issued immediately prior to the start of the selection process; in still others, as we shall see shortly, rules existed but they did not address all aspects related to the choosing of delegates.[11] The Commission therefore recommended that henceforth *all state parties adopt and make readily available rules on how delegates are to be picked.*

Dates and Times of Meeting Places   If you are to participate in the caucus-convention process, you must know when and where the caucuses are going to be held. The McGovern-Fraser Commission found that the party rules in some states were silent on this important procedural question, whereas in other states the party rules authorized local party officials to determine the times and places of caucus meetings. Either way, party officials were left with the power to shape the outcome. In Louisville, Kentucky, for example, a local party leader held his precinct caucus outside in December so as to discourage participation. In neighboring Missouri, Democratic committeemen in four townships refused to disclose when and where they were holding their township caucuses. McCarthy supporters finally managed to learn where one of these caucuses was to be held, but, by the time they arrived, business was already well under way. In another township a local party leader chartered a bus, loaded it with both loyal followers and an ample supply of liquid refreshment, and held his caucus while traveling the interstate at some sixty miles an hour.[12] The Commission recommended that in the future *the times and locations of all caucus meetings be published in advance. In addition, the meetings in any given state must be held on uniform dates, at uniform times, and in places of easy access.*

Proxies and Quorums During the course of their inquiry, the Commission uncovered major abuses in proxy voting, a procedure that allows one person to vote in the name of one or more other individuals. In one township caucus, for instance, McCarthy supporters found themselves in a majority only to be outvoted when the party official chairing the meeting cast 492 unwritten proxies—three times the number of people present—for his own slate of delegates. At the state convention in Hawaii proxies were cast from a precinct which, because of an urban renewal project, consisted largely of vacant lots.

The Commission's fact finding also revealed that quorum requirements for conducting party business were set too low. In Alabama, where the party state committee draws up new delegate selection rules every four years, only 23 percent of the committee had to be present to make this critically important decision. In Arizona, the party state committee was charged with appointing all of its state's delegates to the Democratic National Convention; yet it required a quorum of only 25 percent of the total membership to conduct business.[13] The Commission recommended that *proxy voting be abolished and that quorum requirements at party meetings be set at 40 percent.*

Unit Rule This is a procedure by which the majority is able to bind the minority to vote in accordance with the majority preference. In 1968 some fifteen states using the caucus-convention method employed the unit rule at one or more stages (that is, precinct, county, state convention) in the delegate selection process.[14] Believing that such a procedure prevented a fair reflection of voter preferences, the commission recommended that *the unit rule be abolished.*

Blind Primaries In the states of West Virginia, Illinois, Pennsylvania, Florida, New Jersey, and New York primary laws either prohibited or else did

not require that would-be delegates express a Presidential preference. Consequently, in voting for delegates on the primary ballot the voters had absolutely
no idea how those individuals might vote at the national convention. This
arrangement contributed to an interesting anomaly in Pennsylvania, which has
a delegate/Presidential preference poll type primary; that is, the voters choose
the delegates and also have an opportunity to register their preferences for the
Presidential nomination. Eugene McCarthy won 78.5 percent of the Presidential preference vote and yet garnered only twenty-four of the state's 130 delegates.[15] For 1972, therefore, the Commission proposed that *all delegates be
given the opportunity to list their Presidential preference on the ballot* (including the designation "uncommitted" if appropriate).

Untimely Selection   Certainly one of the most surprising deficiencies
uncovered by the McGovern-Fraser Commission concerned the timing of the
delegate selection process in various states. More specifically, it found that
twenty-four states had picked either all or a significant portion of their delegates prior to the calendar year of the national convention. Thus, on the day
Eugene McCarthy declared his candidacy one-third of the national convention's delegates had already been chosen. As the Commission put it, "By the
time the issues and candidates that characterized the politics of 1968 had
clearly emerged, therefore, it was impossible for rank-and-file Democrats to
influence the selection of these delegates."[16] To correct this problem, the Commission recommended that *all delegates be chosen during the calendar year of
the convention.*

Appointment of Delegates   As noted earlier in this chapter, appointment
constitutes one of the three ways by which delegates may be selected. The
Commission discovered that in four states the party state committee appointed
the state's *entire* delegation. In an additional four states these committees were
authorized to choose anywhere from one-third to one-half of the delegates; and
in two other states the governor alone was empowered to select *all* of the state's
delegation.[17] The Commission thought these proportions excessive in view of
the fact that the appointment system allows for no participation by the electorate. Accordingly, it recommended that henceforth *no more than 10 percent
of a state's delegation be chosen by the appointment method.*

***Ex Officio* Delegates**   This is a practice by which state parties guarantee
delegate slots to certain state party and public officials by virtue of the positions
they hold. In states such as Washington, Maryland, and Colorado, for example,
the proportion of their delegations reserved for these officials was 25, 27, and
14 percent, respectively.[18] Since voters are precluded from having the opportunity to pass judgment on these officials, the Commission recommended that
ex officio delegates be abolished.

Discrimination   Regardless of which method (that is, caucus-convention, appointment, primaries) was employed for choosing delegates, the Commission found that the end result was the same; namely, blacks, women, and the young were substantially underrepresented in state delegations attending the 1968 convention. Thus, whereas blacks constituted 11 percent of the population (and 85 percent of them voted Democratic in 1968), only 5.5 percent of the delegates were black. Similarly, although 53 percent of the adult population was female, they comprised only 17 percent of the delegates. Meanwhile, delegates under the age of thirty constituted only 4 percent of the convention delegates. Having concluded that these data provided clear evidence of discrimination, the Commission issued what was perhaps its most controversial recommendation; namely, that state parties take "affirmative steps to encourage representation . . . of minority groups, young people and women in reasonable relationship to their presence in the population of the state."[19] Thus, for example, if 15 percent of the population of Michigan was black, then every effort must be made to assure that 15 percent of its delegates would be black also; likewise for women and those under the age of thirty. Furthermore, in those instances in which a state's delegation did not realize these quotas, the burden of proof was squarely on the shoulders of the state party to demonstrate that it had made a "good faith effort" to comply with rules on quotas. States that failed to demonstrate their good faith were subject to having their delegation replaced.

Costs, Fees, Assessments   In the course of its inquiry the McGovern-Fraser Commission discovered that the role of delegate could, in some instances, be a very expensive proposition. In the state of Connecticut, for example, the official party slate of delegates gained free access to the primary ballot, whereas any challenge slate was required to ante up more than $14,000 in filing fees. In Iowa and Indiana all members of the state delegation were assesssed $250 by the party, and in the latter state the delegates were tapped for an additional $250 to help pay for its hospitality suite at the national convention. On top of burdens such as these, delegates also had to pay for their hotel accommodations and meals, which in 1968 averaged $445. In view of such costs it should come as no surprise that income levels of delegates to the 1968 convention were considerably higher than for the general population: 40 percent of the delegates made in excess of $20,000 a year, compared with only 12 percent of the population; 47 percent made between $10,000 and $20,000 in contrast with only 18 percent of the population; and, finally, although only 13 percent of the delegates made under $10,000 a year, fully 70 percent of all Americans fell into this income category.[20] Believing that the want of sufficient financial resources should not be an impediment to participating in the nominating process, the Commission recommended that *all costs and fees be limited* *to no more than $10.* It also urged state parties to find other ways to ease the financial burden of being a delegate.

In 1972 the McGovern-Fraser Commission presented all the foregoing findings and recommendations to the Democratic National Committee, which, with one exception, accepted its report as is. (The exception was the National Committee's decision to allow its incoming and outgoing members to be *ex officio* delegates to the 1972 convention.) Since many of these reforms served to reduce significantly the influence of the party leaders in the delegate selection process, some state parties predictably attempted to resist implementing them. On the whole, however, these efforts did not prove successful. Indeed, by the time of the 1972 Democratic convention forty states plus the District of Columbia were in full compliance, and the other ten in substantial compliance. The tardiness of these ten states, moreover, was for the most part due to the fact that legislative as opposed to party action was required to implement some of the Commission's recommendations. In seeking to account for the high level of compliance by the state parties one student of the reform process observed that "much of the credit must be given to the commission staff, a clever newspaper and publicity campaign designed to embarrass local parties into acting, the adroit maneuvering of the national chairman and his staff, and not to be forgotten, the goodwill and desire for improvement of hundreds of regulars and reformers who worked for change at the local levels of the party."[21]

What of reform efforts in the Republican party? The 1968 Republican National Convention also authorized the creation of a Committee of Delegates and Organizations, which, among other things, was charged with looking into the delegate selection process. Their recommendations, however, did not take effect until 1976 since they had to be approved by the party's 1972 convention. The Commission's approved recommendations included a call for open meetings in the selection of delegates by caucus-convention; information systems to apprise individuals of how they could participate in the delegate selection process; and a ban on proxy voting, *ex officio* delegates, and excessive fees. The Commission also urged, but did not require, that efforts be made to encourage greater participation among women, blacks, the young, and senior citizens. That these changes proved to be considerably more modest than those of the Democrats is understandable, for there was no constituency in the Republican party clamoring for reform. The party had, after all, captured the Presidency in 1968 and would do so again in 1972. Moreover, the leader of the party was in the White House and saw little need to make sweeping changes in the process that put him there. Also, given the Republican party's long-standing commitment to "state's rights" on governmental issues, one could hardly expect its national party to dictate to state parties on party matters. Finally, unlike the Democrats, Republican party reforms had to be approved by four separate groups (National Committee Rules Committee, National Committee, Rules

Committee of the national convention, and the convention itself), the first three of which were made up of party establishment types disinclined to institute extensive changes in the delegate selection process.[22]

The Second Round, 1974

The impact of the McGovern-Fraser reforms was readily apparent when the Democrats convened in Chicago for their 1972 convention. Scarcely in evidence were members of Congress, big city mayors, and other prominent state officials, all of whom had liberally populated the floors of previous conventions. On the other hand, among those delegates present 40 percent were women, 15 percent were black, and 22 percent were under thirty.[23] An enraged Richard Daley, mayor of Chicago and long one of the principal kingmakers in the Democratic party, saw his fifty-nine Cook County delegates ousted from the convention and replaced with an alternate slate because they were not in compliance with the quota requirements. Another power broker, AFL-CIO President George Meany, was no less distraught with a quota system that failed to include the mainstay of the Democratic party, namely, the working man. The most dramatic impact of the reforms, however, was the nomination of the liberal insurgent candidate Senator George McGovern. Strongly opposed by most of the party leadership, this fact alone would have been sufficient to doom his candidacy at previous conventions. Not this time, however, for the increase in primaries, the opening up of the caucus-convention process, the limit on appointed delegates, and the ban on *ex officio* delegates, all served to terminate the party leadership's control over delegate selection. But, even though McGovern won the battle, he was destined to lose the war. The party leaders, having played no role in his nomination, felt no obligation to work for him in the general election. Much of organized labor took a similar view, with the AFL-CIO refusing to endorse the Democratic nominee for the first time in twenty years.

The controversy at the convention precipitated by the reforms caused the delegates to mandate another Commission to reassess and refine the changes that had been made. Chaired by Baltimore city council member Barbara Mikulski, the group began its deliberations in April 1973.

Sensitive to the hard feelings generated by the quota requirement, the Commission decided to abandon it. Instead, a state party would be required to take "affirmative action" toward including women, blacks, and the young in reasonable proportion to their numbers in that state's Democratic party. Moreover, in determining whether a state party had made a good faith effort at doing so, the burden of proof would lie with the challenger rather than the party.

Responding to charges that the reforms had organized the party leadership out of the nominating process, the Mikulski Commission made two recommendations which proved to be more cosmetic than real. First, Democratic Governors, Senators, and Representatives were to be given floor privileges at the next convention. They could *not* vote, however. Second, whereas the McGovern-Fraser Commission stipulated that state parties in primary states could appoint no more than 10 percent of their delegates, the number was now to be raised to 25 percent. This change was not as meaningful as it appears, however, for the Mikulski Commission also required that this 25 percent reflect the same distribution of candidate preferences as the delegates chosen in the state's primary.

More significant were the Commission's efforts to ensure that voter preferences would be more accurately reflected in the delegate selection process. Toward this end, it recommended that the winner-take-all primary be abolished, a proposal the McGovern-Fraser Commission had urged on the states, but not required. In a winner-take-all primary the candidate who receives the largest share of the vote wins *all* of a state's delegates. In 1972, for example, Hubert Humphrey won 39.2 percent of the vote in the California winner-take-all primary, and George McGovern garnered 44.3 percent and thereby walked off with all 174 of the state's delegates. Believing that this type of primary essentially disenfranchised those who voted for the loser, the Commission recommended that all delegates henceforth be chosen according to the *rule of proportionality;* that is, the number of delegates received by a candidate would be proportionate to the percentage of the vote won in the primary. This rule was also to be applied to delegates chosen under the caucus-convention system. In order to qualify for a proportional share of the delegates, however, a candidate's support in a given caucus or primary had to reach a minimum threshold of 10 percent. (The Democratic National Committee raised it to 15 percent.) It is important to note here, however, that the Commission did permit one major exception to the rule of proportionality; namely, a state could run its primary on a winner-take-all basis if its delegates were elected at the Congressional district level rather than statewide. Thirteen states, mostly large ones, took advantage of this "loophole" and ran winner-take-all primaries in 1976.[24]

In addition to the rule of proportionality, the Commission sought to ensure a more accurate reflection of voter preferences in another way. It recommended that all individuals running for delegate slots in either the caucuses or the primaries be *required* to declare their Presidential preference. In primary states where state law prohibited listing such preferences on the ballot, parties were required to publicize the names of delegates and their preferred candidates in the newspaper.

Finally, aside from calling for an end to the open primary, the only other major change proposed by the Commission was to allow a Presidential candidate to approve all delegates who intended to run under his or her banner. The need for this change arose because some delegates running in winner-take-all primaries, eager to attend the convention at any cost, allied themselves with the candidate they thought would win the primary rather than with the one they really supported. Once at the convention, they dutifully cast their nomination ballot for the candidate to whom they were formally committed but went on to support "the positions of other contenders (their real choices) on credentials challenges or Platform or Rules committee issues."[25]

In summary, although the Mikulski Commission had made some gestures toward resuscitating the role of the party leadership in the nominating process, these were more symbolic than substantive. Rather, the major thrust of their recommendations was directed toward ensuring that the distribution of delegates at the national convention would reflect the preferences of the voters as accurately as possible. In 1974 these recommendations were presented to the Democratic National Committee, which, apart from raising the proportionality threshold to 15 percent, adopted them largely as is.

At this point, it should be noted that 1974 brought the adoption of another set of reforms also. These, however, dealt with campaign financing rather than delegate selection and were formulated by Congress, not the parties. Moved to action by some of the Watergate revelations, Congress passed several statutes designed to curb the influence of money on the Presidential selection process. Although this legislation will be examined at length later in this book, certain provisions will become relevant to our discussion in this chapter. These include (1) limiting to $1,000 the amount of money an individual may contribute to a candidate; (2) partial public funding of Presidential nomination campaigns on the condition that a candidate first qualify for such funds by raising $5,000 in *each* of *twenty* states in contributions of no more than $250.

The Third Round, 1978

In 1975 the chairman of the Democratic National Committee, reflecting widespread concern over the growing number of primaries, created the Commission on the Role and Future of Presidential Primaries. With minimum debate, the delegates to the 1976 Democratic National Convention expanded the jurisdiction of the group by renaming it the Commission on Presidential Nominations and Party Structure. It was charged with fine tuning the reforms already in place, as well as with considering new ones. This latest reform effort was to take place under circumstances quite different from those of the previous rounds, however, for there was a Democrat in the White House. As leader of his party, Jimmy Carter had considerable influence over both the composition and recommendations of what came to be known as the Winograd Commission, so named after its chairman Morley Winograd.

Pursuant to a decision that had already been made by the delegates to the 1976 convention, the Commission eliminated the last vestige of the winner-take-all primary. More specifically, it abolished the rule allowing states to run their primaries on a winner-take-all basis if delegates were chosen at the Congressional district level rather than statewide.[26] The Commission also raised the 15 percent threshold that had been established for candidates to qualify for delegates under the proportional rule (see p.15). In caucus states it could now be set at 20 percent and in primary states as high as 25 percent. This change came at the urging of Carter supporters who wanted to reduce the risk of challengers to his 1980 nomination bid.[27]

In the past, states typically set their candidate filing deadlines thirty days prior to their primary. The Commission now recommended that states be permitted to set them as early as ninety days prior to the primary. This reform represented a compromise with Carter Commission members who had initially pushed for a mandatory fifty-five day filing deadline. No doubt the President's people sought this change because they wanted to avoid a repeat of 1976 when Senator Frank Church and Governor Jerry Brown entered the race late and defeated Carter in several of the May and June primaries.

Sympathetic to criticism that the delegate selection process was too long— in 1976, for example, it ran for twenty-one weeks—the Winograd Commission recommended it be reduced to thirteen weeks, beginning with the second Tuesday in March and ending with the second Tuesday in June. States would be free to hold their caucuses or primaries on any Tuesday falling within this time frame. The purpose of this change, however, was largely negated by the fact that Iowa, New Hampshire, Massachusetts, and Vermont were all exempted from complying with this calendar. Thus, in 1980 Iowa held its caucus on January 21, New Hampshire scheduled its primary for February 26, and both Massachusetts and Vermont held their primaries on March 4.

Party regulars continued to charge that seasoned politicians were not adequately represented at the reformed conventions. The Commission sought to address this concern by recommending that each state delegation be expanded by 10 percent to provide delegate slots exclusively for state party and elected officials. In states employing the primary these officials were to be chosen by delegates elected in that primary, whereas in states using the caucus-convention system they were to be picked by delegates to the state convention. Bear in mind, however, that these officials would not be coming to the convention as free agents, for the Commission also stipulated that they had to mirror the distribution of preferences among the primary or caucus delegates in their state.[28] Because of this stipulation, most elected officials declined to be included in the 10 percent add on.

In what would later prove to be its most controversial recommendation the Winograd Commission took further steps to ensure that delegates would reflect the preferences of those who had voted for them. In 1976 twenty-two states already had "binding" primaries; that is, delegates with an expressed Presidential preference were bound to vote for that candidate on the first ballot (in some states the binding requirement extended to more than one ballot or until the candidate released them). The Commission now proposed that *all* primary and caucus delegates be bound on the first ballot. Moreover, to protect against the possibility that a delegate might not honor the binding rule, the Commission went along with another proposal suggested by a Carter aide; namely, that a candidate be allowed to replace any delegates on the convention floor who switched their votes to someone else. Clearly, Carter's people were taking no chances.[29]

At its June 1978 meeting, the Democratic National Committee approved the reforms of the Winograd Commission and, under pressure from female activists in the party, added an additional one requiring that one-half of the delegates to the 1980 convention be women. This change was made with the blessing of President Carter, who was eager to please a constituency critical of him for his lukewarm support of ERA and his opposition to federally funded abortions.[30]

The Republican party, meanwhile, had not mandated any of the reforms undertaken by the Democrats in either 1974 or 1978.[31] To the extent that the Democratic reforms applied to the *primaries,* however, the Republicans were in most instances compelled to follow them as well. This is so because state legislative action was required to bring state primary laws into compliance with the reforms, and since most state legislatures were controlled by the Democrats, they usually wrote the legislation to apply to both parties.

A Parallel Development: More Primaries

Before assessing the overall impact of the 1971, 1974, and 1978 reforms, it is first necessary to discuss a development that has accompanied them, namely, the proliferation of primaries.

Although none of the Commissions discussed in this chapter either required or urged states to employ the primary as a mechanism for choosing delegates, nevertheless an increasing number of states have done so over the course of the last decade. Thus, in 1968 there were only seventeen primaries which chose just under 40 percent of the convention delegates that year. The number rose to twenty-three in 1972 and grew again to thirty in 1976. By 1980 there were thirty-five primaries choosing nearly three-fourths of the total number of delegates. The explanations for this increase are varied. Some states, it is argued, felt the complexities of the McGovern-Fraser Commission reforms (1971) were such that they could be implemented more easily in a primary as opposed to a caucus-convention system. It has also been suggested that party leaders felt the primary would be less susceptible than the caucus-convention system to capture by the liberal McGovern wing of the Democratic party. We should not overestimate the importance of these two explanations, however, for there was primary legislation pending in nine states before the McGovern-Fraser Commission had even held its first meeting, and in an additional four states by the time the 1971 reforms were ultimately approved. All of which suggests other considerations had been at work here also. It seems likely that some states, perceiving the broad-based sentiment for greater participation in the selection process, understandably saw the primary as the most democratic method for selecting delegates. Other states such as Vermont appeared to have been motivated by the belief that a switch to the primary would bring greater media coverage and financial benefits to the states. In still other states the decision to opt for the primary was dictated by the desire to provide a political advantage to native son candidates. In 1976, for example, the Texas legislature authorized a state primary after Senator Lloyd Bentsen announced for the Presidency. North Carolina did the same for Presidential aspirant Terry Sanford, as did Georgia for Jimmy Carter.[32]

ASSESSING THE IMPACT OF THE REFORMS

Even the harshest critics of the reforms would acknowledge that some changes were necessary in the nominating process. The total absence of party rules in some states, the failure to publicize times and places of caucus meetings, untimely selection of delegates, abuses of proxy voting, and excessive filing fees and costs all served to impede participation and/or distort outcomes. At the same time, however, these critics maintain that other changes have produced consequences—some intended, some not—which have left us with a nominating process inferior to what existed prior to 1972. We shall now consider the critics' indictments, some of which are compelling and others notably less so.

More Candidates

If we examine the number of Presidential candidates in the out-party (that is, the party not holding the Presidency) since 1968, we discover that eleven Democrats declared for the nomination in 1972, the largest field since 1912. In 1976 there were thirteen announced contenders in the Democratic party, and in 1980 ten Republicans threw their hats into the ring. As for competition within the party holding the Presidency, in 1976 Gerald Ford had to fend off a serious challenge from Ronald Reagan. President Carter also took seriously the challenges to his 1980 renomination by Senator Kennedy and Governor Brown. To be sure, incumbents have not been free of such challenges in the past. Henry Breckenridge decided to run against Franklin Roosevelt in 1936, and John Garner took him on in 1940. In 1964 President Johnson saw his nomination contested by George Wallace and four years later by Senators Eugene McCarthy and Robert Kennedy. In 1972 both Congressmen Paul McCloskey and John Ashbrook decided to take on Richard Nixon. With the possible exception of 1968, however, none of these challenges was regarded as even remotely threatening to the incumbents.

The changes that have occurred in the nominating process since 1968 are largely responsible for the increase in out-party contenders as well as for the more serious challenges to Presidential incumbents. With the proliferation of primaries and the reforms of the caucus-convention system, the nominating process has been taken out of the hands of the party leaders, thereby facilitating insurgent candidacies. In addition, the adoption of the rule of proportionality in the selection of delegates has no doubt provided added incentive for individuals to enter the race since they know they can accumulate delegates even though they may not win a primary or a caucus outright. Finally, the 1974 campaign finance reforms which provide partial public funding of nomination campaigns may also be viewed as a further encouragement to those considering a run for the White House.

It can certainly be argued that an increase in the number of candidates at the starting gates represents a positive development in the nominating process. After all, within limits, a greater number of alternatives is to be preferred over a lesser number. On the other hand, some critics argue that the reforms have made an incumbent President more vulnerable to challenge, and, consequently, he is forced to divert energies from more weighty matters of governing and focus attention on securing renomination.[33] Gerald Ford, for example, claims that in 1976 he was compelled to devote 20 percent of his time to his bid for the Republican nomination.[34]

While this argument is not without merit, it must be weighed against another consideration, namely, that the control of the nominating process by the party leadership prior to 1972 virtually precluded any realistic challenge to an incumbent President. Truman, for instance, despite his low standing in the polls and even some disaffection within the party organization, faced no serious challenge to his nomination bid in 1948. (The same can be said for Hoover in 1932.) By 1954 disapproval of Truman's performance was even more widespread and yet the evidence suggests that had he wanted it, the nomination would have been his once again. And even though public discontent with the Vietnam war rendered Johnson somewhat more vulnerable to being unseated by Kennedy or McCarthy, his continued support among the party leaders would more than likely have led to his renomination as well. In fact, even after his disappointing performance in the New Hampshire primary, Democratic party leaders across the country were still convinced that he would have carried 65 percent of the delegate vote at the 1968 Democratic convention.[35] The point is not that these Presidents either should or should not have been renominated. Rather, it is to suggest that the process should not have foreclosed the opportunity to unseat them. Prior to the reforms, such challenges were all but impossible. Now they are not.

The Process Is Too Long

The reformed nominating process, according to the critics, has become (1) so long and arduous that (2) many able individuals are discouraged from even entering the race and (3) among those who do, the unemployed enjoy a decided advantage over the employed.[36]

Few would dispute the contention that the nominating process now places far greater demands on the time and energy of Presidential contenders. In the old days most of the delegates were chosen by the appointment or caucus-convention systems, both of which were controlled by the party leaders. Candidates, therefore, faced the less time-consuming task of lining up support among this select group of individuals. While primaries were not ignored, they were entered more selectively and viewed principally as a means by which candidates could demonstrate to the party leaders their ability to win votes. In 1960, for example, Kennedy entered only four contested primaries. As the number of primaries grew, however, so did the burden of campaigning, for candidates were compelled to take their case to a much wider audience. In describing his schedule for just one week of his 1972 bid for the Presidential nomination, Senator Edmund Muskie testifies to the frenzied pace of the President-by-primary process: "The previous week I'd been down to Florida, then I flew to Idaho, then I flew to California, then I flew back to Washington to vote in the Senate, and I flew back to California, and then I flew into Manchester (New Hampshire)."[37]

Although the Winograd Commission (1978) attempted to lessen the burden of the primary season by reducing it from twenty-one to thirteen weeks, as noted earlier, this change had little real impact since four states were exempted from complying with it (see p.17). Moreover, it is also important to note that the demands of the primary process over the last decade have actually increased because circumstances require candidates to prepare for it much earlier. In 1967, for example, no one had yet declared for the race of the following year. On the other hand, as of June 1975 six individuals had already announced for the 1976 contest, and by June 1979 seven Presidential hopefuls had tossed their hats into the ring for the 1980 contest.[38] The necessity for these early declarations has been occasioned primarily by three factors: first, the proliferation of primaries; second, the increased importance of the *early* primaries; and, third, the 1974 campaign finance reforms requiring a candidate to raise $1,000 in each of twenty states to qualify for partial public financing—an undertaking which, as candidates have repeatedly pointed out, requires elaborate planning and organization.

If the nominating process is far more demanding than it used to be, can it also be said that this reality has had an impact on the quality of individuals seeking the Presidency? Some critics have answered this question in the bluntest of terms. Writing in the midst of the 1980 primary season, former

Under Secretary of State George Ball observed that "Participation in the embarrassing pageants (primaries) we are now observing can be stomached only by second-raters."[39] In a similar vein, another critic wrote that: "The primary system has made it so that nice guys, including the competent ones, stay out of the whole ordeal. Right from the start, the primary system means that only those who possess nearly psychopathic ambition and temperament will get involved and stay involved."[40]

Whether the current breed of Presidential candidate is more disturbingly ambitious than those of the past is, of course, a matter of speculation. We do not purpose adding to it here except to say it is not readily apparent that Jimmy Carter, Ronald Reagan, or George Bush, for example, evinced any greater level of ambition than did Lyndon Johnson, Richard Nixon, or John Kennedy. The lack of empirical evidence also makes it difficult to assess the extent to which presumably able individuals may have been deterred from entering the race *solely* due to the grueling nature of the primary process. It seems probable, however, that Adlai Stevenson, a widely admired and reluctant Presidential candidate, would have had little taste for the hurly burly of the primary process as it now functions. Although he has since had a change of heart, the ordeal of the campaign apparently precipitated Walter Mondale's early withdrawal from the Presidential race in 1976: "I found I did not have the overwhelming desire to be President which is essential for the kind of campaign that is required. . . . I don't think anyone should be President who is not willing to go through the fire. . . . I admire those with the determination to do what is required to seek the presidency, but I found I am not among them."[41]

Yet even if the arduous nature of the primary process *may* serve to discourage some able people, nevertheless it would be difficult to sustain the charge that the process failed to attract men of experience and accomplishment in 1980. Among the more serious contenders on the Republican side were John Anderson, with twenty years of service in the U.S. House of Representatives and ten years as chairman of the Republican Conference; Howard Baker, with fourteen years in the Senate and Minority Leader since 1977; Ronald Reagan, a two-term Governor of the largest state in the nation; George Bush, a two-term Congressman, U.S. Ambassador to the United Nations, chariman of the Republican National Committee, Director of the Central Intelligence Agency, and Chief of the U.S. Liaison Office in the People's Republic of China; John Connally, one time Secretary of the Navy, three-term Governor of Texas, and Secretary of the Treasury; Philip Crane, with eleven years as a member of Congress; and Robert Dole, twelve years a U.S. Senator, chairman of the Republican National Committee, and a Vice Presidential nominee. On the Democratic side Jimmy Carter was being challenged by Edward Kennedy, long a formidable figure during his eighteen years in the Senate; and Edmund Brown, Jr., Governor of California since 1975. Moreover, others would no doubt have taken on the vulnerable Carter as well had it not been for the fact that Kennedy was initially perceived as being the odds on favorite. To be sure, the candidates identified here were not all equally accomplished; nor was any one of them wholly free of liabilities. Taken as a whole, however, the field is notable for the depth and, in some instances, the breadth of government experience.

More persuasive is the critics' charge that the demanding nature of the nominating process gives a distinct advantage to candidates with a good deal of free time on their hands. Note, for example, that the out-party nominees in our last two Presidential elections were both unemployed at the time they entered the Presidential sweepstakes. Having finished his stint as Governor of Georgia in 1972, Jimmy Carter was able to devote full time to his 1976 campaign, a campaign which, by the way, he began planning as far back as late 1972. Likewise, Ronald Reagan was free of official obligations after completing his tenure as Governor of California in 1974. Moreover, his major competition for the 1980 Republican nomination came not from Congressional incumbents (Baker, Dole, Crane, and Anderson) but rather from George Bush who was also unemployed at the time. Although it would be oversimplifying matters to argue that free time by itself guarantees success—it did not save Reagan in 1976, nor Connally in 1980—nevertheless, the investment of time that the nominating process now requires of candidates certainly puts a premium on being unemployed. Any incumbents, then, who are reasonably conscientious about meeting their official responsibilities are likely to be at a serious disadvantage in competing for the Presidential nomination. This is a regrettable development, for as Howard Baker pointed out: "With a system that requires you to be unemployed to be a successful candidate, you lock out virtually every person that has current information about the problems that confront the country. What we've done is create a core of professional candidates for President, and I think that's bad because it means they will necessarily be perennial outsiders."[42]

Premature Closure

Earlier in this chapter we noted that the presence of a greater number of candidates at the starting gate represents a positive development in the reformed nomination process. But a wider field of contenders matters little if they are eliminated from the race before they have an adequate opportunity to make their case. Unfortunately, as the process now functions, the number of candidates is reduced very quickly because events occurring early in the race have taken on much greater importance. In 1976, for example, the caucuses and primaries held in the first three weeks effectively eliminated all Democratic candidates except Carter, Udall, and Jackson. Moreover, the momentum generated by Carter in this early period was instrumental in preventing Udall and Jackson from posing any realistic threat to his nomination. As Udall put it,

> We had thirty primaries, presumably all of them equal. After three of those primaries, I'm convinced it was all over. The die was cast. . . . If there was a state in America where I was entitled to relax and feel confident, it was Wisconsin. . . . Well, I take a poll two weeks before the primary and [Carter's] ahead of me, two to one, and he has never been in the state except for a few quick visits. That was purely and solely and only the product of that narrow win in New Hampshire and that startling win in Florida.[43]

By March 19, 1980, after only four primaries, such Republican notables as Howard Baker, John Connally, Robert Dole, and Philip Crane had been eliminated; and as of the end of March the nominations in both parties had for all practical purposes been decided. This despite the fact that no primary had yet taken place west of the Mississippi;[44] indeed, slightly more than half of the primary season remained. Sensing where the action is, it should come as no surprise that an increasing number of states have moved their primary dates closer to the start of the primary season (see Table 1-1). Parenthetically, it is worth noting that the states of Maine and Florida went these states one better by deciding to hold straw polls as early as November 1979. Although both of these events were totally meaningless in terms of winning delegates, the candidates were well aware that establishing momentum early was more important than ever in the reformed nominating process. Consequently, they flocked to both states and spent thousands of dollars in an effort to make a creditable showing.

While one would expect some early eliminations in a multicandidate race, the increased importance of early campaign events has accelerated the process. In seeking to account for their pivotal role, part of the blame can be laid at the doorstep of the campaign finance reforms of 1974. More precisely, the $1,000 limit on individual contributions has severely curtailed the ability of candidates to raise money at a time when the proliferation of primaries and inflation requires more money than ever. Accordingly, it has become all the more essen-

TABLE 1-1

DEMOCRATIC PRESIDENTIAL PRIMARIES HELD IN EACH PHASE OF THE NOMINATING PROCESS, 1968–1980

	1968	1972	1976	1980
First phase (February to early April)	2(12%)	4(17%)	8(27%)	13(37%)
Second phase (Late April through June 1)	10(59%)	14(61%)	19(63%)	14(40%)
Third phase (Rest of June)	5(29%)	5(22%)	3(10%)	8(23%)
TOTAL	17 (100%)	23 (100%)	30 (100%)	35 (100%)

Source: Congressional Quarterly Weekly Report, December 26, 1981, p. 2567.

tial to do well early in order to establish momentum and thereby bring in more funds.[45] Candidates, particularly the less well known, who do not fare well during this early period find it extremely difficult to make a comeback because their already limited financial resources become even more so; and, given the $1,000 limit, they can no longer turn to a few wealthy contributors who could provide them with an infusion of funds to keep their campaigns going. Add to this the fact that under the 1974 campaign finance reforms, a candidate receiving less than 10 percent of the vote in two consecutive primaries becomes ineligible to tap matching public funds and can requalify only by winning at least 20 percent of the vote in a subsequent primary. This fate befell candidates Dole, Brown, and Crane in the 1980 election.[46] Finally, the initially unsuccessful candidate is put at a further disadvantage since more successful opponents are not only able to raise more money, but also have that money doubled by matching public funds.

The influence of early contests in the delegate selection process has also been enhanced by a development not directly related to the reforms, namely, increased media attention. The CBS television network is a case in point. Whereas it featured only two stories on the Iowa caucus in 1972, this number had grown to twenty-three in 1980. Likewise the number of stories devoted to New Hampshire rose from nineteen in 1972 to thirty-three in 1980.[47] This kind of media coverage is no doubt encouraged by the Democratic party's decision to exempt these two states from complying with the March to June time frame for selecting delegates (see p.17). Were they required to hold their contests in this time period, they would have to compete with other states for the media's attention.

That these early events can exert influence out of proportion to their importance in the greater scheme of things is illustrated by the case of New Hampshire. It contains less than 1 percent of the nation's population and sends only nineteen Democratic and twenty-two Republican delegates to the national conventions. In 1976, moreover, 82,381 New Hampshire citizens went to the polls and Jimmy Carter won with a plurality of 23,373 votes, only 4,443 more than his closest challenger, Morris Udall. Yet in the week following this primary "*Time* and *Newsweek* put Carter's face on their covers and his story in 2,600 lines of their inside pages. The second place finisher, Udall, received 96 lines; all of Carter's opponents together received only 300 lines. The television and newspaper coverage given Carter that week was about four times the average amount given each of his major rivals."[48] Such an election result in a state the likes of New Hampshire scarcely justifies elevating a candidate to front-runner status, along with the increase in money and exposure that typically comes with it.

The problem of premature closure is not only one of candidates being forced out of the race too early but also of inhibiting their entry into the race after it has begun. The reforms are a key factor in accounting for this development.

You will recall that at the urging of the Carter supporters, the Winograd Commission (1978) recommended that states be permitted to set their primary filing deadlines as early as ninety days prior to the day of their primary. Many states did precisely that. Consequently, by January 21, 1980, the day of the Iowa caucus, the filing deadlines had already passed in four states, with New Hampshire, Massachusetts, and Illinois among them. By the day of the first primary in New Hampshire, filing deadlines had expired in nearly one-half the states, including New York, Pennsylvania, and Florida. As of the end of March, and with more than half of the primary season remaining, a candidate would have been able to get on the ballot in just seven states, only one of which (New Jersey) was of any major consequence.[49]

Unrepresentative Primary Results

Many critics maintain that while a nominating process heavily laden with primaries gives the appearance of being more democratic than the old system, in fact it is not. In the words of Newton Minow:

> Presidential primaries were designed to take the nomination away from the party bosses in the back room and to give the decisions to the voters. But they haven't worked out that way. Instead, the current version of primaries turns the decisions over to a new kind of boss. Today, a small, unrepresentative handful of party activists, often concerned only with one issue or with narrow, special interests, dominate the primaries. Because the broad center of moderate and independent voters seldom vote in the primaries, the decisions are abdicated to small groups of motivated extremists of the left or the right.[50]

Several points are in order concerning this indictment. First, primary turnout is not very impressive. Approximately 33 percent of the eligible voters participated in the 1972 and 1976 Presidential primaries, and in 1980 the number rose slightly to 36 percent. Moreover, these participants are older, more educated, more well-off, and more interested in politics than the population as a whole.[51] This is hardly surprising, however, for such people have always been overrepresented in all types of elections as well as other kinds of political activity. The more critical question is do these primary voters reflect an ideological persuasion that is also unrepresentative of the general population? The most recent and extensive study on this matter, conducted by the Center for Political Studies at the University of Michigan, finds little evidence to support such a claim. More specifically, in the last three Presidential elections there were no significant ideological differences between primary voters and party identifiers in primary states; nor, for that matter, between a party's primary voters and its rank-and-file membership nationally. The Michigan study also revealed that in two of the last three elections the ideology of rank-and-file party identifiers "matched most closely with that of primary voters who supported the party's front runner." The exception was in 1972 when George McGovern's primary voters were in fact more liberal than Democratic rank-and-file party identifiers, who were ideologically more attuned to primary voters supporting Hubert Humphrey.[52] While the critics may point to this exception as confirming their concern about the primaries, we should also bear in mind that the pre-1972 nominating process was not immune to being captured by ideologues either. To demonstrate that this is so we need look no further than the nomination of Senator Barry Goldwater by the Republican party in 1964. Although he had not won a single contested primary prior to California, a highly organized grass roots effort allowed his supporters to dominate the caucus-conventions and walk off with the nomination.[53]

Even if it were demonstrably clear that primaries had become the play-ground of a single-issue enthusiasts and ideological extremists, more caucus-convention states and fewer primaries—proposed by some critics—would not necessarily be an appropriate corrective. To a far greater extent than the primaries, the caucuses are likely to attract the intensely committed activitst. Primaries, after all, make only a minimal demand on voter motivation, namely, going to the polls and spending a few minutes pulling a lever or marking a ballot. Caucuses, on the other hand, require individuals to surrender an evening of their time and state publicly their Presidential preference. Finally, in terms of number of participants, it is difficult to see how caucuses would yield results more reflective of rank-and-file preferences than the primaries. In 1980, for example, participation in the Democratic primaries averaged 532,727 voters per primary, whereas an average of 29,944 citizens participated in each of the party's eighteen caucuses. This amounts to a ratio of approximately eighteen to one.[54]

The Decline in Quality Control

Beyond any question, changes in the nominating process between 1971 and 1978 brought to an end the crucial role once played by party and elected officials in the selection of Presidential nominees. These changes included not only the proliferation of primaries but also such McGovern-Fraser Commission (1971) reforms as the requirement for written party rules governing delegate selection, publication of times and places of caucus meetings, elimination of *ex officio* delegates, and the reduction in the number of delegates who could be appointed by state party committees. Nor was the impact of these reforms less-ened to any significant degree by the Winograd Commission's (1978) decision to increase each state's delegation by 10 percent to provide delegate slots exclusively for its party and elected officials. For you will recall that the Commission also stipulated that the distribution of Presidential preferences among these officials must mirror those of the delegates elected in their state. Thus, these officials could not come to the 1980 Democratic National Convention as free agents.

Certainly one of the most serious and widely shared criticisms of the reformed nominating process is that by curtailing the role of party and public officials, we have lost an important element of quality control over the selection of Presidential nominees. James Sundquist exemplifies this concern in the following:

> When the state presidential primaries became the mode rather than the exception after 1968, a basic safeguard in the presidential election process was lost. Previously an elite of party leaders performed a screening function. They administered a kind of competence test; they did not always exercise the duty creditably, but they could. More important, they could—and did—ensure that no one was nominated who was not acceptable to the preponderance of the party elite as its leader. Even if a candidate swept the limited number of primaries, he could still be rejected, as Senator Estes Kefauver was in 1952. Usually, then, the nominee was an insider in the political system, a person who had established some credentials as a politician or an administrator, or both, of national stature and of demonstrated competence. The party leaders who approved the nomination were prepared to follow the nominee, and to mobilize the party on his behalf.[55]

While the quality control function attributed to the party leaders is not wholly unpersuasive, it is, at the very least, overstated. Writing about the American political system in the late 1800s, James Bryce observed that "What a party wants is not a good president but a good candidate. . . . The Party managers have therefore to look out for the person likely to gain most support, and at the same time excite the least opposition."[56] Although he exaggerates the point, the fact remains that a party unable to win elections fails in its primary reason for being. Thus, it should come as no surprise that from 1936 through 1968, a period when the party leaders were in firm control of the nominating process, the national conventions on all but one occasion nominated the candidate most preferred by the rank-and-file of their party.[57] These data invite one of two conclusions: the rank-and-file were fully as discerning as the party leaders; or, alternatively, the party leaders were as unenlightened as the rank-and-file. Either way, the alleged screening function of the party leaders would appear to be of questionable importance. Moreover, let us consider the one instance when the choice of the party leaders did diverge from rank-and-file members. Senator Estes Kefauver arrived at the 1952 Democratic National Convention after having entered thirteen of seventeen primaries and won twelve of them. He also enjoyed a decisive lead in the polls (Kefauver, 45; Stevenson, 12; Russell, 10; Harriman, 5).[58] Yet because Adlai Stevenson was the clear preference of the party leaders, Kefauver was passed over for the nomination; and incidentally, Stevenson went on to lose the election in the fall.

The rejection of Kefauver, however, does not appear to have been based on the belief that he was not Presidential timber. Indeed, one long-time chronicler of American elections states that "he seemed most qualified for the leadership denied him."[59] Rather, the party leadership's rejection of Kefauver was motivated primarily by the fact that his Senate crime committee investigations had uncovered connections between organized crime and some big-city Democratic machines. To make matters worse, he also fell out of favor with Truman because he announced his candidacy before the President had made his own decision on whether or not to seek another term.[60]

With some justification, the critics argue that the results of the reformed nominating process have not been especially encouraging. As one put it, "The old rules—the old bosses—gave us Franklin Roosevelt. The new rules gave us McGovern and Carter and Reagan."[61] George McGovern was nominated in the face of strong opposition from party leaders, who favored Hubert Humphrey, and he went on to lead the Democratic party to its greatest election defeat in this century. In 1976 the reformed nominating process gave us Jimmy Carter, an avowed political outsider of limited experience, whose tenure in office manifested both of these limitations. It is still too early to assess Ronald Reagan's performance. These nominations, however, should not necessarily make us nostalgic for the days when the party leaders were instrumental in the nominating process. For one thing, they constitute a very small sample on which to judge the efficacy of the reforms. For another, in the cases of Carter and Reagan, at least, it is far from clear that they would have been denied nomination by the party leadership under the old system. Carter did, after all, come into the convention with a hefty 53 percent of the rank-and-file Democrats favoring his nomination. As for Ronald Reagan, he had led in the polls since September 1978 and arrived at the convention with 46 percent of the Republican party identifiers favoring his nomination. On the other hand, although McGovern led in the polls by the time he arrived at the convention, it was with a plurality of only 30 percent.[62] Third, if the reformed nominating process has yielded "questionable" nominees, we should also bear in mind that the record of the party leadership has not been unblemished in this regard either. Warren Harding proved to be the most inept President in this century. Herbert Hoover's first four years in the White House scarcely justified an additional four. And, while Barry Goldwater certainly did not command the support of most state and national officials—only four of the nation's sixteen Republican governors publicly endorsed his candidacy—nevertheless, he was strongly favored by 48 percent of the Republican county chairmen throughout the country; his closest rival, Richard Nixon, finished a distant second with only 21 percent.[63] Still more recently, we have the case of Richard Nixon who, along with Franklin Roosevelt, is the only individual in our entire political history to be nominated for national office five times; twice for Vice President and three times for President. In each of his three Presidential bids he commanded the support of the party leadership as well as the Republican rank-and-file. Needless to say, his tenure in office demonstrated that we were not well served by the screening function of the party elite, even though his previous track record in politics ought to have generated considerable skepticism among those alleged to be most astute in identifying Presidential timber.[64]

In short, the contention that party and public officials provided an important element of quality control over the nominating process is not a thoroughly convincing one. However, this is not to say that there are no compelling reasons for increasing the input of party elites. The critics persuasively argue that a candidate should have to come to terms with the party's elected officials (most notably, Senators and Representatives) if only because their support will be needed after the election. Yet in view of their diminished influence over the selection of delegates and their declining numbers at the conventions themselves (see Table 1-2), Presidential candidates no longer have much incentive to cultivate the support of Senators and Representatives. The sharp decline in legislators attending the 1972 and 1976 Democratic conventions was attributable primarily to the ban on *ex officio* delegates. They were, of course, free to run for delegate slots along with everyone else, but members of Congress have traditionally been reluctant to do so for political reasons. As one Congresswoman put it, "If I had to run against our district leader for one of our seats, I would win, but I wouldn't do it. I wouldn't want to risk her being upset at me and making my own re-election more difficult a few months later."[65] Although the Winograd Commission (1978) subsequently expanded each state delegation for the sole purpose of providing delegate positions for state party and elected officials, as noted earlier, this 10 percent had to mirror the distribution of Presidential preferences existing among the state's elected delegates. Since most members of Congress are reluctant to make an early commitment to a Presidential candidate—again, for political reasons—this reform failed to increase their ranks at the 1980 convention[66] (see Table 1-2).

TABLE 1-2
ELECTED OFFICIAL PARTICIPATION IN NATIONAL CONVENTIONS

Delegates to national conventions (Democrats)	Pre-reform, % (1956–1968)	Post-reform, % (1972–1976)	1980
U.S. Representatives	41	15	14
U.S. Senators	75	27	14
Governors	82	64	74

Source: William Crotty, "Two Cheers for the Presidential Primaries," in Thomas Cronin (ed.), *Rethinking the Presidency* (Boston: Little, Brown, 1982), p. 68.

The Rubber Stamp Convention

When delegates arrived at the 1960 Democratic National Convention, most were not legally bound to vote for a given candiate, and many had not even been required to indicate a Presidential preference when they ran in the primary. The independence enjoyed by these delegates, however, was gradually eroded by the reforms implemented between 1971 and 1978. The first move in this direction came in 1971 when the McGovern-Fraser Commission stipulated that delegates chosen in the primaries must be given the opportunity to list their Presidential preference, unless state law prohibited doing so. In 1974 the Mikulski Commission went further by requiring that all delegates chosen in caucuses and primaries state their Presidential preference; where state law prohibited the listing of Presidential preferences on the ballot, parties were required to publicize the names and preferences of delegates in the newspaper. In addition, the Commission also gave a candidate the right to approve any delegate intending to support him. In 1978 the Winograd Commission tied the knot when it stipulated that all delegates must vote for their stated Presidential preference on the first convention ballot and authorized a Presidential candidate to replace any delegate who failed to do so (rule F 3c). Although the adoption of rule F 3c generated no controversy within the Commission, it became the subject of heated debate at the 1980 Democratic convention where, in the hope of shaking loose some Carter delegates, Kennedy supporters mounted an unsuccessful campaign to change it.

Many have charged that these reforms fundamentally changed the convention from a deliberative body to nothing more than a rubber stamp for decisions already made in the primaries and the caucuses.[67]

Whether the conventions have ever been deliberative bodies is open to question. Writing as far back as 1940, for example, one of the most astute scholars of American party politics noted that "To expect bands of local chieftains and their henchmen to come together and act as a deliberative national unit every four years is to expect the impossible."[68] Bound or unbound, it is even more improbable that delegates to the 1980 convention could have deliberated in any *collective* sense if only because their numbers were so great—3,331 as compared with 1,521 in 1960 and 1,154 in 1940. At the same time, however, the binding rule clearly does impede *individual* deliberation. Our nominating process spans a period of several months during which time delegates have the opportunity to take the measure of a candidate. Presidential contenders who, in terms of ability and electability, appear formidable at the start of the race may prove to be decidedly less so by the time of the convention. To lock delegates into supporting a given candidate is to deny them the opportunity to factor into their decision how he or she performed subsequent to the time those delegates were chosen by the caucuses or primaries. In 1980, for example,

Jimmy Carter was a far weaker candidate at the end of the primary process than he was at the start. Several indicators substantiate this conclusion. A Gallup poll taken just prior to the start of the convention revealed that only 21 percent of the American people approved of the way he was handling his job as President. This was not only the lowest approval rating of his entire four years in office but also the lowest score ever recorded by Gallup for a sitting President. In another poll taken at approximately the same time, Gallup found that were the election held then, Reagan would have defeated Carter soundly (Reagan, 53; Carter, 37; undecided, 10). Furthermore, while Carter had fared far better than his opponent Edward Kennedy during most of the primary season, nevertheless, of the eight primaries taking place in June, Kennedy won five of them.[69] Thus, despite the fact that available indicators cast serious doubt on Carter's viability as a candidate, the binding rule prevented any Carter delegates from reconsidering their announced preference had they wanted to do so.

Finally, the binding rule carries with it a peculiar irony when viewed in the context of another commitment of the Democratic party, namely, increasing the role of minorities in the nominating process. Of the delegates in attendance at the 1968 convention, 13 percent were women, 5 percent black, and 3 percent under thirty. In 1980, on the other hand, 49 percent were women, 15 percent black, and 11 percent under thirty.[70] Yet although the reforms had increased the representation of these groups significantly, this advantage was to a considerable extent diluted by the fact that the binding rule denied them any independent bargaining power vis-à-vis candidates.

REFORMING THE REFORMS, 1982

Even before the 1980 election had run its full course, there was mounting pressure in and outside the Democratic party to begin an agonizing reappraisal of the reforms undertaken over the course of the last decade. The decisive defeat of Jimmy Carter at the hands of Ronald Reagan only served to further intensify this call for self-examination. Accordingly, the chairman of the Democratic National Committee constituted yet another reform Commission on Presidential Nominations, this time headed by Governor James Hunt of North Carolina. The group began its deliberations in August 1981 and reported its recommendations to the Democratic National Committee some seven months later. After making only one significant change in these recommendations, the Committee gave its stamp of approval in March 1982.

In an effort to restore a measure of independent judgment to the delegates, the Commission unanimously voted to abolish the infamous rule F 3c which had allowed candidates to replace unfaithful delegates. In addition, whereas all delegates to the 1980 convention had been required to vote for their Presidential preference on the first ballot, this was now replaced with more permissive language stating that delegates "shall in good conscience reflect the sentiment of those who elected them."[71]

Certainly one of the most persistent indictments against the reformed nominating process was its failure to provide a meaningful role for party and elected officials, thereby leading to a loss of quality control over candidates as well as diminishing the need for contenders to court the support of those who share in the governing process. As a corrective, the commission recommended that 14 percent of the delegate slots—561 of the 3,923 delegates expected at the 1984 convention—be reserved exclusively for elected and party officials who would go to the 1984 convention *unpledged* to any candidate. Included in these 561 delegates would be up to two-thirds of the Democratic Senators and Representatives in Congress, to be chosen by the party membership in their respective chambers. (The Democratic National Committee subsequently changed this number from two-thirds to three-fifths.) The remainder of these 561 *unpledged* delegate slots were to be distributed by state party and elected officials.[72] While the increased presence of members of Congress at the 1984 convention should enhance the chances of forging a closer relationship between the Presidential nominee and his Congressional party, whether or not these unpledged party and elected officials can provide much in the way of quality control is problematic. They will, after all, constitute only one-seventh of the total number of delegates. Moreover, even though this number could be enough to tip the balance in a close contest, we have no assurance that they would necessarily coalesce behind or against the same candidate. And, if the contest is not close at all, these officials will more than likely throw their support behind the inevitable winner.

The Commission also tried to respond to charges that the delegate selection season was too long and that events occurring early in the process exercised a disproportionate influence over the outcome. Thus, while Iowa and New Hampshire were once again exempted from the second Tuesday in March to second Tuesday in June calendar, Iowa was prevailed on to move its caucus from January 21 to February 27, and New Hampshire was likewise persuaded to shift its primary from February 26 to March 6. Moving these states back is designed in part to shorten the process; and in part to lessen their impact, since they will now be selecting their delegates closer to the official starting date of March 13. Whether these changes will accomplish their intended purpose is also debatable. The grueling nature of the nominating process has less to do with length and a lot more to do with the *number* of primaries, a problem the Commission did not address in its reforms. Moreover, what makes Iowa and New Hampshire so influential is that they start the delegate selection process and face no competition for media and public attention. In other words, each is the only show in town on that day. The Hunt Commission reforms have not changed this fact. Note also that while five weeks intervened between the Iowa caucus and the New Hampshire primary in 1980, only eight days separate these two events in 1984. Consequently, the winner of the Iowa caucus could well come into the New Hampshire primary with even greater momentum than in the past.

In 1974 The Democratic party had instituted the rule of proportionality to ensure that delegate strength would reflect voter preferences as accurately as possible. The Hunt Commission, however, concluded that proportional representation did not serve either the party or the candidates very well in 1980. More specifically, this rule denied Carter the opportunity to deliver a knockout punch to Ted Kennedy and as a result the divisive contest dragged on, preventing the party from uniting behind the front-runner. At the same time, although the rule of proportionality enabled Kennedy to do well enough to stay in the race, it denied him the ability to register a big win even when Carter appeared to be running out of steam. With these considerations in mind, the Commission decided to restore to the states the "loophole" option (see p.15) which allows primaries to run on a winner-take-all basis if delegates are selected at the district level rather than statewide. We can expect many states to take advantage of this option as they did in 1976. For those states that choose to retain proportional representation, the Commission has provided a "winner-take-more" option whereby the highest vote getter in a Congressional district receives a bonus of one extra delegate. Unfortunately, for those concerned with the problem of premature closure, these reforms are not free of potential difficulties either. The candidate who emerges the clear winner from the early contests, as Carter did in 1976, is already accorded a significant advantage in terms of momentum—momentum that would become even more irresistible with winner-take-all contests added to it. In addition, such an early resolution of the contest would thwart another Hunt Commission goal, namely, the opportunity for the 561 *unpledged* delegates to exert some influence over the convention outcome. Finally, as pollster Pat Caddell warned, restoring the winner-take-all system "could help develop a quick consensus around a fringe candidate unpopular with the vast majority of Democratic voters."[73]

In summary, whether these latest reforms serve the purposes, and only those purposes, intended by the Hunt Commission, remains to be seen. If the history of election reform in the last decade has taught us anything, however, it is to expect the unexpected.

OTHER REFORM PROPOSALS

Before concluding this chapter, it is worth considering other proposals for reforming the nominating process, some of which represent variations on what we have now while one entails a major departure from it.

Primary Clusterings

Some suggestions for reforming the nominating process include primary clusterings of one kind or another. One such plan calls for grouping primaries by region, with each holding its primaries on a given day. This arrangement would help to conserve a candidate's energy and financial resources, since he would be able to focus his attention in one area rather than hopping about the country as he must do now. Futhermore, given the fact that the primary season would open with a group of primaries, the potential influence of any one would be diluted. Consequently, we would no longer face the problem of a candidate being catapulted into the lead by virtue of having won in the single state of New Hampshire. The major limitation of this proposal, however, is that a candidate could be either advantaged or disadvantaged, depending on which region goes first. In 1976, for example, had the primaries begun in the West instead of the East, Jimmy Carter would have been knocked out of the race early. Likewise, had this region begun the primary season in 1980, Reagan would have eliminated George Bush from the race even sooner than he did.

Others have suggested that primaries be clustered according to the four time zones in the continental United States, with each cluster being scheduled at one-month intervals. This arrangement would mitigate the problem of regional bias for or against a given candidate. Moreover, unlike the current system in which primaries are scheduled every Tuesday over a thirteen-week period (see page 33), the interlude of one month would lessen the fallout of the previous round of primaries and provide candidates with more time to prepare for the next round. But this proposal has its drawbacks as well. For one thing, several states are located in more than one time zone. For another, nearly one-half the primary states, including a majority of the big ones (New York, New Jersey, Pennsylvania, Ohio, and Florida), fall into the eastern time zone. Thus, campaigning for this particular cluster would be a formidable task indeed. Furthermore, if this time zone led off the primary season, the candidate of limited visibility and financial resources would probably be hard pressed to wage an effective campaign in even half of the states involved.

National Primary

Others have come out in favor of a reform that would expand public participation even beyond what exists under the current system.[74] Known as the national primary, it would allow the rank-and-file in each party to vote directly for their nominee in a single nationwide election. The national conventions would then convene primarily for the purpose of drawing up the parties' platforms. This proposal is attractive for several reasons, not the least of which is that 66 percent of the American people favor it.[75] In addition, since the proliferation of primaries in the last decade has brought an increase in the number of people participating in the nominating process a nationwide primary could reasonably be expected to swell the ranks still further. Third, such an arrangement would eliminate one of the major deficiencies in the existing nominating process, notably, the disproportionate impact of the early primaries. Fourth, although Presidential candidates currently face their first contest in February, under a national primary the election would not come before May or June. Conceivably, this postponement of the contest would alleviate the need for candidates to begin their campaign a year or more prior to election year as they do now. Finally, all voters would have the opportunity to vote for the same candidates in a national primary. Under the present system this opportunity is frustrated not only because candidates may enter the primaries selectively, but also because some contenders get knocked out of the race early, and others may enter it late. By March 15, 1980, for example, Baker, Connally, Dole, and Pressler had withdrawn and thus voters in the twenty-eight remaining primary states had no opportunity to vote for them. Similarly, in 1976 Brown and Church did not throw their hats into the ring until the middle of March, thereby preventing residents in New Hampshire, Massachusetts, Vermont, Florida, and Illinois from passing judgment on their candidacies.

If the benefits associated with a national primary are compelling, so too are the liabilities. Certainly for those who think the nominating process is already too demanding and expensive, a national primary would merely be making a bad situation worse. In addition, since party leaders and public officials would have no formal role in the selection process, this plan would deal a further blow to the already diminished position of political parties in the American political system. A nationwide primary would also place less well-known candidates at a distinct disadvantage. Under our current system of discrete primaries, Presidential aspirants with limited national visibility have an early opportunity to demonstrate their viability as candidates. They would have no opportunity to do so under a national primary because it is a one-shot affair. We also face the problem of what to do in the event that no candidate receives a majority of the vote. You will recall that in 1976 thirteen individuals initially announced for the Democratic nomination, and in 1980 ten Republican hopefuls threw their hats into the ring. With fields as large as these a national primary winner could well finish with no more than 20 or 30 percent of the vote. This eventuality would presumably necessitate a runoff. Thus, we would be faced with three nationwide elections (national primary, runoff, general election), which would not only be a very expensive proposition but also impose a heavy burden on the stamina of the candidates and the attention span of the voting public. Moreover, there is another potential problem associated with a runoff election; in a large field of candidates, those falling near the middle of the political spectrum could split the vote, leaving the candidate on the extreme right and the extreme left with the largest pluralities. Thus, these two candidates would go into the runoff even though they might be least preferred by the largest number of voters. This problem is not unique to a national primary, however. Nor does a national primary necessarily have to be accompanied by a runoff. As Stephen Brams has suggested, the runoff could be mitigated if a system of "approval voting were instituted whereby a voter may choose or approve of as many candidates as desired in a multicandidate election. For example, a voter might vote for just one candidate, or for several candidates if more than one is found acceptable. However, only one vote may be cast for every approved candidate. . . . The candidate with the most votes wins."[76]

CONCLUSION

Since the nominating process determines the alternatives from which we ultimately choose, it may rightly be regarded as the most crucial stage in the electoral process. This reality was not lost on the famous Boss Tweed who is reputed to have said, "I don't care who does the electing, so long as I do the nominating."

For some time many have expressed profound dissatisfaction with the way this process has functioned at the Presidential level. Much of this chapter has been devoted to an examination of their indictments. Some of those, we believe, are not fully persuasive; namely, that capable individuals are no longer seeking the Presidency; that primary electorates are ideologically atypical of the general electorate; or that the current system affords substantially less quality control over candidates than the unreformed nominating process did. At the same time, however, other charges leveled against how we select our Presidential nominees are very compelling indeed. Nominating a Presidential candidate has in fact evolved into such a lengthy, demanding undertaking that leisure time has become a highly prized, if not indispensable, campaign resource. Consequently, public officeholders are placed at a serious disadvantage in competing against their unemployed opponents. In addition, contests occurring early in the primary season have assumed an importance out of proportion to what they deserve, thereby providing a not wholly warranted boost to the winners and a frequently fatal setback to the losers. Our national conventions, meanwhile, have been reduced to little more than echo chambers of results registered in the primary and caucus contests. And, finally, Presidential candidates have little incentive to come to terms with those individuals—most especially, members of Congress—whose support they will need once elected.

Unfortunately, the Democratic party's latest effort at reforming the reforms constituted only a marginal move in the direction of correcting these problems. To be sure, convention delegates will have a freer hand at the convention, but the length of the process will not be lessened significantly; the primaries will not necessarily be fewer in number; and the importance of early contests will be at least as great or, perhaps, even greater than before. Moreover, although the inclusion of Representatives and Senators as *ex officio* delegates represents an improvement over their modest presence at recent conventions, the fact remains that they will still constitute a very small percentage of the total number of delegates.

The deficiencies associated with the current system of nominating candidates prompt us to offer an alternative procedure for consideration, namely, having Presidential nominees chosen by the members of their party in Congress. While a detailed examination of this proposal must await the final chapter on the interface of Presidential selection and Presidential leadership, its benefits may be briefly summarized here. First, this plan would eliminate all the major defects attributed to the current nominating process. Second, the number of participants in the decision would be small enough to ensure more meaningful deliberation on the choice of candidates. Third, we believe such a system would substantially increase the element of quality control over candidates well beyond what has even been claimed for the prereformed nominating process. Fourth, those making the selection would be more accountable to their constituencies than convention delegates, most of whom are unknown to the electorate in their states, as are the votes these delegates cast on the convention floor. Finally, and perhaps most important, this method of selection would go a long way toward ensuring that Presidential candidates will have gained the confidence of those whose support will be most crucial in governing. One eminent student of the Presidency rightly points out that "The classic test of greatness in the White House has been the chief executive's capacity to lead Congress."[77] This mode of selection increases the likelihood that Presidents will be able to pass that test, for to lead Congress, a President must be able to lead his own party in Congress.

NOTES

1 Terry Sanford, *A Danger of Democracy: The Presidential Nominating Process* (Boulder, Colo.: Westview Press, 1981), pp. 100, 101.

2 *The Washington Post,* June 8, 1980, p. B7.

3 Jeane Kirkpatrick et al., *The Presidential Nominating Process: Can It Be Improved?* (Washington, D.C.: American Enterprise Institute, 1980), p. 14.

4 Martin Plissner, "Reforming Presidential Primaries," *Public Opinion,* 5 (February/March 1982), p. 58.

5 Austin Ranney, *Participation in American Presidential Nominations, 1976* (Washington, D.C.: American Enterprise Institute, 1977), pp. 2, 3.

6 William Crotty, *Political Reform and the American Experiment* (New York: Thomas Y. Crowell, 1977), pp. 201, 202.

7   Ranney, *Participation in American Presidential Nominations, 1976*, p. 4.
8   James W. Davis, *Presidential Primaries: Road to the White House*, 1st ed. (New York: Thomas Y. Crowell, 1967), pp. 28, 29.
9   Ranney, *Participation in American Presidential Nominations, 1976*, p. 4.
10 *Mandate for Reform*, A Report of the Commission on Party Structure and Selection to the Democratic National Committee (Washington, D.C.: Democratic National Committee, 1970), p. 9.
11 William Crotty, *Decision for Democrats: Reforming the Party Structure* (Baltimore: John Hopkins University Press, 1978), p. 84.
12 Crotty, *Decision for Democrats*, p. 84; Kenneth Bode and Carol Casey, "Party Reform: Revisionism Revised," in Robert A. Goldwin (ed.), *Political Parties in the Eighties* (Washington, D.C.: American Enterprise Institute, 1980), p. 7; *The New York Times*, January 17, 1980, p. A26.
13 *Mandate for Reform*, pp. 23, 25.
14 Ibid., p. 22.
15 Bode and Casey, "Party Reform: Revisionism Revised," p. 9.
16 *Mandate for Reform*, p. 30.
17 Ibid., p. 19.
18 Crotty, *Decision for Democrats*, p. 94.
19 *Mandate for Reform*, pp. 26–28, 34; Crotty, *Decision for Democrats*, p. 77.
20 *Mandate for Reform*, pp. 30, 31; Crotty, *Decision for Democrats*, p. 81.
21 Crotty, *Decision for Democrats*, pp. 145, 133.
22 Donald Fraser, "Democratizing the Democratic Party," in Robert A. Goldwin (ed.), *Political Parties in the Eighties* (Washington, D.C.: American Enterprise Institute, 1980), pp. 119,120.
23 Warren Mitofsky and Martin Plissner, "The Making of the Delegates, 1968–1980," *Public Opinion*, 3 (October/November 1980), p. 43.
24 *Congressional Quarterly Weekly Report*, April 3, 1982, p. 751.
25 Crotty, *Decision for Democrats*, p. 229.
26 Two states, Illinois and West Virginia, were exempted from this rule.
27 *The Washington Post*, June 10, 1978, p. 2.
28 *Congressional Quarterly Weekly Report*, August 4, 1979, p. 1609.
29 *Congressional Quarterly Weekly Report*, December 26, 1981, p. 2563.
30 Mitofsky and Plissner, "The Making of the Delegates, 1968–1980," p. 40.
31 Congressional Quarterly Inc., *Elections '80* (Washington, D.C.: Congressional Quarterly Inc., 1980), p. 60.
32 Bode and Casey, "Party Reform: Revisionism Revised," pp. 16, 17; James W. Ceaser, *Presidential Selection: Theory and Development* (Princeton, N.J.: Princeton University Press, 1979), p. 263; Ranney, *Participation in American Presidential Nominations, 1976*, pp. 6, 7.
33 See, for example, Robert S. Hirschfield (ed.), *Selection Election: A*

Forum on the American Presidency (New York: Aldine Publishing Co., 1982), p. 168.

34 Jack Walker, "Reforming the Reforms," *The Wilson Quarterly,* 5 (Autumn 1981), p. 98.

35 William Keech and Donald Matthews, *The Party's Choice* (Washington, D.C.: Brookings Institution, 1976), pp. 40–42, 106.

36 See, for example, Anthony King, "How Not to Select Presidential Candidates: A View from Europe," in Austin Ranney (ed.), *The American Elections of 1980* (Washington, D.C.: American Enterprise Institute, 1981), pp. 321, 322.

37 Cited in Theodore White, *The Making of the President 1972* (New York: Atheneum, 1973), p. 81.

38 *Congressional Quarterly Weekly Report,* June 16, 1979, pp. 1168.

39 *The Washington Post,* February 29, 1980, p. A13.

40 Cited in Anthony King, "How Not to Select Presidential Candidates: A View from Europe," p. 322.

41 Cited in Arthur Hadley, *The Invisible Primary* (Englewood Cliffs, N.J.: Prentice-Hall, 1976), p. 38.

42 *The New York Times,* August 31, 1980, p. 43.

43 Cited in Jules Witcover, *Marathon: The Pursuit of the Presidency, 1972–1976* (New York: Viking Press, 1977), pp. 649, 650.

44 Gerald Pomper, with colleagues, *The Election of 1980: Reports and Interpretations* (Chatham, N.J.: Chatham House, 1981), pp. 13, 34.

45 Congressional Quarterly Inc., *Elections '80,* p. 76.

46 Ibid., p. 130.

47 Michael Robinson, with Nancy Conover and Margaret Sheehan, "The Media at Mid-Year: A Bad Year for McLuhanites?," *Public Opinion,* 3 (June/July 1980), p. 43.

48 Thomas Patterson, *The Mass Media Election: How Americans Choose Their President* (New York: Praeger Publishers, 1980), p. 45.

49 Congressional Quarterly Inc., *Elections '80,* p. 68.

50 *The Wall Street Journal,* August 13, 1979, p. 14; see also, Edward Banfield, "Party 'Reform' in Retrospect," in Robert A. Goldwin (ed.), *Political Parties in the Eighties,* p. 27; Byron Shafer, "Anti-Party Politics," *The Public Interest,* No. 63 (Spring 1981), p. 101.

51 Barbara G. Farah, "Convention Delegates: Party Reform and the Representativeness of Party Elites, 1972–1980." (Prepared for delivery at the Annual Meeting of the American Political Science Association, New York City, September 3–6, 1981), p. 3.

52 Ibid., pp. 7, 9, 11.

53 Sanford, *A Danger of Democracy,* p. 25.

54 William Crotty, "Two Cheers for the Presidential Primaries," in Thomas

Cronin (ed.), *Rethinking the Presidency* (Boston: Little, Brown, 1982), pp. 67, 68.

55 James Sundquist, "The Crisis of Competence in Government," in Joseph Pechman (ed.), *Setting National Priorities: Agenda for the 1980s* (Washington, D.C.: Brookings Institution, 1980), p. 543.

56 James Bryce, *The American Commonwealth,* Vol. 1 (London: Macmillan and Co., 1889), p. 187.

57 William Ludy, "Polls, Primaries, and Presidential Nominations," *Journal of Politics,* 35 (November 1973), p. 837.

58 Keech and Matthews, *The Party's Choice,* p. 185; George Gallup, *The Gallup Opinion Poll: Public Opinion, 1935–1971,* Vol. 2 (New York: Random House, 1972), p. 1075.

59 Theodore White, *America in Search of Itself: The Making of the President 1956–1980* (New York: Harper and Row Publishers, 1982), p. 75.

60 James W. Davis, *Presidential Primaries: Road to the White House* (New York: Thomas Y. Crowell, 1967), p. 176.

61 Hirschfield, *Selection Election: A Forum on the American Presidency,* p. 107.

62 *The Gallup Opinion Index,* December 1980, Report No. 183, pp. 13, 16; Pomper, with colleagues, *The Election of 1980: Reports and Interpretations,* p. 33; Keech and Matthews, *The Party's Choice,* p. 202.

63 Keech and Matthews, *The Party's Choice,* p. 193.

64 See, for example, Theodore White, *Breach of Faith: The Fall of Richard Nixon* (New York: Atheneum Publishers, 1975), p. 65.

65 Cited in *National Journal,* January 2, 1982, p. 27.

66 Mitofsky and Plissner, "The Making of the Delegates, 1968–1980," p. 37; *National Journal,* January 2, 1982, pp. 27, 28.

67 See, for example, Kirkpatrick et al., *The Presidential Nominating Process: Can It Be Improved?,* p. 14.

68 Pendleton Herring, *The Politics of Democracy: American Parties in Action* (New York: W. W. Norton, 1940), p. 225.

69 *The Gallup Opinion Index,* Report No. 182, October/November 1980, p. 13; *The Gallup Opinion Index,* Report No. 183, December 1980, p. 13; Appendix C in Ranney (ed.), *The American Elections of 1980,* pp. 363, 364.

70 Mitofsky and Plissner, "The Making of the Delegates, 1968–1980," p. 43.

71 *The Washington Post,* January 16, 1982, p. A3.

72 *Congressional Quarterly Weekly Report,* April 3, 1982, p. 751.

73 Ibid., p. 750.

74 See, for example, Michael Nelson, "Two Cheers for the National Primary," in Thomas Cronin (ed.), *Rethinking the Presidency,* pp. 55–63; Godfrey Hodgson, *All Things to All Men: The False Promise of the Mod-*

ern Presidency (New York: Simon and Schuster, 1980, p. 250); *Congressional Quarterly Weekly Report,* July 8, 1972, pp. 1650–1654.

75 Nelson, "Two Cheers for the National Primary," p. 62.

76 Steven J. Brams, "Approval Voting: A Practical Reform for Multi-Candidate Elections," *National Civic Review,* 68 (November 1979), p. 549.

77 James M. Burns, *Roosevelt: The Lion and the Fox* (New York: Harcourt, Brace, 1956), p. 186.

THE MEDIA IN
PRESIDENTIAL SELECTION

The presence of the media in American society is pervasive. Seven of ten people read a daily newspaper and two of ten, a weekly news magazine of some kind; the number of radios in use is nearly double the size of our population; 97 percent of the households in the U.S. have a television set, which is turned on an average of six hours and forty-four minutes a day, up from four hours and thirty-five minutes in 1951. On a given evening anywhere from 50 to 60 million people are tuned to one of the three network evening news programs, and for 64 percent of the citizenry television is the primary source of information for learning what is happening in the world.[1] Given their ability to reach a wide audience, Presidential contenders have understandably come to view the media—particularly television—as the key variable in determining the success or failure of their candidacies. For this reason media related activities typically consume one-half or more of a candidate's budget, and the ranks of his campaign staff are heavily populated with individuals whose responsibilities interface with the media in one way or another. These include a media advance person, radio and TV writer, radio and TV producer, film documentary producer, radio and TV time buyer, newspaper space buyer, and television coach.[2]

In the course of the last twenty years or so, television especially has insinuated itself into the Presidential selection process more and more. This has happened for several reasons. Technological developments such as the portable TV camera have greatly facilitated the network's ability to cover Presidential campaigns. Even more important, the major television networks have steadily expanded their commitment to news programming in general. Beginning in 1963, they increased their evening news programs from fifteen to thirty minutes, and local stations followed suit not long thereafter. For some time the networks have also featured morning news programs as well as news "updates" periodically throughout the day; and in December 1979, ABC instituted a late night news program running from 11:30 PM to 12:00 AM. Apparently convinced that there was an audience for late night news, in 1982 CBS initiated an extended news telecast running from 2:00 AM to 7:00 AM, and NBC scheduled one from 1:30 to 2:30 AM. Cable television has also gotten into the act with twenty-four hour news channels.

Last, but not least, the increase in both the number and importance of primaries has also contributed to television's growing presence in the Presidential selection process. Since this method of delegate selection requires that candidates appeal to a much wider audience, they have been forced to rely more heavily on paid television advertising. Furthermore, primaries are precisely the kinds of events that television networks like to cover because they involve drama, conflict, and concrete results. Anyone watching the three networks in the last two Presidential elections, for example, saw news specials on the evenings of the Iowa caucus and New Hampshire primary and on every Tuesday evening during the regular primary season, beginning in the middle of March and ending in early June.

If the media are more heavily involved than ever in the Presidential selection process, has their influence on the process been commensurate with this level of involvement? This question will constitute the central focus of this chapter. More specifically, we shall be concerned with what impact, if any, the media have on the behavior of candidates, the outcome of the nominating contest, and, finally, on the information voters acquire about candidates and issues.

THE MEDIA PRESENCE

We are inclined to view the media's influence as flowing from what they report about people and events. Less appreciated is the fact that the media, by virtue of their presence, can have an impact on people and events even before they report on them. Stated another way, they can affect the very phenomena they are observing.

If a Presidential candidate is to stand any chance of winning the nomination and the general election, he must attain and maintain national visibility. Attention by the written and electronic press is indispensable to achieving these goals. Moreover, this kind of *free* coverage is a greater necessity than ever before, for both inflation and campaign spending limits have impeded the candidate's ability to purchase television time. To maximize the possibility that a watching media will report on their candidacies, Presidential contenders organize their campaigns to suit the needs of the media. This means handling travel arrangements and hotel accommodations, as well as providing telephones and typewriters for the television correspondents and newspaper reporters following their campaign.[3] It also means that candidates must gear their own activities and schedules to meet the news deadlines of the various media. As one campaign consultant put it, "You're running around constantly making sure you do something for the first editions of the major papers and you've got something to say that makes the wires and making sure you've got another story that's timely enough to be able to be transmitted back to New York to make the evening news."[4]

In securing coverage *what* a candidate does is every bit as important as *when* he does it. Presidential hopefuls fully recognize that whereas the print media may be content to report on a candidate's speech or a press release detailing his position on a given issue, the television networks are not so easily satisfied. Recounting a candidate's issue position or showing his "talking head" on the screen are, in the networks' judgment, not exciting enough to hold audience attention.[5] Accordingly, providing an exciting, colorful "visual" becomes a daily imperative for Presidential contenders in order to increase the likelihood of making the evening news. These events may include everything from jousting with hecklers, touring factories, or talking with senior citizens, to climbing mountains and shooting rapids as Robert Kennedy did in his 1968 nomination campaign. These visuals, it should be noted, are usually filmed by the candidate's own staff also and supplied to local television stations that may lack the resources to cover a campaign. As we shall see later in this chapter, television's preoccupation with the visually dramatic and the candidates' willingness to accommodate it have some not insignificant implications for the Presidential selection process.

In addition to what candidates do in the campaign, as well as when, the media presence can also have an impact on *where* they choose to do it. In 1976, for example, the Iowa caucus did not figure importantly in Morris Udall's campaign strategy, for he and his staff had concluded that New Hampshire would be the first contest to draw significant media coverage. To their surprise, the media did in fact decide to focus their spotlight on Iowa. Fearing that he would lose out on valuable media attention, the Udall staff made an about face and decided to commit $80,000, as well as ten campaign days, to the Iowa caucus. Although there is no way of knowing for certain whether this diversion of time and money hurt Udall in the New Hampshire primary, clearly his staff thought so. In the words of his press secretary:

Iowa was regrettable in that we had no inclination or desire to devote resources and time and money to Iowa. But it became such a media event that I think some of our staff people—national staff and Iowa staff—panicked in the face of it and we rushed in headlong. . . . The worse thing was we took ten days away from the New Hampshire schedule.

In 1980 the media decided to give considerable coverage to an event occurring well before the Iowa caucus, namely, the November 18, 1979 straw poll in Florida. Consequently, Presidential hopefuls descended on the sunshine state trying to drum up support, with one candidate (John Connally) going so far as to plough a quarter of a million dollars into this effort. Had the media not decided to focus on this event, which had little relevance to the selection of delegates in that state some three months later, it hardly seems likely that most of the candidates would have either.[7]

In a decidedly different way, media presence also influenced Gerald Ford's campaign strategy in 1976. As President he was guaranteed extensive media coverage whether on the campaign trail or in the White House. Aware of this fact and convinced as well that Ford was not a very effective campaigner, his staff adopted what came to be known as the "Rose Garden" strategy—"the president campaigning from the sheltered confines of the White House lawn, making presidential announcements against backdrops conducive to television coverage, while Carter plunged on in the pit of public exposure at the mercy of the wolves of the press."[8] Believing that he too had more to gain by being "Presidential," Jimmy Carter pursued this same strategy running against Senator Edward Kennedy in the 1980 nominating contest. He was forced to abandon it in mid-April of that year, however, when his insulation behind the White House walls became a campaign issue.

THE MEDIA AS ARBITERS AND INTERPRETERS

Identifying Serious Candidates

While braving the elements in New Hampshire during the 1980 nominating contest, one Presidential aspirant came upon NBC correspondent Tom Petit and his camera crew. The candidate proceeded to lodge a vigorous protest over the lack of coverage given to his candidacy thus far in the campaign. To which Petit wryly replied, "Well, today you are within the zone of coverage."[9]

Embedded in this amusing encounter is an important point. Declaration of candidacy is no guarantee that it will necessarily be viewed with the degree of seriousness candidates think is warranted. On the contrary, well before a single vote is cast in a primary or caucus, judgments are made concerning the viability of Presidential candidacies. In the days when the party leaders controlled the nominating process, they played the key role in making this determination. With their declining influence, however, the media have become the principal arbiters of which candidates are to be taken more or less seriously. The pressure to make such judgments is considerable since resource constraints prevent the media from giving equal coverage to all candidates, particularly given the large field of contenders in each of the last three elections. Television networks face an additional constraint, for unlike the print media, which have greater flexibility in terms of space, the evening newscasts are limited to thirty minutes (including commercials).

According to media specialist Michael Robinson, the networks are content to let the print journalists take the lead in deciding who is a serious candidate partly because "network people still believe that print people know more"; and in part also because "Network people worry more about making a candidate credible in the public eye because they know how much more 'powerful' they can be than the print as the campaign moves along."[10] Not all print media are created equal, however. Newspapers such as *The New York Times, The Washington Post,* and *The Wall Street Journal,* along with the three major news weeklies *(Time, Newsweek, U.S. News and World Report),* speak with the loudest voices as mentioners of Presidential candidates.

The crucial question in all this is, of course, the criteria applied in determining the seriousness of a Presidential candidacy. Although this subject has never been systematically examined, several factors appear to be involved: whether or not a candidate has sought the nomination before; his standing in the national polls; and his ability to attract financial support, most notably by qualifying for public financing.[11] Finally, a carefully planned attempt to cultivate relationships with members of the media apparently can help to be taken seriously also. In 1976, for example, there were no compelling reasons why Jimmy Carter ought to have received any more media attention than some of his opponents prior to the primaries. He was, after all, a former one-term Governor from the state of Georgia whose national recognition standing in the polls hovered around 2 percent. But Carter took to heart the advice given him by campaign strategist Hamilton Jordan:

> "Stories in the *New York Times* and *Washington Post* do not just happen but have to be carefully planned and planted," Jordan wrote. He submitted a list of nationally known writers "who you know or need to know," and advised: "You can find ample excuse for contacting them, writing them a note complimenting them on an article or column and asking that they come to see you when convenient. Some people like Tom Wicker or Mrs. Katherine Graham are significant enough to spend an evening or leisurely weekend with."[12]

Accordingly, the invitations were issued and soon a steady stream of journalists made their way to Plains to meet with the former Governor. This strategy appears to have met with some success, for a study of *The Washington Post* and *The New York Times* between November 1975 and February 1976 revealed that Carter received substantially more coverage than his opponents.[13]

Quite obviously, the media's judgment on who is a serious candidate—and allocating coverage accordingly—can have a significant impact on the ability of Presidential hopefuls to wage an effective campaign, for voters are not likely to vote for, or otherwise support, candidates about whom they know little. The point was well made by a federal judge for the U.S. Court of Appeals (District of Columbia), commenting on a suit brought against CBS by independent and third-party candidates seeking the Presidency in the 1976 election:

> Under present practices, as outlined by CBS, a candidate is doomed at the very beginning to having his *personal significance* as a candidate judged by the broadcasters practically before he ever starts his campaign. Thereafter the coverage of the issues he raises is effectively frozen out of the political campaign by the media. While the present candidates, who are appellants in this proceeding, may by general estimates be far removed from having any chance to win, the media can just as effectively, behind the screen of "news judgment," by exercising their claimed evaluation of a candidate's personal *significance,* reduce its coverage of candidates who might have a chance to win, given fair coverage. And for CBS to argue that the petitioners have not "submitted any specific information to show that CBS's news judgments are unreasonable," merely compounds the error. Candidates (whom) the media freezes out from the beginning will practically never be able to demonstrate that the media's news judgments are unreasonable because they can *never* show how significant their campaigns might have become if they had received fair coverage from the beginning for the issues they raised. Thus, the media's early "evaluation" becomes a self-fulfilling phrophecy.[14]

The Media as Interpreters of Results

The media's impact on the nominating process does not end with their role as arbiter of who is and is not a credible candidate. Once the delegate selection process is under way, they also report and interpret the results of the primary and caucus contests. How they choose to do so has consequences both for their own behavior and also a candidate's campaign.

As the April 4th Wisconsin primary approached in 1972, one might have expected the Presidential candidacy of Senator Edmund Muskie to be on solid ground. In the preceding six weeks he had run ahead of Senator George McGovern on each of the five occasions in which they had contested (Iowa, Arizona, New Hampshire, Florida, Illinois). Moreover, four of those five times, he had come out ahead of all other contestants as well. In actuality, however, Muskie's Presidential bid was in desperate straits, and his loss in Wisconsin proved to be the nail in the coffin.[15] The media played no small part in bringing about his demise, even though there was no conscious intent to do so. An accumulation of endorsements as well as his standing in the polls earned the Maine Senator clear front-runner status coming into the 1972 election. Consequently, he was expected to do well in the primaries. When he failed to live up to these expectations, the media interpreted his performance as a setback, even when he won. While New Hampshire was not the only contest in which Muskie became the victim of expectations, it was probably most damaging to his candidacy. On the eve of this the opening primary, he was well ahead in the national polls and, more to the point, a poll of New Hampshire voters revealed that he would take the state with 60 percent of the vote to McGovern's 25. After the votes had been counted, however, Muskie won 45 percent of the vote and McGovern came in second with only 37 percent. Although on paper, this result represented a comfortable victory for Muskie, the media actually interpreted the numbers as a serious setback to his candidacy and a moral victory for the little known McGovern. This judgment was based primarily on his failure to live up to preprimary poll predictions. To have judged him by this yardstick was hardly fair, however. The results of preprimary state polls are of questionable reliability because the samples are typically small, primary turnout is low, and voter attitudes are often quite unstable during the early part of the nominating process.[16]

Muskie's failed candidacy was not, of course, solely the consequence of interpretations attached to his showing in New Hampshire and some of the other primaries. His failure to identify himself with any single issue, the crying scene outside a New Hampshire newspaper building, and his decision to run in all the primaries hurt him as well. But even after one allows for these considerations, the fact remains, as pollster Burns Roper put it, "The effect of the press's touting of McGovern's strong showing (in New Hampshire) was to administer a near mortal blow to Muskie's candidacy."[17]

Smarting somewhat from criticism of the way they reported the New Hampshire primary, the electronic media resolved that in the next Presidential election they would declare winners on the basis of votes won, not expectations.[18] As the following illustrations suggest, however, making such a determination on numbers alone could be misleading also.

The 1976 Presidential selection process opened with the Iowa caucus on January 21st. At the conclusion of these first-stage precinct caucuses, Jimmy Carter had finished ahead of the other candidates. Roger Mudd of CBS weighed in with the observation that Jimmy Carter "was the clear winner in this psychologically crucial contest."[19] To assert that the Georgian was the "clear winner" was at the very least extravagant when one considers the overall context of the Iowa caucus. For one thing, these precinct caucuses were only the first stage in the state's caucus-convention process. For another, only 45,000 people had participated in this process, with Carter having garnered less than 15,000 of their votes. Third, the largest number of votes, some 40 percent, was actually cast for the "uncommitted" option. Finally, Carter was being cast in the role of front-runner even though a poll taken one week later showed him to be the choice of only 4 percent of the rank-and-file Democrats nationally.[20] Four years later the media were to treat George Bush's Iowa victory in a similar fashion. Some 106,608 Iowa Republicans participated, and Bush came in 2,182 votes ahead of Ronald Reagan, who had scarcely campaigned in the state. In the following week Bush received two to three times the amount of coverage accorded any other Republican contenders.[21] Even one of Bush's top campaign aids acknowledged that the fallout from Iowa was far out of proportion to the nature of the victory: "Then, the ride we got out of Iowa gave us an enormous boost—probably undeserving. It projected us into a front-runner status, a status we did not deserve. But there is no doubt about it; a ride by the press makes a lot of converts."[22]

In 1976 the numbers game was also apparent in the media's treatment of New Hampshire, the super bowl of early primaries. Of the 82,381 voters who went to the polls, Jimmy Carter finished first with a plurality of 23,373 votes, just 4,443 more than Morris Udall. Yet, once again, the media declared Carter to be the unqualified winner, and in keeping with this judgment both television and the press gave him most of the coverage the following week. This included placing his face on the covers of *Time* and *Newsweek* as well as according him 2,600 lines of space inside, compared with only ninety-six lines for the close second, Morris Udall. Television networks took a similar tack, giving Carter four times the amount of attention given to each of his opponents.[23] On the other hand, while journalists appear to have been overly generous in interpreting the magnitude of Carter's victory, it may also be said that they were unduly modest in their assessment of Reagan's defeat in New Hampshire by President Ford. Although he barely lost to an incumbent President by 1.4 percent (1,587 votes), Reagan was declared to be the loser and thus did not benefit from any added coverage the following week.[24] This judgment stands in marked contrast to 1968 when Eugene McCarthy was declared the real winner despite having lost to President Johnson by 7.7 percentage points; and to 1972 when George McGovern was declared the moral victor, although Muskie had defeated him by 9.3 percentage points. Clearly, the decision to define winners solely in terms of the raw vote could lead to overestimating losses as well as wins.

The New York and Wisconsin primaries, both of which occurred on April 6, were also subject to media interpretations not wholly justified by the results. New York was selecting four times the number of delegates being chosen in Wisconsin. Udall trounced Carter in New York, walking away with seventy delegates to Carter's thirty-five. Yet because New York's delegate selection process was so complicated and, unlike Wisconsin, provided no drama in the form of a Presidential preference vote, the media chose to focus on the Wisconsin primary. Here Carter defeated Udall by the slimmest of margins, 36.6 to 35.6 percent, which converted into twenty-nine delegates for the former and twenty-five for the latter. Consequently, Carter came away from these two primaries receiving more coverage than his opponent even though Udall, as a result of his total performance that day, had won ninety-five delegates and Carter only sixty-four.[25]

The media's interpretative role in the nominating process extends not only to the results of individual primaries but also to when the race has, in effect, been won. On June 8, 1976, the last day of the primary season, primaries were held in the heavyweight states of Ohio, California, and New Jersey. In Ohio Carter garnered a healthy 52 percent of the votes, whereas Udall managed only

21 percent. In California, however, the Georgian was soundly beaten by Jerry Brown, 59 to 29.4 percent; likewise, in New Jersey an uncommitted slate of delegates hastily put together by Brown attracted 42 percent of the vote and the Carter slate only 28 percent. Whether he acted on his own or through a prior arrangement with Carter is not clear, but Chicago Mayor Richard Daley proclaimed Ohio to be the ballgame and endorsed the Carter candidacy. The media also allowed as how Carter had now locked up the nomination, despite the fact that he had barely the required number of delegates needed and appeared to be losing steam as well.[26] Although the media proved to be correct in their judgment, one cannot help but wonder if their saying so helped to make it so. Four years later they would render a similar judgment, this time even earlier in the process. There were two primaries on May 20, 1980; one in Michigan with eighty-two delegate votes at stake and the other in Oregon where twenty-nine delegates were to be chosen. Reagan defeated Bush decisively in Oregon, receiving 54.5 percent of the vote to Bush's 34.7. Bush, however, beat Reagan even more decisively in Michigan where he won 57.5 percent of the vote to Reagan's 31.8. Although a substantial win in a state the size of Michigan would normally be expected to attract considerable attention, in reality it was largely ignored by the media. Instead, the major story proved to be ABC's declaration that Reagan had amassed enough votes to win the nomination, even though there were twelve primaries remaining. Well aware that such a declaration would destroy any momentum yet remaining in his candidacy, Bush decided to withdraw shortly thereafter. The ABC network defended its actions, arguing that they based their assessment on "a careful, deliberate delegate count."[27] Others, including *Newsweek*'s chief political correspondent, felt that the network had behaved inappropriately: "It's one thing to say that a candidate is leading and appears to have enough delegate votes for the nomination; it's another thing to imply he is the nominee. That can have an enormous impact and create a bandwagon effect."[28]

The role of the media as interpreters of results has several implications for the Presidential selection process. First, as the above illustrations have attempted to show, media verdicts on winners and losers do not always do justice to the full context of a given primary or group of primaries. More important, the reporting of these verdicts across the country can affect the viability of a Presidential candidacy, for there is evidence to suggest that voters tend to adopt the media's view of winners and losers and, not surprisingly, regard losers less favorably.[29] Thus, the candidate saddled with a loser image, *particularly if he is not well known to begin with,* is likely to experience a decline in the polls and a loss in financial support.

Second, the media's judgment on winners and losers determines how much coverage they decide to give a candidate. More precisely, the candidate who wins the most votes in a primary receives coverage far in excess of his opponents (see Table 2-1). Moreover, this tends to be the case regardless of how

TABLE 2-1
WEEKLY NEWS COVERAGE OF THE DEMOCRATIC CANDIDATES, DEPENDING ON THEIR
ORDER OF FINISH IN THAT WEEK'S PRIMARY (PERCENT)

Position candidate finished in	Network evening newscasts	Erie Times/ News	L.A. Herald- Examiner	L.A. Times	Time/ Newsweek
First place	59	58	52	60	62
Second place	17	18	29	19	14
Third place	16	16	17	15	13
Fourth place	8	8	2	6	11
Total	100	100	100	100	100

Note: Based on average for the thirteen primary weeks of 1976.
Source: Thomas E. Patterson, *The Mass Media Election: How Americans Choose Their President* (New York: Praeger, 1980), p. 45.

close the win might have been. Thus, the Presidential hopeful who is not well known to begin with and who does not win early is likely to experience great difficulty in getting his name before the public; this fact in turn impedes his ability to succeed in subsequent primaries, since voters do not support candidates they do not know. For example, in the important 1976 Pennsylvania primary practically all voters cast their ballot for a candidate about whom they had some knowledge. Since Jimmy Carter was known to 90 percent of the state's electorate and Udall and Jackson were known to only 50 percent, Carter enjoyed a distinct advantage over his opponents: "Carter received about 12 percent more votes than he would have received if each candidate had been equally known to the voters."[30] In short, the candidate with little national visibility, who does not win early, faces a "catch 22" situation: in order to gain coverage he must win, but in order to win he must receive coverage. What all this means is that in deciding whom to cover and how much coverage to give, the media play a crucial role in shaping the alternatives that voters consider, even though they may not necessarily influence which one of those alternatives the voters select.

Third, for the candidate who does not win early, the problem of coverage appears to be one of quality as well as quantity, for the media tend to treat winners more favorably than losers. More specifically, in his insightful study of the media in the 1976 Presidential campaign, Thomas Patterson found that

Carter's performance also provided him with news coverage that was more favorable than that received by his opponents. Evaluations of the candidates were keyed primarily to their success. A winning candidate was said to be an effective campaigner and organizer while a loser was normally presented as lacking in these talents. Moreover, since popular support is considered a *sine qua non* of success, a winning candidate was usually described by such adjectives as likeable and appealing. Although a losing candidate was normally not described in opposing terms, it was often stated or implied that voters were not particularly attracted by his personality or style.[31]

The less favorable coverage accorded losers would not necessarily affect voter preferences if the candidate is already well known, with a firm base of support, for voters would already have accumulated information and impressions against which such coverage would be weighed. For the candidate who lacked national visibility, however, this kind of media coverage might well affect voters' assessments of the candidate, since their knowledge base would in all likelihood be quite limited.

Finally, it should be noted at this point that one study of media coverage in the 1980 election found television taking a tougher, more critical approach to front-runners: "if he leads the pack or starts to pull away from it, chances are near certain the networks will get tougher with him. And the better he does, the tougher they get."[32] Although this finding may signal an attempt by the media to provide a corrective to their coverage in the previous election, its significance must be tempered by two considerations: first, the study represents a systematic analysis of only one television network, namely, CBS; in addition, even though each of the more critical stories on front-runners consumed several minutes, these reports were rare occurrences. Indeed, more than 99 percent of the stories run on CBS between January and June 4, 1980, refrained from making any explicit comments about any candidate's competence or personal integrity.[33]

THE MEDIA AS INFORMERS

Although one would probably find considerable disagreement on how much weight should be attached to each, most would probably acknowledge that experience, issue positions, political skills, and character are all relevant to formulating judgments about a candidate's fitness for office. We now consider the media's role in educating the electorate to these various dimensions of a Presidential candidate. In doing so we shall first examine the media in the context of their reporting function and then focus on them as a vehicle employed by candidates to convey information through political advertising.

Informing by Reporting

Those who look to the media, particularly television, to play a crucially important role in educating the voters about the candidates and the issues are likely to be somewhat disappointed. In their study covering the last seven weeks of the 1972 election campaign, Patterson and McClure found that the three networks gave only limited coverage to the candidates on twelve important "personal and leadership qualities."[34] To be specific, ABC devoted less than twenty minutes, CBS only sixteen minutes, and NBC a mere eight minutes. All of this coverage taken together constituted only 1 percent of the total news time available to the networks during this seven-week period. The record on covering the candidates' twenty-six issue positions was only slightly better, with CBS giving them 46 minutes of attention, and ABC and NBC according them 35 and 26 minutes, respectively. Once again, if one views the issue coverage of all three networks in terms of the total amount of news time available to them during this period, it comes to a modest 3 percent. Moreover, if one excludes the issue of Vietnam peace negotiations, which were ongoing during the campaign, this figure drops to only 2 percent.[35]

If candidate qualities and issue positions received such limited coverage during the 1972 general election, to what aspects of the campaign did the networks turn their attention? According to Patterson and McClure, they focused mostly on the "horse race" and "hoopla" dimensions of the contest—strategies, tactics, rallies, motorcades, polls, etc. In fact, television news gave nine times more coverage to this subject matter than it gave to candidates' personal and leadership qualities, and four times more coverage than was given to issue positions.[36]

Thomas Patterson's study of the media's reporting role in the 1976 election campaign is even more instructive because it included newspapers as well as television and also emcompassed the entire campaign period (January 1– November 2). His findings, some of which appear in Table 2-2, are revealing in several respects. First, with the exception of the *Los Angeles Times* during the general election stage, both the networks and the print media gave greater coverage to the campaign game (that is, horse race and hoopla) than they did to substance, and they did so at *every* stage of the Presidential selection process; second, the difference in coverage given to the game and substance was substantial in most instances, particularly during the primary season; third, at each of the three election stages, television on the average gave even greater coverage to the game than did the print media; finally, for both the networks and newspapers, the focus on horse race and hoopla declined in the general election period. Although there have thus far been no comparable studies of media coverage in the 1980 election, Michael Robinson did undertake a content analysis of CBS news coverage from January 1 through June 4 and found that no less than 66 percent of its stories were devoted to "hoopla" and "campaign activity." *If* these findings are any indication of coverage by the rest of the media, it would appear that their preoccupation with the game of Presidential selection continues unabated.[37]

To say that the media choose to emphasize the game rather than the substance of the campaign does not tell the whole story, however, for even when the issues receive attention, it is "campaign issues" which are given the most extensive treatment. They constitute remarks or behavior by the candidates during the course of the campaign that are viewed as having the potential to

TABLE 2-2
NEWS COVERAGE OF SUBSTANCE AND GAME DURING THE PRIMARY, CONVENTION, AND GENERAL ELECTION PERIODS (PERCENT)

Period	Network evening newscasts	Erie Times/ News	L.A. Herald- Examiner	L.A. Times	Time/ Newsweek
Primaries					
Game	64	64	62	59	62
Substance	24	26	24	28	24
Other	12	10	14	13	14
Total	100	100	100	100	100
Conventions					
Game	58	59	55	52	54
Substance	29	28	28	33	31
Other	13	13	17	15	15
Total	100	100	100	100	100
General Elections					
Game	51	52	51	42	46
Substance	35	36	36	42	41
Other	14	12	13	16	13
Total	100	100	100	100	100

Source: Thomas Patterson, *The Mass Media Election: How Americans Choose Their President* (New York: Praeger, 1980), p. 29.

affect their prospects for success (for example, Carter's *Playboy* interview and "ethnic purity" remark, Ford's comment on Eastern Europe, Bush's behavior in the New Hampshire debate, and Kennedy's statement on the Shah of Iran). In 1976, for example, more than 50 percent of the campaign issues were heavily reported by television and newspapers as compared with only 15 percent of the policy issues. If television alone is considered, the percentage of heavy coverage for campaign issues rises to 70 percent, and the coverage for policy issues drops to 10 percent.[38] It is hardly surprising that the media in general, and television in particular, give such intense coverage to campaign issues, for they are usually more colorful grist for the media mill. Yet one may certainly question whether such issues merit the quantity and/or quality of coverage they received.

That Jimmy Carter chose to grant an interview to *Playboy,* and state during it that he had lusted after other women, were both rather trivial matters when juxtaposed with the issues of war and peace, energy, and the economy. The interview, however, became a major media event as soon as the magazine hit the newsstands. The same overreporting followed President Ford's observation, made in the second of the 1976 Presidential debates, that the Soviet Union did not dominate Eastern Europe. This was an obvious misstatement, one he immediately tried to clarify, and flew in the face of what he had said on the subject during his two years in office. Nor apparently did voters attach great importance to this remark since a poll taken by Robert Teeter immediately afterward showed President Ford winning the debate by 11 percentage points. The media, however, made Ford's remark a lead story, noting that it represented a major blunder. Polls taken on the heels of this reporting showed Ford losing the debate by 45 percentage points.[39] George Bush's altercation with Ronald Reagan over who was to participate in the Nashua, New Hampshire, debate certainly deserved some media coverage. But did it merit seventeen minutes on the weekend news programs to the exclusion of any mention of what both men actually said in the debate iself?[40]

For other campaign issues, the problem lay with the quality rather than the quantity of coverage. Jimmy Carter's remark about preserving the "ethnic purity" of neighborhoods had potentially important policy implications and thus merited the attention it received. Unfortunately, although this remark was the subject of some thirty stories on the evening new programs, all but six concentrated on how this gaffe would impact on his chances of winning the Presidency.[41] Likewise, Edward Kennedy's controversial criticism of the Shah and his opposition to granting him asylum, dealt with issues that were by no means trivial. Yet once again, the reporting focused primarily on how his remarks would affect the campaign. As one national correspondent for the *Los Angeles Times* observed: "What was discussed was whether this was a dumb move, whether he had screwed up his campaign, was back in the game; did Kennedy stumble, commit an error, was this lousy strategy? The question of whether this statement was accurate, whether this should change our view was not discussed."[42]

Given how the media report on the Presidential selection process, what possible consequences does this have for the candidates and the voters? For one thing, to the extent that reportage emphasizes the game over substance, Presidential candidates are encouraged to do so as well. Speaking to this problem one political consultant noted:

> I have been associated with many candidates who made a serious effort to present substantive policy statements on a variety of issues and I have seen 100 page documents presented for solutions on the Middle East and energy crisis and so forth. And there was a deliberate effort not to hype it, to present it as a serious substantive statement. It got virtually no coverage. What happens after a while if you have been through this on a regular basis, you begin to deal with television in that you need a good visual. You have to present a visual backup to get the story on the evening news, and it does become a bit cynical.[43]

As to the impact of news reporting on the electorate, Patterson and McClure found that regular newspaper readers substantially improved their knowledge over nonreaders on all but one of the major issues in the 1972 general election campaign. At the same time, however, on only one-half of these issues did regular viewers of the evening news programs learn more than those who failed to tune in. Moreover, when questioned about what they had seen on television, some 54 percent of the viewers recalled some aspect of the game. This is in contrast with newspaper readers, only 31 percent of whom mentioned hoopla and horse race stories.[44] In his examination of the 1976 Presidential race Patterson also found that regular readers of newspapers learned more about the issues, but regular viewers of the evening news programs did not significantly increase their information levels. In addition, the majority of stories recalled by both readers and viewers were game related, with the percentage reaching 80 during the primary season and dropping to 60 in the general election period. Finally, not only were game stories recalled most frequently, but respondents regarded one or another facet of the campaign game as the "election's most important feature."[45] That the media have chosen to emphasize the game is unfortunate, particularly since some of the candidates emerging as front-runners in recent elections were initially unknown quantities. Such was the case, for example, in both the 1972 and 1976 Democratic nominating contests. George McGovern had served one and a half terms in the U.S. Senate and during this time had not attained any degree of national prominence. Jimmy Carter enjoyed similar anonymity and had an even more modest track record, one term as Governor of Georgia. Yet during the crucial nominating phase, when most voters had little information about these individuals, electronic and print journalists were telling us more about how the candidates were doing than where they stood on the issues.

Given the media's emphasis on the game of Presidential selection, one might well conclude that they have fallen considerably short of meeting their responsibility to inform the electorate. Such a judgment must be tempered by several considerations, however. For one thing, the focus on the game is partially due to the fact that the proliferation of primaries (from seventeen in 1968 to thirty-seven in 1980) has made the game a more prominent feature of the Presidential selection process. Prior to this growth, candidates entered fewer primaries and spent most of their time lining up support among party leaders, an activity that lacked the drama of the primary contests we have now. Moreover, even though voters feel that stories on the game do no adequately prepare them to make voting decisions, they also admit that this kind of reportage interests them.[46] Media outlets, whose viability quite obviously depends on capturing an audience, cannot ignore this reality.

We should also bear in mind that Presidential candidates do not make it easy for the media to report on their issue positions, for they typically remain deliberately vague on many policy issues, focusing instead on "descriptions of problems, promises to attain general goals, criticism of the opponent's past performance, and lavish praise for the past performance of the candidate's own party."[47] This strategy of calculated ambiguity is readily understandable from the candidate's point of view, since the more specific he becomes the greater the risk of dissatisfying some portion of the electorate as well as rendering himself more vulnerable to attack by his opponent. Also, a hard and fast stand on an issue may leave him with little room to maneuver after the election when, if victorious, he faces the realities of governing.

In reporting on candidates' issue positions the media face the problem of newsworthiness, in addition to ambiguity. Once a Presidential aspirant has articulated his position on a given issue, it thereafter declines in news value— unless he changes—for journalists are interested in what is changing, not what remains constant. As CBS correspondent Bill Plante put it, "[Candidates] have an agenda which they want to follow. We are more interested, many times, in getting the candidate to react to the day's news, to world events that are going on, than we are in hearing what he has to say for the twenty-seventh time . . . out of his standard speech."[48] Furthermore, the problem with the news value of issues has been further exacerbated by the lengthening of the Presidential selection process, for the media now have a longer time frame in which to present a limited number of issues.[49]

Finally, in the case of television, at least, its suitability for covering issues in some depth is impeded by factors beyond those already mentioned. To a greater extent than any other medium, "its audience is an *inadvertent* one— which, in large proportion, does not come purposely to television for news, but arrives almost accidentially, watching the news because it is 'on' or because it leads into or out of something else."[50] Add to this the fact that for some 87 percent of the population, the motives for watching the evening news are "nonpolitical."[51] Add further the fact that, unlike newspapers, television can be and often is watched while the viewer is doing something else. All of which suggests that the evening news audience may be less than fully attentive to what is being presented on the screen. And, even if television news were assured thoroughly attentive viewers, time constraints would inhibit its ability to provide in-depth treatment of complex issues. The networks are, after all, presented with the formidable task of squeezing the day's news into a thirty-minute time slot (including commercials). Thus, as Walter Cronkite noted, the evening news can function as little more than "a headline service."[52] Newspapers, on the other hand, do not face this space limitation. Consequently, they can and do provide more in-depth treatment of candidates and issues. This no doubt helps to explain why newspaper readers gain more information about the campaign than do television viewers.

Television Advertising

Media news coverage is one major way by which voters are exposed to Presidential candidates. The other is through paid political advertisements, including newspaper advertisements, billboards, literature, and radio and television commercials of varying length and format. Of all these media outlets, however, it is clear that candidates attach greatest importance to television as a vehicle for projecting their candidacies. First employed in the Eisenhower Presidential campaign of 1952, television advertising has grown to the point that it typically constitutes the single largest campaign expenditure, often consuming as much as one-half of the candidates's financial resources. In 1976, for example, each Presidential nominee, in accordance with public funding provisions of the Federal Election Campaign Act, was given $21.8 million to spend for his campaign. Carter allocated $10.3 million for media, $7.6 of which went for the purchase of television time. President Ford spent $10.8 million on media, and $6.3 million of the amount was funneled into television advertising. In 1980 the general election public funding allotment was raised to $29.4 million for each nominee. Carter and Reagan each spent approximately $19 million of this sum on radio and television commercials, with most of the money again going to the latter.[53]

The importance that candidates attach to television commercials has been matched by a long-standing concern in some quarters that this form of communication may be used to manipulate rather than inform the electorate. Manipulation is, of course, scarcely new to American electoral politics. Turning out crowds, balancing tickets, seeking endorsements from celebrities, tailoring remarks to suit particular audiences, to name but a few, all smack of manipulation to one degree or another. Employing television for this purpose has evoked special alarm, however, not only because of its capacity to reach a mass audience but also because of the very nature of the medium. Being visual, many fear that it necessarily emphasizes appearance over substance and encourages the viewers to do likewise in forming their judgments. Thus, what becomes important is not what the candidate says but the subliminal impressions that register from his looks, demeanor, personality, and the context in which he is presented. Candidates are portrayed as dutifully surrendering themselves to public relations experts who, after extensive polling designed to tap voter sentiment, contrive an image for a candidate and merchandise it on television much like a product.[54] Moreover, the television campaign commercial is seen as a highly suitable vehicle for the image makers to work their will since the content is essentially theirs to determine:

Political advertising—now the principal means of communication and persuasion between candidates and voter—is without peer as the most deceptive, misleading, unfair, and untruthful of all advertising, especially on television, the most powerful of our advertising media. Today the sky is the limit in political advertising with regard to what can be said, what can be promised, what accusations can be made, what lies can be told. Short of libel or slander—charges that are almost never pursued legally during or following an election—the only restriction upon political advertising is that it is identified as such.[55]

Although the concern voiced over the merchandising of candidates is not wholly unwarranted, we should not attach greater significance to this development than it deserves. For a variety of reasons, voters may not be as easily hoodwinked by the image makers as some suppose.

Conditions for Propaganda   For one thing, propaganda, of which political advertising is one form, is most likely to succeed when it is constant, intense, and not recognized as such. Presidential campaign advertising does not meet any of these conditions very well. Political commercials occur only over a nine-month period and become relatively intense only during the last two weeks or so of the campaign. Moreover, campaign advertisements are blatantly obvious to the viewer, for they represent an abrupt departure from the standard bill of fare on television, to say nothing of the fact that all such advertising must be so labeled on the screen. Thus, aware that they are about to be propagandized as soon as a commercial appears, voters are automatically put on their guard. This does not mean that efforts to influence voters in this way will inevitably fail. Rather, it is to suggest that image makers must overcome the formidable obstacle of voters who, from the start, are likely to be wary of what they are about to see and hear on the screen.[56]

Sources of Information   Those who seek to contrive a particular image for a candidate must be able to control the information voters receive about him. While the image makers do in fact have complete control over the content of televised commercials, they have little or no control over other sources of information available to the electorate—personal contacts, print, radio and television news, television public affairs and talk show programs. Of course, a candidate could seek to minimize as much as possible his exposure to uncontrollable media formats, but this strategy is not likely to meet with much success. If a Presidential hopeful is not very well known to begin with, he will in all likelihood lack the financial resources that would allow him to gain national exposure primarily through controlled advertising appeals. Accordingly, he must scramble for exposure any way he can get it, including appearances on public affairs, talk show, and news programs. The luxury of being able to pursue the controlled exposure strategy lies only with the candidate who is already well known and well financed. But herein also lies his problem, for since he is already well known, he already has an established image; one which cannot be altered significantly by media advertising. This fact became apparent in what has become known as the classic case of trying to sell a Presidential candidate, namely, Richard Nixon's 1968 bid for the Presidency. Following the advice of campaign consultants, he assiduously avoided uncontrollable media formats from early 1967 until shortly before the election. By controlling the environment in which he appeared, aides hoped to fashion a new Nixon image, notably, one of warmth and humor. Although he ultimately succeeded in winning the 1968 election, the evidence suggests that his expensive image campaign had very little to do with it. Indeed, his aides were so unimpressed with the results of the 1968 image effort that they greatly reduced (from $12.6 million to $4.3 million) the money targeted for broadcasting in the 1972 campaign, diverting it instead into direct mailing.[57]

Predispositions   The analogy drawn between selling candidates and selling products is a familiar one in the writings of those who express alarm over political advertising: "You cannot merchandise candidates like soap and hope to preserve a rational democracy."[58] In reality, however, it is probably much easier to sell a product than a candidate. Consumers are likely to approach new products with few preconceived notions. Voters, on the other hand, do not come to their assessment of Presidential candidates *tabula rasa,* but rather carry with them a cargo of predispositions shaped by such factors as personal associations, ideology, socioeconomic status. and party identification. Moreover, voting research conducted from the late forties through the early sixties revealed party identification to be an especially strong influence on how voters perceived candidates. Depending on the strength of this partisan commitment, individuals were found to engage in *selective exposure, selective perception,* and *selective retention,* all of which posed formidable obstacles for those seeking to move an individual from one candidate to another.[59] More specifically, individuals were likely to expose themselves only to those sources of information that reinforced their predispositions. When confronted with circumstances that rendered selective exposure impossible, partisan identification induced selective perception and retention of what was being read or seen. In the 1960 Presidential debates, for example, supporters of Kennedy and Nixon not only saw their man as the winner, but also were inclined to attribute candidate remarks with which they disagreed to the opposition candidate, even when it was their own who made them. In addition, they tended to recall only the statements of their candidate with which they agreed, and only those of his opponent with which they disagreed.[60] Because of the strong influence of party identification, it was not uncommon for anywhere from 60 to 75 percent of the electorate to reach a voting decision before the general election campaign even got under way.[61]

All this is not to say that political advertising was found to have no impact on voters. Such influence, however, most often took the form of activating and reinforcing voter predispositions rather than converting a voter from one candidate to another. Of course, those who came into the general election campaign undecided on how to vote were more susceptible to political advertising, but they were also likely to be least interested in politics and, consequently, least likely to expose themselves to political communications.[62]

In the last fifteen years, however, not only has television advertising become a more prominent feature of Presidential campaigns, but research has also recorded an erosion in partisan commitment, with the most sustained decline occurring between 1962 and 1972 and leveling off thereafter.[63] In addition, although more recent studies continue to find voters engaging in selective perception, there is little evidence to suggest that they practice selective exposure as well.[64] In the case of television, at least, this latter finding is hardly surprising. Unlike reading a newspaper, an individual cannot easily self-edit what appears on the television screen, be it a political advertisement or an item about a candidate on the evening news.

With the decline in attachment to party and the growing presence of television advertising, have voters become more vulnerable to the image makers? The available evidence suggests that this is not the case. In 1972 Richard Hofstetter and others interviewed more than 1,000 individuals between October 3 and November 4 in order to ascertain the impact of television and print media on the electorate. They concluded that for all kinds of television presentations, including political commericals, "Very little relationship between kinds of favorable and unfavorable perceptions of the major party candidates and exposure to any of the types of television programming was present during the 1972 campaign." Television viewing did, however, increase "both the amount and variety of thinking about candidates."[65] Patterson and McClure interviewed more than 600 people from September 18 to November 6, 1972, and found that television advertising had no detectable impact on those who had a candidate preference: "whether people watched television regularly, and constantly saw the advertised images of Nixon and McGovern, had no influence on their impressions of the two candidates; whatever people were getting from political spots, it was not their images of the candidates."[66] More significant, perhaps, the authors also examined the impact of political ads on the undecided voters, those who would presumably be most susceptible to influence. Among the respondents falling into this category, only 16 percent were found to be influenced by the ads. Furthermore, of this 16 percent only 7 percent (this converts into approximately 1 percent of the national electorate) were actually manipulated by what they saw in the political commercials; that is, they were persuaded to vote against their own self-interest. The other 9 percent made use of the information provided in the commercials but were not manipulated by them.[67]

The limited impact of television advertising during the general election period is not altogether surprising. By the time this stage in the Presidential selection process arrives, voters have already accumulated some information about the candidates during the nominating and convention periods. This information constitutes a knowledge base against which political advertisements are weighed. Second, even though party identification does not have the hold on voters it once did, more than one-half of the electorate still identifies with a political party to one degree or another. Furthermore, if DeVries and Tarrance are correct, even the new breed of voters (that is, ticket splitters) for whom the party is distinctly less important may not be all that vulnerable to television advertising. These voters are more educated and politically active than the average citizen and, although they rely on television as their primary source of information, they are attacted to media formats that cannot be easily manipulated by the candidate. Indeed, of thirty-five information sources used by ticket splitters, TV advertising ranked twenty-fourth in order of importance.[68] To be sure, it is regrettable if even 1 percent of the electorate is, as Patterson and McClure found, manipulated by television advertising. At the same time, however, this finding suggests a problem different in magnitude from those who contend that "If they so desire, these new managers—acting rationally from their own point of view all the while—can play upon the voters like virtuosos. They can push a peddle here, strike a chord there. And presumably, they can get precisely the response they seek."[69] Finally, we should also bear in mind that those most susceptible to manipulation are so because they have so little information about the candidates and the issues. This fact in turn results from their low level of interest in the campaign, which means that in all likelihood they will not even come to the polls on election day.

It is important to note at this point that all the studies discussed here focus exclusively on the influence of political commercials at the general election stage. During the nomination period, however, party identification cannot come into play as a mediating factor between voter and candidates, since all the candidates one might contemplate voting for are within the same party. Nor during this earlier period are voters likely to have as much information about the candidates as they do later in the campaign. Thus, the potential impact of television advertising would appear to be greater at this stage of the Presidential selection process. On the other hand, those who vote in the primaries are more highly educated and more interested in politics than the average citizen, and consequently, we could reasonably expect them to be more discerning and critical in evaluating the commercials to which they are exposed. Unfortunately, it is not possible at this time to go beyond these conjectures since there is little empirical evidence on the impact of television advertising during the nomination period.[70]

Advertising Content   The critics of campaign advertising view its content as deceptive, superficial, and generally lacking in any capacity to inform and enlighten the electorate:

> The dominant goal of political broadcasts paid for by a political party is obviously the promotion of a candidate, not the enlightenment of the voter. This promotion takes its very worst form in the thirty-second or one minute spot commercial where political issues are so oversimplified or ignored that the voter is given no information or, even worse, misleading information.[71]

This is an argument for an idea whose time has not yet come. It is, however, an idea whose time had better come soon for the health and welfare of American democracy. For if there is one legislative remedy that might reverse the growing and pervasive American distrust with politics and the increasing desertion of Americans from the polling booth, it is this, abolish the paid political television commercial.

Abolish the marching drummers, swinging to the tune of I'm feeling good about America. Eliminate the fast-paced clips of the strong man with his shirt-sleeves rolled up, his tie at half-mast, jacket slung over his shoulder . . .

Blow away the radioactive mushroom-shaped cloud hovering over the little girl picking daisies or the rooster-shaped weathervane whose 180-degree swings meter the candidate's expressed view. Cancel the starstudded galas and send the glamorous back to Hollywood to endorse the soaps and shampoos, their experience with which may make them qualified to serve as judges for the rest of us.[72]

Although political advertisments are certainly not free of the imagery, gimmickry, and hoopla described above, neither are they wholly lacking in substance. Of the spot commercials appearing in the 1972 general election campaign, for example, 42 percent were concerned primarily with issues and an additional 28 percent contained a good deal of issue content. In fact, the issue content of political advertisements was decidedly greater than the amount of time devoted to issues by the three television networks. On Nixon's twelve policy issues, the networks together spent anywhere from five to fifteen minutes, whereas the time given to these issues in the spots ranged from twenty-five to sixty-five minutes. As for McGovern's political advertisements, they devoted a total of sixty-five minutes to his five major policy issues, whereas the networks allocated only ten minutes to them.[73] Jeff Greenfield, in his analysis of television advertising in the 1980 general election, also found the issue content of campaign commercials to be superior to that of the news media: "For the voter trying to decide between Jimmy Carter and Ronald Reagan, the political advertising provided much clearer arguments about the nature of the choice than did the overall coverage of the campaign on television and in the mainstream press."[74]

Not only do political advertisements contain more substantive content than many had presumed, but voters appear to benefit from this content as well. Thus, while Patterson and McClure found that viewers were little moved by the image appeals contained in television campaign commercials, these same viewers did learn from the issue content presented. More precisely, those with high exposure to ads became more knowledgeable about every issue treated than did those with low exposure. Other studies also confirm that television campaign commercials, far from fostering an evaluation of candidates based on personality and appearance as some had feared, actually serve to increase the issue consciousness of the voter. Furthermore, these advertisements appear to be particularly beneficial for those segments of the population least interested in and least informed about the campaign. Because of their low political motivation, these individuals do not seek out political information about Presidential candidates, but since the appearance of the commercials on television is unpredictable, they can hardly avoid them. Consequently, as a result of this exposure, their information base is increased beyond what it would be otherwise.[75]

Having said that television commercials increase the information levels for those who watch them, one should not presume that their content is free of exaggeration, oversimplification, omission, and even some distortion. It is not. Since candidates engage in this kind of behavior out on the stump, one would hardly expect them to refrain from doing so in their advertising. They are, after all, attempting to put the best possible face on things. But voters are well aware that commercials are by their very nature designed to present one side, and for precisely this reason, assess what they see with a skeptical eye, weighing it against other information and their own experience.

Nor should we overlook the fact that such exaggerations and omissions as do occur in commercials are likely to be kept within fairly narrow limits, for to do otherwise is to run the risk of being exposed by the opposition and the watching media. In 1964, for example, the Johnson campaign ran a spot showing a little girl picking daisies in a field as a mushroom cloud ascended in the background. Although this spot made no mention of Barry Goldwater by name, its import was clear—the Republican Presidential candidate was not to be trusted with the matter of war and peace. The cries of protest, which were immediate, intense, and widespread, led to the withdrawal of the commercial after one airing. In the more recent 1980 election the media zeroed in on several television commercials, the most notable of which was a spot put together by the campaign staff of Senator Howard Baker. The film showed the Senator addressing an audience at the University of Iowa, where an Iranian student suddenly rose and asked the Senator why he had not denounced the oppressive regime of the Shah. Baker replied, "Because, my friend, I'm interested in *fifty Americans,* and when they are released." Thunderous applause followed. Shortly after the ad began running, Baker appeared on *Face the Nation* and pointed out that the Iranian student and others had been trying to take over the meeting. This commercial, as well as the Senator's subsequent remark, became the subject of a seven minute CBS investigative report which, among other things, pointed out that the Iranian student had not been part of a group; that he actually opposed the takeover of the American embassy in Teheran; and that the thunderous applause, which actually came ten minutes after Baker's response to the student, had been edited to immediately follow it. Three days after this report, the ad was withdrawn. A George Bush commercial showing him stepping off a plane and moving toward a hangar full of eager supporters also drew media attention when it was learned that the whole scene had been staged. Nor did Ronald Reagan's commercials escape scrutiny. As seen in one commercial, Reagan both reduced taxes and saved the state of California from bankruptcy. This drew not only an in-depth critical analysis by *The New York Times* but also a rebuttal commercial from the Carter campaign.[76]

Although none of the 1980 campaign commercials described here was even remotely as inappropriate as the infamous "daisy" ad of 1964, nonetheless, the coverage they received signaled that the media will be taking a closer look at this feature of the Presidential selection process. This fact should caution future Presidential contenders and their campaign advisors to be even more careful about what they put on the television screen.

Presidential Debates

In our discussion of the media as informers during the Presidential selection process we have thus far focused on their reporting of the campaign, as well as their use by candidates for paid political advertisements. At this point some mention should be made of a third way in which the media may be employed to educate the electorate on the candidates and issues, namely, Presidential debates. It differs from the first two in that the format allows a candidate to speak to the voters without having his remarks edited by the networks, and yet at the same time denies him the kind of control he enjoys over his own political advertisements.

First instituted in 1960, when Kennedy and Nixon agreed to face each other in four one-hour programs, the practice was not renewed again until 1976 at which time Carter and Ford met in three ninety-minute appearances. While Carter and Reagan followed suit in 1980, they agreed to only a single debate lasting one hour. Since the 1960 debate was sponsored by one of the television networks, Congress was required to pass legislation temporarily exempting the network from section 315(a) of the Communications Act, which requires television networks to afford equal time to all candidates seeking a given office. The debates of 1976 and 1980 presented a different situation, for the sponsor on these two occasions was the League of Women Voters rather than the networks. The networks, however, were once again exempted from complying with the equal time requirement because the Federal Communications Commission ruled that the debates were a legitimate news event and thus deserving of live coverage by the networks.

The desirability of holding Presidential debates has itself been the subject of considerable debate in both academic and political circles. For those who question their usefulness in the Presidential selection process, the bill of particulars includes several criticisms. In the first place, there is no opportunity for a free exchange of views and questions *between* the candidates themselves. Instead, questions are posed by panelists and the candidate responds to them rather than to his opponent. Characterizing this format as a debate is thus a misnomer. Second, well aware of the high stakes involved, candidates are suitably cautious in their presentations and responses, revealing little that is not already known. Third, at least in the case of the 1960 and 1980 Presidential debates, there was not sufficient time to plumb the candidates' views on complex issues. When one subtracts from all three of the 1960 Presidential debates the time taken by the panelists and moderator, Kennedy and Nixon each had less than one and a half hours to make his case. In 1980 the time problem was even more acute, with Carter and Reagan each having less than one-half hour. Fourth, the debates highlight the superficial at the expense of substance. A premium is placed on the quick answer as opposed to the more reflective, if sometimes, more halting response. Stage presence, not substance, is what wins points. In 1960, for example, it was widely thought that Nixon lost the first debate not so much because of what he said but rather because of the way he looked—tired, no make-up, a five o'clock shadow, and poor lighting.[77]

In defense of Presidential debates on the other hand, it may be argued that they serve to mitigate the national exposure that any incumbent President enjoys over his challenger; they present voters with one of the few opportunities to observe candidates in a context in which their remarks are not subject to editing by the media and where the candidates themselves cannot control the agenda; and they provide voters with means for *comparing* candidates' positions on the issues. In the final analysis, however, the justification for Presidential debates must rest on whether or not they inform the electorate. Although the evidence on this question is still out for the 1980 debate, studies of the 1960 and 1976 debates are instructive. The thrust of the research findings on the Kennedy/Nixon encounter suggests that viewers improved their understanding of issues to some extent but reacted primarily to the personalities of the candidates.[78] Studies conducted on the 1976 debate not only found that voters *perceived* it as a highly useful source of information but, more important, that this perception was essentially correct: "A variety of studies statistically traced a substantial increase in election-relevant knowledge to the debates."[79] Viewers came away from these encounters with a clearer view of how the candidates differed on policy issues. Reflecting, perhaps, a more issue-conscientious electorate than existed in 1960, the findings also suggest that viewers were more concerned with what the debates conveyed about issues as opposed to candidate image.[80] In short, on the crucial point of whether or not the debates inform, the weight of the evidence would appear to argue for their continuance.

There is certainly room for improvement, however. A single hour-long debate such as occurred in 1980 is scarcely enough time to probe where the candidates stand on major policy issues. A more appropriate model to emulate would be the 1976 debates in which there were three ninety-minute encounters, the first focusing on the economy, the second on foreign policy and defense, and the third reserved for any and all issue areas. Furthermore, at least one of these sessions, probably the last, should take place in a format consisting solely of a moderator and the candidates, where each contender would be free to ask questions of the other. As two seasoned political observers aptly point out, "There are few better, tougher critics of any politician than his opponent."[81] The import of the debates would also be enhanced if the media changed the emphasis of their coverage. In 1976, for example, more than half of the television and newspaper coverage of the Carter/Ford face-off dealt with how they performed, how they projected, and how their performance would affect their campaigns. Although these facets of the debate cannot be ignored, greater emphasis on *what* the candidates had to say would certainly be more beneficial to the public.[82]

To argue that Presidential debates deserve a future is, of course, no guarantee that there will be one. In the past the decision to debate has always rested with the nominees and, understandably, they have agreed to face their opponents only if convinced that they had more to gain than to lose. While the occurrence of debates for two elections in a row might place some added pressure on the 1984 nominees to continue the practice, this alone is not very good insurance. Candidates can obfuscate their firm intention not to debate by agreeing in principle to face their opponent and then proceeding to haggle endlessly over details. A variety of proposals have been put forth which call for either Congress or the political parties to require Presidential nominees to square off against each other. The most intriguing of these suggestions is one offered by political scientist Malcolm Moos, namely: Congress should ask the networks to set aside a block of time for the debates and specify that if either candidate declines to participate, his time will be given to his opponent.[83] Faced with the prospect that his challenger would be accorded valuable national exposure at no cost, perhaps debating an empty podium, it hardly seems likely that any Presidential candidate would refuse.

CONCLUSION

The role of the media in the Presidential selection process presents us with a paradox of sorts. It appears to be least influential when being used for precisely that purpose (political advertising) and most influential when it is not (reporting).

Although television campaign commercials have often been portrayed as the *bête noire* of the Presidential selection process, their persuasive powers would appear to be considerably less than some would have us believe. Attempts to seduce voters through carefully contrived image appeals must overcome a variety of obstacles, including voter skepticism, attitudinal predispositions, countervailing sources of information, and a growing concern for issues. On the other hand, as reporters of people and events, the media's impact on the Presidential selection process is very significant indeed. Their pervasive presence affects much of what candidates do in the campaign, as well as when and where they do it. More important, with the declining role of party leaders in the nominating process, the media have become the key force in shaping the alternatives presented to the electorate:

> What is new is not mass communication as one of the major forces in politics, but rather its emergence to fill virtually the whole gap in the electoral process left by the default of other independent elites who used to help manage the choice. Their power is all the stronger because it looks, to the casual observer, like no power at all. Much as the old party bosses used to pass themselves off as mere "coordinators" and powerless arrangers, so some modern-day titans of journalism want themselves thought of as mere scorekeepers and messenger boys. Yet the signs of journalists' key role as the major advancers and retarders of presidential ambitions are all around us.[84]

Even before the process of Presidential selection is officially under way, journalists decide which candidates merit their attention, thereby determining in large measure those we find out about and those we do not. Moreover, as the nominating process gradually plays itself out in a sequence of primaries and caucuses, the media also tell us who is winning and who is losing. How they choose to interpret a candidate's performance in these contests can affect not only the flow of support to him, financial and otherwise, but also the amount of media coverage he receives. To this extent, then, their judgments can serve to advance, impede, or even terminate a Presidential candidacy. As noted earlier in this chapter, primary and caucus outcomes have not always warranted the interpretations given them by the media, nor the degree of coverage granted or denied candidates based on those interpretations.

Back in the days when the party professionals were instrumental in the nominating process, they played the key role in judging the significance of primary and caucus results. Now the media do. As a consequence of this change, we run a greater risk of eliminating some capable candidates prematurely. This risk exists not because the media are biased against qualified contenders, but rather because their decisions on coverage are so heavily determined by who is winning and losing. Consider the candidacies of Muskie (1972), Udall (1976), and Baker (1980). All were individuals with considerable experience in public affairs. All enjoyed wide respect among their fellow politicians. Each was arguably more qualified for his party's nomination than the man who ultimately won it. Yet because they did not start out winning (Udall, Baker), or winning big (Muskie), each suffered in quantity and/or quality of media coverage. This in turn contributed to a loss of momentum in a process in which establishing momentum early is crucial. Baker was knocked out of the box after only two weeks. Muskie hung on for a while and Udall for still longer, but neither one was able to recuperate enough to mount a serious challenge. Had the party professionals been performing their traditional role when these individuals ran, things might well have been different. Although party leaders did not ignore primary and caucus results, neither were their judgments wholly determined by them, particularly in the early going. An individual's qualifications for office were also factored into their overall assessment of his viability. Consequently, a Presidential contender of demonstrated ability was not necessarily placed at a serious disadvantage merely because he did not get off the mark quickly enough.

All this is not to argue that the media either can or should refrain from judging election results—Presidential selection is, after all, ultimately about who wins and loses. Rather, it is to suggest that the voters and candidates would be better served were journalists to strike a better balance in the amount of coverage they accord competing candidates in the early stages of the nominating process.

NOTES

1   *U.S. News and World Report,* August 2, 1982, pp. 28, 29; Burns Roper, "Emerging Profiles of Television and Other Mass Media," *Public Attitudes* (New York: Television-Information Office, 1967); William Crotty and Gary Jacobson, *American Parties in Decline* (Boston: Little, Brown, 1980), p. 68; Theodore White, *America in Search of Itself: The Making of the President 1956–1980* (New York: Harper and Row, 1982), p. 165.

2   Robert Agranoff, *The New Style in Election Campaigns* (Boston: Holbrook Press, 1972), p. 17.

3   Ibid., p. 366.

4   John Foley et al. (eds.), *Nominating a President: The Process and the Press* (New York: Praeger, 1980), p. 75.

5   William E. Bicker, "Network Television News and the 1976 Presidential Primaries: A Look from the Networks' Side of the Camera," in James David Barber (ed.), *Race for the Presidency* (Englewood Cliffs, N.J.: Prentice-Hall, 1978), p. 105.

6   F. Christopher Arterton, "Campaign Organizations Confront the Media-Political Environment," in James David Barber (ed.), *Race for the Presidency,* p. 17.

7   Foley et al., *Nominating a President: The Process and Press,* p. 119; *Newsweek,* November 26, 1979, p. 50.

8   Jules Witcover, *Marathon: The Pursuit of the Presidency, 1972–1976* (New York: Viking Press, 1977), p. 533.

9   Cited in Jonathan Moore (ed.), *The Campaign for President: The Managers Look at '76* (Cambridge, Mass.: Ballinger Publishing Co., 1981), p. 130.

10 Michael Robinson, "TV's Newest Program: The 'Presidential Nominations Game,'" *Public Opinion* (May/June 1978), p. 44. See also, Rich-

ard Stout, "The Pre-Pre-Campaign-Campaign," *Public Opinion,* 5 (December/January 1983), p. 18.

11 Donald Matthews, "Presidential Nominations: Process and Outcomes," in James David Barber (ed.), *Choosing the President* (Englewood Cliffs, N.J.: Prentice-Hall, 1974), pp. 42, 43; Arterton, "Campaign Organizations Confront the Media-Political Environment," pp. 13–15.

12 Witcover, *Marathon,* p. 113.

13 Robinson, "TV's Newest Program: The 'Presidential Nominations Game,'" p. 44.

14 Cited in Eugene McCarthy, *The Ultimate Tyranny* (New York: Harcourt Brace Jovanovich, 1980), pp. 147, 148.

15 Lanny J. Davis, *The Emerging Democratic Majority* (New York: Stein and Day, 1974), pp. 123, 124.

16 Burns W. Roper, "Distorting the Voice of the People," *Columbia Journalism Review* (November/December 1975), pp. 31, 32.

17 Ibid., p. 29.

18 Bicker, "Network Television News and the 1976 Presidential Primaries: A Look from the Networks' Side of the Camera," p. 93; Michael Robinson, "Media Coverage in the Primary Campaign of 1976: Implications for Voters, Candidates and Parties," in William Crotty (ed.), *The Party Symbol: Readings on Political Parties* (San Francisco: W. H. Freeman, 1980), p. 179.

19 Thomas E. Patterson, *The Mass Media Election: How Americans Choose Their President* (New York: Praeger, 1980), p. 44.

20 George Gallup, *The Gallup Poll: Public Opinion, 1972–1977,* Vol. 2 (Wilmington, Del.: Scholarly Resources, 1978), pp. 648, 649.

21 *Christian Science Monitor,* February 20, 1980, p. 1; *Congressional Quarterly Weekly Report,* January 26, 1980, p. 187.

22 Cited in *National Journal,* July 12, 1980, p. 1134.

23 Patterson, *The Mass Media Election,* p. 45.

24 Patterson, *The Mass Media Election,* p. 48; Moore (ed.), *The Campaign for President,* p. 170.

25 Rhodes Cook, "Media Coverage of the 1976 Nominating Process," in Crotty (ed.), *The Party Symbol,* pp. 173, 174; Patterson, *The Mass Media Election,* p. 46.

26 Cook, "Media Coverage of the 1976 Nominating Process," in Crotty (ed.), *The Party Symbol,* pp. 173, 174; Patterson, *The Mass Media Election,* p. 46.

27 Cited in *National Journal,* July 12, 1980, p. 1134.

28 Cited in ibid.

29 Patterson, *The Mass Media Election,* pp. 119, 126.

30 Ibid., pp. 115, 116.

31 Ibid., p. 48.

32 Michael Robinson, "A Statesman Is a Dead Politician: Candidate Images on Network News," in Elie Abel (ed.), *What's News* (San Francisco: Institute for Contemporary Studies, 1981), p. 160.

33 Michael Robinson, with Nancy Conover and Margaret Sheehan, "The Media at Mid-Year: A Bad Year for McLuhanites?," *Public Opinion,* 3 (June/July 1980), p. 42.

34 These qualities included political experience, foresight, understanding of the electorate, clarity of intentions, compassion, trustworthiness, personal appeal, political expediency, control, ability to inspire confidence, tendency toward political extremism, and political conviction.

35 Thomas E. Patterson and Robert McClure, *The Unseeing Eye: The Myth of Television Power in National Elections* (New York: G. P. Putnam's Sons, 1976), pp. 35, 38–40.

36 Ibid., p. 41.

37 Robinson, with Conover and Sheehan, "The Media at Mid-Year: A Bad Year for McLuhanites?," p. 43.

38 Patterson, *The Mass Media Election,* p. 36.

39 C. Anthony Broh, "Horse-Race Journalism: Reporting the Polls in the 1976 Presidential Election, *Public Opinion Quarterly,* 44 (Winter 1980), pp. 515, 516; Witcover, *Marathon,* pp. 598, 601; Patterson, *The Mass Media Election,* p. 36.

40 Michael J. Robinson, "The Media in 1980: Was the Message the Message?," in Austin Ranney (ed.), *The American Elections of 1980)* (Washington, D.C.: American Enterprise Institute, 1981), p. 208.

41 Patterson, *The Mass Media Election,* p. 38.

42 Foley et al. (eds.), *Nominating a President: The Process and the Press,* p. 38.

43 Ibid., p. 76.

44 Patterson and McClure, *The Unseeing Eye,* pp. 49–51, 79–82; for similar findings see Patterson, *The Mass Media Election,* pp. 156, 157.

45 Patterson, *The Mass Media Election,* pp. 86, 98, 156, 157.

46 Doris A. Graber, *Mass Media and American Politics* (Washington, D.C.: Congressional Quarterly Press, 1980), p. 183.

47 Benjamin I. Page, *Choices and Echoes in Presidential Elections: Rational Man and Electoral Democracy* (Chicago: University of Chicago Press, 1978), p. 153.

48 Cited in Jeff Greenfield, *The Real Campaign: How the Media Missed the Story of the 1980 Campaign* (New York: Summit Books), p. 290.

49 Patterson, *The Mass Media Election,* p. 30.

50 Michael Robinson, "Television and American Politics," *The Public Interest,* No. 48 (Summer 1977), p. 15.

51 Ibid., p. 15.

52 Cited in Greenfield, *The Real Campaign,* p. 31.

53 Graber, *Mass Media and American Politics,* p. 161; White, *America in Search of Itself,* p. 166.

54 See, for example, Sidney Blumenthal, *The Permanent Campaign* (Boston: Beacon Press, 1980), pp. 4, 5; Larry J. Sabato, *The Rise of the Political Consultants* (New York: Basic Books, 1981), pp. 143–153; Melvyn H. Bloom, *Public Relations and Presidential Campaigns: A Crisis in Democracy* (New York: Thomas Y. Crowell, 1973), chap. 7.

55 Robert Spero, *The Duping of the American Voter* (New York: Lippincott and Crowell, 1980), p. 3.

56 Harold Mendelsohn and Irving Crespi, *Polls, Television, and the New Politics* (Scranton, Pa.: Chandler, 1970), pp. 251–254.

57 Jack W. Germond and Jules Witcover, *Blue Smoke and Mirrors* (New York: Viking Press, 1981), pp. 198, 212; Joe McGinniss, *The Selling of the President 1968* (New York: Pocket Books, 1970), pp. 30, 31, 104; William Flanigan, *Political Behavior of the American Electorate,* 4th ed. (Boston: Allyn and Bacon, 1979), p. 132; Herbert Alexander, *Financing Politics: Money, Elections and Political Reform* (Washington, D.C.: Congressional Quarterly Press, 1980), p. 11.

58 Cited in Mendelsohn and Crespi, *Polls, Television and the New Politics,* p. 290.

59 Dan Nimmo, *The Political Persuaders: The Techniques of Modern Election Campaigns* (Englewood Cliffs, N.J.: Prentice-Hall, 1970), pp. 168, 169.

60 Elihu Katz and Jacob J. Feldman, "The Debates in the Light of the Research: A Survey of Surveys," in Sidney Kraus (ed.), *The Great Debates* (Bloomington, Ind.: Indiana University Press, 1962), p. 201.

61 Dan Nimmo and Robert L. Savage, *Candidates and Their Images* (Pacific Palisades, Calif.: Goodyear, 1976), p. 17.

62 Joseph T. Klapper, *The Effects of Mass Communication* (New York: The Free Press, 1960), chap. 2–5; Walter Weiss, "Effects of the Mass Media of Communication," in Gardner Lindzey and Elliot Aronson (eds.), *Handbook of Social Psychology,* Vol. V, 2d ed. (Reading, Mass.: Addison-Wesley, 1969), pp. 77–195; Philip E. Converse, "Information Flow and the Stability of Partisan Attitudes," *Public Opinion Quarterly,* 26 (Winter 1962), pp. 578–599.

63 John Kessel, *Presidential Campaign Politics: Coalition Strategies and Citizen Response* (Homewood, Ill.: Dorsey Press, 1980), p. 224.

64 Drury R. Sherrod, "Selective Perception of Political Candidates," *Public Opinion Quarterly,* 35 (Winter 1971–1972), pp. 554–562; Patterson, *The Mass Media Election,* pp. 77–84, 86–91; David O. Sears and Johnathan L. Freedman, "Selective Exposure to Information: A Critical Review," *Public Opinion Quarterly,* 31 (Summer 1967), pp. 194–213.

65 C. Richard Hofstetter, Cliff Zukin, and Terry F. Buss, "Political Imagery in an Age of Television: The 1972 Campaign." (Prepared for delivery at the Annual Meeting of the American Political Science Association, Chicago, September 2–5, 1976), p. 25.

66 Patterson and McClure, *The Unseeing Eye,* p. 113.

67 Ibid., pp. 133–136.

68 Walter DeVries and V. Lance Tarrance, *The Ticket-Splitter: A New Force in American Politics* (Grand Rapids, Mich.: William B. Eerdmans, 1972), pp. 61, 74, 77, 78.

69 James M. Perry, *The New Politics: The Expanding Technology of Political Manipulation* (New York: Clarkson N. Potter, 1968), pp. 213, 214.

70 Michael Robinson reports that an unpublished study on the influence of the media in four 1980 primaries (New Hampshire, Massachusetts, New York, Connecticut) and the Iowa caucus "found little evidence that they (the ads) influenced the votes of anyone." See Robinson, "The Media in 1980: Was the Message the Message?," p. 183.

71 Cited in Patterson and McClure, *The Unseeing Eye,* p. 109.

72 Cited in Foley et al. (eds.), *Nominating a President: The Process and the Press,* p. 57.

73 Patterson and McClure, *The Unseeing Eye,* pp. 103, 104.

74 Greenfield, *The Real Campaign,* p. 248.

75 Patterson and McClure, *The Unseeing Eye,* p. 117; Hofstetter et al., "Political Imagery in an Age of Television: The 1972 Campaign," p. 11; Charles Atkin et al., "Quality versus Quantity in Televised Political Ads," *Public Opinion Quarterly,* 37 (Summer 1973), p. 223.

76 Greenfield, *The Real Campaign,* pp. 136, 137, 249, 254; Robinson, "A Statesman Is a Dead Politician: Candidate Images on Network News," p. 167.

77 See Evron M. Kirkpatrick, "Presidential Candidate 'Debates': What Can We Learn from 1960?," pp. 1–50; Nelson W. Polsby, "Debatable Thoughts on Presidential Debates," pp. 175–186; both in Austin Ranney (ed.), *The Past and Future of Presidential Debates* (Washington, D.C.: American Enterprise Institute, 1979).

78 Katz and Feldman, "The Debates in the Light of the Research: A Survey of Surveys," pp. 200–205.

79 Steven H. Chaffee and Jack Dennis, "Presidential Debates: An Empirical Assessment," in Austin Ranney (ed.), *The Past and Future of Presidential Debates,* p. 87; see also, Patterson, *The Mass Media Election,* pp. 157, 163, 165.

80 Ibid., p. 88.

81 Jack W. Germond and Jules Witcover, "Presidential Debates: An Overview," in Austin Ranney (ed.), *The Past and Future of Presidential Debates,* p. 202.

82 Chaffee and Dennis, "Presidential Debates: An Empirical Assessment," p. 84.

83 Germond and Witcover, "Presidential Debates: An Overview," pp. 197, 198.

84 James David Barber, *The Pulse of Politics: Electing Presidents in the Media Age* (New York: W. W. Norton, 1980), p. 8.

THE ROLE OF MONEY IN PRESIDENTIAL SELECTION

Apart from his own talents, the volunteers he is able to draw to his cause, and whatever free media coverage he manages to secure, virtually everything else connected with a candidate's quest for the Presidency requires money—staff, consultants, transportation, lodging, headquarters, fund raising, polls, etc. The old saying that "Money is the mother's milk of politics" may have become a hackneyed expression, but it is no less valid for being so.

The role of money in the Presidential selection process has long captured the attention of political observers, with many concluding that it has done more to debilitate the process than to nourish it. Their concerns fall into three major areas: *access, outcomes,* and *influence-buying.* Most would agree that access to the selection process, as well as who ultimately wins, ought to be a function of criteria deemed relevant to executing the office of President. Since personal wealth or connections to wealth have absolutely no bearing on competency to assume the Presidency, they should play no role in the process. To the extent that money does in fact inhibit entry into the race and to the extent that it proves decisive in determining the outcome of the competition, the Presidential selection process may be judged deficient. The third concern generated by money stems not from its impact on the selection of Presidents but rather on what happens afterward. More precisely, those candidates who receive large contributions to finance their campaigns may, once elected, feel special obligations to make policy decisions in the interests of their financial benefactors to the exclusion of the greater public interest.

At various points throughout our history, Congress has attempted to regulate the role of money in the electoral process. That its efforts had not met with much success was apparent as late as 1967 when President Johnson accurately referred to the accumulated legislation as "more loophole than law."[1] Indeed, not until the early seventies did Congress make a serious effort to address this issue. First came the Federal Election Campaign Act and the Revenue Act, both passed in 1971. Three years later, in the aftermath of the Watergate revelations, Congress was moved to enact the most comprehensive campaign finance reforms in our history. Further adjustments in this legislation were to be made in 1976 and, again, in 1979. We have lived under these reforms for two Presidential elections, and it is fair to say that the cure has evoked as much controversy as the disease. Thus, there is every reason to believe that Congress will once again be called on to legislate in this area.

In this chapter, we shall first examine the role of money in Presidential selection prior to the historic reforms in 1974; and second, assess the impact of these reforms on the process and suggest what further changes ought to be contemplated.

MONEY IN PRESIDENTIAL CAMPAIGNS: PRE-1974

Laws and Loopholes

The first mild attempt to deal with money in elections dates back to 1867 when Congress passed a naval appropriations bill stipulating that no naval officer or federal employee could solicit political contributions in the navy yards. Thirteen years later Congress enacted the Civil Service Reform Act. This legislation not only prohibited federal employees from collecting contributions from fellow workers, but also protected all employees of the United States government from being harassed or otherwise punished for declining to give to any candidates' election campaign. Not before the late 1800s, however, did corporate giving become the subject of Congressional attention. Reacting to the huge sums of money that both banks and corporations had given to bankroll William McKinley's first Presidential bid (1896), the muckrakers of the period launched a campaign for election reform. They had a valuable ally in the person of Theodore Roosevelt whose first annual message to Congress stated that "All contributions by corporations to any political committee or for any political purpose should be forbidden by law."[2] Congress responded two years later by passing the Tillman Act (1907), which barred both corporations and banks from contributing to any federal candidate in the general election. The next Congressional foray into the campaign finance area did not come until 1925, when it passed the Federal Corrupt Practices Act. However, although this legislation succeeded in establishing expenditure limits and disclosure requirements for House and Senate candidates, no such restrictions were required for candidates seeking either the Presidency or Vice Presidency. The year 1940 saw Congress for the first time place a limit on individual contributions. In an amendment to the Hatch Act (1939), the legislators prohibited individuals from giving more than $5,000 to any federal candidate or *national* political committee in a single year. Note, however, that state and local committees were exempt from this limitation. This amendment contained two other restrictions as well, namely, individuals or businesses under federal contract were barred from giving to federal candidates and political committees; and political committees operating in two or more states were limited to spending $3 million in a single year.[3] In 1945 Congress decided to bring labor unions under the umbrella of regulation just as it had done for banks and corporations back in 1907 (Tillman Act). Specifically, labor unions were to be prohibited from giving money to any federal candidate or political committee in the *general election*. Two years later the Taft-Hartley Labor Management Act (1947) went one step further by preventing corporations, banks, and labor unions from making contributions at the *nominating* as well as the general election phase of the campaign.[4]

Although these regulations, taken together, may appear to represent a significant assault on the influence of money in the electoral process, in actuality contributors quickly found numerous ways to circumvent their intent. Corporations, for example, began the practice of increasing the expense accounts, salaries, and bonuses of their management employees on the condition that these increases were to be given as campaign contributions. In addition, businesses attempted to skirt the law by placing their goods and services at the disposal of a candidate, including office equipment, airplanes, automobiles, office space, and public relations firms.[5] Political parties provided businesses with yet another surrogate for contributions by inviting them to take out advertisements in party publications—advertisements that sold at prices ranging from $5,000 to $15,000 per page. In 1966 Congress finally sought to curb this practice by instructing the Internal Revenue Service not to permit corporations to deduct these advertisements as legitimate business expenses. Two years later, however, this prohibition was modified to allow such deductions as long as they were associated with the parties' nominating conventions.[6]

Like corporations, labor unions also proved highly adept at finding ways around the prohibition against giving. They merely set up committees—the AFL-CIO's Committee on Political Education (COPE) being a notable example—which were legally separate from their unions. These committees solicited contributions from their union membership. In 1968, for example, thirty-seven labor political committees spent $7.1 million on elections at all levels, and in 1972 thirty-five committees spent more than $14.8 million. It should also be noted here that while labor contributions to candidates cannot come out of union treasuries, educational activities related to elections can. These include registration drives, getting out the vote on election day, and publishing material on candidates' past voting records. Needless to say, given labor's long-standing attachment to the Democratic party, these kinds of activities typically operate to the beneift of Democratic rather than Republican candidates.[7]

The campaign finance regulations not only provided organizations with opportunities to skirt restrictions on contributions, they enabled individuals to do so as well. The $5,000 limit on individual contributions to candidates or political committees was eluded in several ways. For one thing, since this limit applied only to national political committees, individuals could simply give whatever they wanted to state or local committees, which in turn forwarded the money to the candidate's national organization.[8] Candidates also created numerous national political committees, each under a different name, thereby allowing an individual to give up to $5,000 to each one. In 1968, for example, the Humphrey-Muskie campaign created no less than ninety-five such separate committees. Consequently, had an individual availed himself of the opportunity to give the $5,000 maximum to each one, the Humphrey-Muskie campaign would have been the beneficiary of $475,000. Nor were there any provisions in the existing laws to prevent a wealthy individual from giving $5,000 in the name of family members, including children, wife, aunts, and uncles. Finally, of course, if givers made use of all the circumventions noted here, they would be able to inject very large sums indeed into a candidate's campaign war chest. No doubt, it was the use of these loopholes in combination which enabled Mrs. John D. Rockefeller, Jr., to contribute $1,482,625 to Nelson Rockefeller's Presidential bid in 1968, and insurance executive W. Clement Stone to channel $2.8 million into Richard Nixon's 1972 reelection campaign.[9]

The Role of Money: Access and Outcomes

If the laws on the books between 1867 and 1972 provided the opportunity for money to flow freely into Presidential campaigns in sums both large and small, it is far less clear that money alone was sufficient to determine the outcome of general election campaigns. Indeed, from 1900 through 1972 there were nineteen Presidential elections, with the biggest spender winning eleven and losing eight.[10] Moreover, even in those instances when the biggest spender won, we should not necessarily conclude that it was because he enjoyed the advantage of more funds. Consider, for example, the 1972 McGovern/Nixon contest, in which the latter spent $61 million in his quest for a second term. This sum was not only the largest ever recorded for a Presidential candidate, but it also represented a two-to-one advantage over the $31 million spent by McGovern. Substantial though this expenditure gap was, it did not prove to be the key variable in explaining why McGovern failed to carry all but the single state of Massachusetts. For one thing, there is a point at which additional expenditures of money yield diminishing returns, and one suspects that Nixon reached this threshold well before he had spent the last of his $61 million. More important, the evidence suggests that the greatest impediment to George McGovern's election was himself. More precisely, he was closer to the electorate than Nixon on only three of the fourteen major issues in the campaign. Add to this the fact that public reaction to him as a person was so low as to make him "the least popular Democratic presidential candidate of the last twenty years."[11] In short, his issue positions and image were liabilities that no amount of money could overcome.

What of the influence of money at the nominating stage of the Presidential selection process? It has often been asserted that you have to be wealthy to make a run for the Presidency. This generalization oversimplifies a rather complex issue. To be sure, there have in the past been several candidates who enjoyed considerable personal wealth (Stassen, Stevenson, Kennedy, Symington, Rockefeller, Scranton, Romney), but they were the exception rather than the rule. Nor is it likely that these individuals were judged serious contenders merely because they had money. Rather, they were viewed as such because they occupied important, visible positions in our society, and managed to establish records of achievement. No doubt, their wealth and/or social background played an important role in helping them gain these positions.[12]

If personal wealth was not a prerequisite for entering the Presidential sweepstakes, certainly connections to big money was. But even this statement requires some qualification, for several Presidential candidates managed to fuel their nominating campaigns largely from small contributions. In 1964, for example, Barry Goldwater raised $4.5 million, more than any of his opponents, from some 300,000 contributors. In challenging Lyndon Johnson for the Democratic nomination in 1968, Eugene McCarthy managed to secure $11 million. Although $2.5 million came from 50 contributors, the remainder was garnered from 150,000 small contributors. More broad-based still was George Wallace's 1968 nomination campaign which, between February and October, reported raising $6.7 million from 750,000 donors, 85 percent of whom gave $100 or less. In 1972 George McGovern accumulated some $3 million, with most coming from contributions of under $100.[13] Of course, the ability of these candidates to raise substantial sums in small contributions was largely due to the fact that they were appealing to highly committed constituencies on the left or right of the political spectrum. More moderate candidates appeal to more moderate voters who are less intensely committed to the issues, and consequently, are less motivated to give. These candidates, therefore, must rely on more substantial donations from a smaller number of contributors. Thus, in 1968 Nixon raised $8.5 million, with more than one-half of this amount coming from 1,200 contributors; Nelson Rockefeller amassed $1.5 million from only twenty-four individuals and an additional $5.5 million from members of his own family;

and George Romney's short-lived campaign secured 85 percent of its funds from a mere three individuals, one of whom was himself.[14]

While nominees could secure the financial support of their parties in the general election campaign, Presidential contenders had to rely exclusively on their own sources for funds at the nominating stage. Thus, it was during this period that money conferred its greatest advantages. The candidate who was not widely known and lacked access to wealth might experience considerable difficulty in meeting the crucially important start-up costs associated with his campaign. In addition, once the contest was under way, a few poor showings might send a candidate's campaign into a slump. At such times, the flow of money into the coffers typically declines as potential donors become fearful of backing a loser. The candidate with access to money would be in a better position to keep his candidacy afloat, perhaps by injecting his own money into the campaign, or turning to a few wealthy backers, or taking out loans, or all three of these. On the other hand, the candidate who was neither wealthy nor well connected might find his quest for the Presidency quickly terminated. Finally, of course, it should be noted that those with access to wealth have been aided by the fact that to a greater extent than any other resource, money is *convertible;* that is, it can be used to purchase other essential campaign resources such as advertising, staff, polls, office space.

If access to wealth carries with it certain advantages in the nominating process, we should not suppose that money alone is sufficient to ensure victory. Were this the case, the campaigns of such candidates as Rockefeller, Stassen, Symington, and Romney would have met with greater success. Not only did each fail to win his party's nomination, but none of these individuals even attained the status of "front-runner." Far more decisive in determining a contender's prospects for victory were such factors as experience, issue positions, and image. If a candidate was perceived positively on these factors and had wealth besides (for example, John Kennedy), then he was in a very advantageous position indeed. If he was not blessed with a personal fortune but was judged favorably in these other areas (for example, Humphrey, Nixon), he stood a good chance of attracting the necessary financial support. Finally, if he lacked a record of accomplishment, a positive image, and compelling issue positions, money alone could not save him. This reality was once again confirmed by the Presidential candidacy of John Connally in the 1980 election. Although the new campaign finance reforms were already in place by this time, he was exempt from complying with the new spending limits because he decided to finance his campaign exclusively from private sources. Had he opted for the new system of public matching funds, he would have been obliged to abide by the spending limits then in effect. At any rate, his personal wealth and ties into the corporate establishment enabled him to raise and spend the substantial sum of $13.8 million. With the primary season scarcely one month old, however, he was forced to withdraw from the race following a series of poor showings.

Indeed, despite his best efforts, he managed to win the support of only one delegate to the Republican National Convention. Apparently, no amount of spending was able to allay continuing public doubts about his character and personal style.

THE ROLE OF MONEY: INFLUENCE-BUYING

People may decide to contribute to a candidate's campaign for any one of a number of reasons. Some may be motivated by nothing more than a sense of civic responsibility. Others may see a sizable contribution as a means of enhancing their own status in the community; perhaps by being included in a small gathering with the candidate or having him put in an appearance at a social function given by the donor. Still others may decide to give because they believe his overall philosophy will lead to decisions that will benefit them and/or the nation. Contributions may also come from individuals who, although having no specific claim to make on a candidate, nevertheless want to ensure their ready access to him should the need arise. Finally, there are those who may donate substantial sums because they do in fact seek to influence a candidate's position on one or more policy issues. While few would be terribly upset with the first three motives, the fourth and fifth should be a source for concern. Clearly, if big contributions can significantly affect access to public officials, as well as the decisions they make, then those who cannot give, cannot give enough, or choose not to give are all placed at a serious disadvantage in the policy-making process.

That big money may contaminate government decision-making was demonstrated by the irregularities uncovered in connection with Richard Nixon's 1972 reelection campaign. As previously noted, the Nixon campaign had raised some $61 million, the largest sum ever generated for a Presidential campaign, and $51.3 million of which came from individuals giving $10,000 or more:[15]

Item: After the Nixon administration decided *not* to increase price supports for milk in March 1971, milk producers sought and received a meeting with the President. At this meeting, they pledged $2 million to his campaign (ultimately, they gave only $682,500). The President reversed his decision and on March 25 the Department of Agriculture announced that it would *increase* price supports for milk.

Item: Applications by American Airlines for additional and more profitable routes were approved by the government shortly after the company made a substantial and illegal contribution to the Nixon reelection campaign.

Item: Despite a recommendation from a Cabinet task force calling for the abolition of oil import quotas, President Nixon decided in 1970 to retain them. Several oil executives gave a total of $5 million to his campaign.

Item: A construction worker, Calvin Kevens, was convicted and jailed for mail fraud. He contributed $30,000 to the Nixon reelection campaign and was pardoned by the President in January 1972.

Item: After his reelection President Nixon nominated 319 people to federal positions, fifty-two of whom had contributed a total of $703,654 to his campaign. A Nixon aide was ultimately tried and imprisoned, in part, for having promised some of these positions in return for a generous contribution.[16]

The revelations associated with giving in the 1972 election also served notice that the problem of influence-buying is not only one of donors seeking to influence candidates, but also one of candidates attempting to pressure potential donors. Indeed, several of Nixon's key lieutenants, including then Secretary of Commerce Maurice Stans, approached various large corporations and informed them that they were expected to give $100,000. A lesser sum was set for smaller companies. Although some declined these solicitations, many complied. Still others did not even need to be asked. Ultimately, some twenty-one corporations were found guilty and fined for making illegal contributions that totaled approximately $842,500. While it is unclear whether Nixon aides were attempting to extort money from corporations, certainly corporate executives believed this to be the case. In subsequent testimony before Congress, several stated that they felt failure to give would lead to government decisions unfavorable to their companies.[17] At the very least, it can be said that corporate contributors would be favored with special access to the administration. As President Nixon's personal lawyer later testified, "[I]n return for that ($100,000) contribution it would be possible for me to arrange for several appointments with various people within the White House."[18]

THE MOVEMENT TOWARD REFORM

Although the transgressions just described, and more, would prove to be the catalyst for realizing the most comprehensive campaign finance reforms in our history, Congress had begun to act even before this. The momentum for legislation of some sort had been building ever so gradually over the previous ten-year period. In 1961 President Kennedy established the Commission on Campaign Costs and, based on its recommendations, submitted five reform proposals to Congress. President Johnson also moved in this area placing before Congress his own election reforms in May 1967. Although neither President's recommendations were enacted into law, their efforts had served to elevate the level of awareness regarding the role of money in campaigns. Circumstances surrounding the elections of 1968 and 1970 gave a further boost to reform efforts. More specifically, campaign costs for media had skyrocketed and a growing number of wealthy candidates were challenging incumbents. Sensing their vulnerability to well-heeled challengers who could afford to bankroll an expensive media campaign, Congressional incumbents felt additional pressure to make changes.[19] Accordingly, in 1971 legislators enacted the Revenue Act, which provided for government financing of Presidential general election campaigns. Shortly thereafter, Congress passed the Federal Election Campaign Act (FECA). It established new disclosure requirements, limits on media spending, and limits on how much of their own money candidates could spend on their campaigns. The major provisions of each act are outlined below:

Revenue Act:

• Allowed a tax credit of $12.50 ($25 for a married couple) or deduction of $50 ($100 for married couple) for political contributions to candidates running for federal, state, or local office. (In 1978 the tax credit was raised to $50 and the tax deduction was eliminated.)

• Provided taxpayers with option of contributing $1 of their taxes to a Presidential general election fund.

• Money from the general election fund was to be distributed equally to each major party nominee based on a formula of 15 cents times the number of United States citizens eighteen years or older. (Formula was subsequently changed to $20 million plus adjustments for inflation.)

• No Presidential nominee who chose to finance his campaign from the general election fund could receive any private contributions.

• Minor parties could qualify for money from the general election fund if their candidates had received at least 5 percent of the vote in the previous Presidential election.

Federal Election Campaign Act:

• A Presidential candidate and his family could each give no more than $50,000 to his campaign. (Primaries and general election counted as separate campaigns.)

• Presidential candidates were limited to spending no more than 10 cents times the number of eligible voters on mass media advertising (that is, radio, newspapers, billboards, television, magazines).

• Any candidate or political committee in a federal election campaign was required to file quarterly spending and receipt reports, noting all contributions of $100 or more, as well as the name, place of business, and address of the contributors. In an election year additional reports were required fifteen and five days before the election. Any contribution of $5,000 or more recieved after the final report had to be reported within 48 hours.

• Reporting requirements applied to primaries, runoffs, conventions, and general elections. For Presidential candidates reports were to be submitted to the comptroller general.

The Revenue Act, it should be noted, did not take effect until 1976. President Nixon insisted on delaying the implementation as a condition for signing the bill into law. No doubt, he did not want to provide his Democratic opponent with the opportunity to finance his campaign from public funds. The FECA, however, did take effect in time for the 1972 Presidential campaign. Clearly its most significant changes proved to be in the disclosure area, for candidates were not only required to make more frequent and detailed reports, but they had to do so at all stages of the Presidential selection process. The Act was not without its limitations, however. For one thing, the amount of information generated by the disclosure requirements was so voluminous that it could not be carefully examined and released in a timely fashion. Fortunately, the public interest group Common Cause came to the rescue. At an expense of $250,000 and thousands of hours of volunteer work from its members, the organization went over the disclosure reports and presented summary findings to the press. Second, the prosecution of violators was hampered by the fact that only one Justice Department lawyer was given full-time responsibility in this area.[20] Third, although the amount of money spent on media at the Presidential level was approximately one-half the 1968 level ($20.3 million), it is less clear that the FECA was instrumental in bringing about this decline. As two students of the subject have pointed out, "The media rate reductions helped lower costs. So did prevailing doubts about the effectiveness of saturation radio and television advertising in 1972."[21] Finally, for those who hoped that more stringent disclosure requirements would serve to discourage large contributions, the Act proved to be a disappointment. Of the $43.3 million raised by the Nixon campaign after the FECA took effect on April 7, 1972, $4.4 million was given by no more than thirty-seven contributors each donating $50,000 or more. Incidentally, prior to April, the Nixon forces had already raised $19.9 million, $12.4 million of which came from eighty-seven contributors.[22]

In 1973–1974 both the Congress and the Justice Department conducted extensive investigations into the 1972 Presidential election campaign. Based on these inquiries, along with information gained from the new disclosure requirements, it became apparent that: the Committee to Re-Elect the President (CREEP) had been the recipient of large sums of money from a small group of individuals; administration officials had, in some instances, promised favors in return for sizable donations; many corporations had contributed to the campaign illegally; and, finally, some money raised for the Nixon reelection campaign had been used to finance political espionage activities, including the break-in at the Democratic party national headquarters and the use of assorted "dirty tricks" against Democratic Presidential candidates. Indeed, had it not been for the fact that CREEP had so much money to spend, these espionage activities might never have been undertaken in the first place. In any event, this veritable waterfall of abuses convinced Congress and the public that more stringent campaign finance regulations were necessary.

In 1974 Congress acted by passing several amendments to the FECA of 1971. Although the details of these reforms will be outlined later, their major dimensions included (1) *contribution limits:* limits were placed on how much individuals and groups could give directly to candidates, how much individuals could spend on behalf of candidates, and how much candidates could spend on their own campaigns; (2) *public financing:* candidates were given the option of financing part of their nomination campaign through a system of public matching funds; (3) *spending limits:* overall spending limits were established both for nomination and general election campaigns; (4) *disclosure:* candidates were required to establish a central campaign committee and periodically disclose receipts and expenditures; (5) *enforcement:* a Federal Election Commission was created to supervise, interpret, and enforce campaign finance regulations. It is fair to say that these reforms taken together constituted the most ambitious attempt ever made by Congress to control the influence of money on elections.

Enter the Court: *Buckley v. Valeo*

Opposition to these latest charges was not long in coming, however. A group of otherwise improbable allies (conservative Senator James Buckley, liberal Eugene McCarthy, New York Conservative party, New York Civil Liberties Union, Libertarian party, Mississippi Republican party) joined to file suit charging that these new regulations severely restricted freedom of expression. The case of *Buckley v. Valeo* ultimately came before the Supreme Court, which rendered its decision on January 2, 1976. With respect to limits imposed on contributions given *directly* to the candidates, the Court saw no significant infringement on free speech because "the transformation of contributions into political debate involves speech by someone other than the contributor."[23] On the other hand, the judges did strike down the limitation on how much an individual could spend *on behalf of* a candidate (for example, taking out a newspaper advertisement). Such activity constituted a legitimate exercise of free speech as long as it was not *coordinated* with the candidate on whose behalf it was being spent. Also struck down as an abridgment of free speech was the limit on how much of their *own* money candidates could spend on their campaign. According to the Court, the government could impose this limit only on candidates who chose to finance their campaigns with public funds. As for the overall spending limits established at the nominating and general election stages, the Court ruled that these violated the first amendment also: "A restriction on the amount of money a person or group can spend on political communication during a campaign necessarily reduces the quantity of expression by restricting the number of issues discussed, the depth of their exploration, and the size of the audience reached."[24] At the same time, however, the judges went on to note that government could impose such expenditure limits on those candidates who chose to finance their campaigns with public funds. Finally, although the Court upheld the concept of a Federal Election Commission, it ruled that the method of appointment to this body violated the separation of powers. Under the 1974 reforms, the Commission was to consist of eight members, two appointed by the President, two by the House, two by the Senate. In addition, the Secretary of the Senate and the Clerk of the House of Representatives were to serve as *ex officio* nonvoting members. However, since the commission would be exercising executive powers, the Court ruled that Congress could not participate in nominating the members.

Congress amended the reforms in 1976 and, again, in 1979. This was done to bring the new regulations into compliance with the Supreme Court ruling and also to make additional adjustments that Congress thought necessary. These changes are incorporated into the major provisions of the 1974 reforms outlined in an appendix to this chapter (see pp. 101–104).

ASSESSING THE REFORMS

Fundamental changes rarely command universal support and the campaign finance reforms have proved no exception. For some critics, the objections are philosophical in nature; that is, they are in principle opposed to one or more of the various approaches incorporated into the reforms (disclosure, contribution limits, spending limits, public financing). For most, however, their concerns lie not with the approaches themselves, but rather with how they have been implemented. We shall now consider these criticisms in greater detail.

Disclosure

There is general agreement among those associated with Presidential campaigns that the disclosure provisions work reasonably well.[25] To be sure, following the 1976 election there were numerous complaints that some of the information required was both unnecessary and needlessly time-consuming. Congress, however, remedied most of the problem when it amended the FECA in 1979. These changes included raising from $100 to $200 the threshold for reporting names of contributors; increasing the threshold for reporting independent expenditures from $100 to $250; raising from $100 to $200 the threshold requirement for itemizing expenditures; and reducing from eleven to six the categories of information required on registration statements filed by political committees.

Some, however, continue to find the disclosure requirement offensive on the ground that it intrudes on the individual's right to privacy. Independent and third-party candidates in particular charge that this reform has discouraged people from contributing to their campaigns. Eugene McCarthy, for example, maintains that as soon as the press began to point out how his 1976 Presidential candidacy might influence the outcome of the election "we found people who said they would like to contribute but could not go on record."[26] Parties falling outside the political mainstream (for example, Socialist Workers party) have likewise charged that disclosure deters financial support for their candidates.[27] Although the Supreme Court argued (*Buckley v. Valeo*, 1976) that the benefits of disclosure outweighed possible threats to individual privacy, it was not unmindful of the problem this regulation might pose for third-party candidates. Indeed, the judges noted that minor parties might be entitled to some flexibility in meeting this requirement if they could show "a reasonable probability that the compelled disclosure of a party's contributors' names will subject them to threats, harassment or reprisals from either government officials or private parties."[28] In a ruling handed down in December 1982 *(Brown v. Socialist Workers '74 Campaign Committee)*, the Supreme Court found that the Socialist Workers party had made such a showing. Pointing to the FBI's "massive" campaign to disrupt the party in the sixties and seventies, the judges concluded that it was entitled to conceal both its contributors and expenditures.[28a]

Limits on Contributions

Under the new regulations, individuals may give no more than $1,000 per election (nomination and general election campaigns are treated as separate elections) directly to a Presidential candidate, and no more than $5,000 to a political committee. Political action committees (PACs), on the other hand, may give up to $5,000 to a candidate. Most would acknowledge that these changes have terminated the ability of individual "fat cats" to exert leverage through huge contributions given *directly* to Presidential contenders. Speaking to this point in November 1975, one prominent journalist noted that "When Jimmy Carter takes the oath next January, his situation will differ from that of other recent newly elected Presidents in one interesting respect: He will not be obligated to a single large campaign contributor."[29] Even PACs, which can give a more sizable contribution than individuals, have had only a modest impact on campaign war chests. In 1980 PAC money constituted no more than 3 percent of the funds raised by a Presidential contender. (This figure is in sharp contrast to Congressional elections in which PAC money represents one-fourth of all the money spent by candidates.)[30] Moreover, to avoid alienating a prospective President, PACs typically withhold most of their contributions until it becomes clear who is going to win. Thus, although Jimmy Carter had received only a single PAC contribution during the first six months of 1975, by June 1976 he had accumulated $200,000 in donations from PACs. Similarly, whereas Reagan had garnered only $30,000 in PAC contributions by the end of February 1980, by convention time he had become the recipient of more than a quarter of a million dollars from these sources.[31]

There are those, however, who oppose the very idea of singling out money for regulation in the Presidential selection process.[32] A doctor, for example, may be too busy to devote his time and energy to a candidate's campaign, and consequently, may choose to show his support by making a sizable contribution. On the other hand, a college professor may lack the money but does have the time and, perhaps, the expertise to place at the disposal of a candidate. Since both obviously constitute a contribution, why should one be restricted, and the other not? Three reasons come immediately to mind. For one thing, unlike other resources, money is easily quantifiable and therefore more susceptible to being regulated. More important, as a campaign asset money carries a special advantage because it can be converted into other resources more easily than other resources can be transformed into money. Finally, as noted earlier, the motivation behind giving may be to buy influence. Since money is easily quantifiable, a candidate can readily assess its significance as a contribution. The giving of one's time and expertise may well have the same motivation, but its import is not so easily calculated by a candidate and thus its ability to buy influence will likely be more problematic.

The more pervasive and compelling criticism of the contribution limits is directed not at the principle of limitation itself but rather at the excessively low ceiling placed on individual contributions. Bear in mind that while Congress allowed overall spending limits to be adjusted for cost-of-living increases, it made no such provision for the $1,000 contribution limit. Adjusted for the rate of inflation, a $1,000 contribution in 1980 had the buying power of $641 in 1975, when the law went into effect. To make matters worse, the cost of goods and services associated with campaigning (for example, travel, advertising, polling) has accelerated at an even faster rate than the Commerce Department's market basket of consumer goods.[33] Complicating the problem still further has been the increase in the number of primaries, a delegate selection method requiring a much greater outlay of funds than the caucus-convention process. In 1976, for example, primary spending by candidates outdistanced caucus spending by a margin of five to one.[34] In short, the $1,000 contribution limit meant that candidates running in 1980 were able to raise less money at a time when the increase in inflation and primaries necessitated more.

Gone are the days when a candidate could, as Muskie did in 1972, get his campaign off the ground by raising $600,000 from a mere forty contributors, each giving between $50,000 and $100,000.[35] On the contrary, the contribution limit now forces candidates to devote far more time to raising money, thereby restricting their opportunities to meet and persuade voters. As one campaign official put it, "Now you talk to a person to raise $250 the same amount of time that you talked to a person who gave you $50,000 or $100,000 in the past. That's not very cost effective."[36] Moreover, given the investment of time demanded for fund raising, candidates are virtually compelled to begin their campaigns much sooner. Note, for example, that five prospective candidates for the 1984 race had established exploratory committees well before the 1982 midterm election had even taken place.[37] Such a development is unfortunate, for not only does it further extend an already lengthy nominating period, but it forces a President to turn his attention to reelection sooner as well.

In addition to more time, the stringent contribution limit has had the ironic effect of requiring candidates to spend more money to raise money. They must now make a broad-based appeal to voters which necessitates expensive mass mailings and the hiring of consultants with expertise in this approach to fund raising. According to one Reagan campaign operative, it took one dollar to raise four in the 1980 Presidential election.[38]

Finally, the burden of generating funds under the new limit has encouraged "creative" efforts to circumvent the spirit if not the letter of the law. One of these, the "candidate political action committee," originated with Reagan campaign officials who in 1977 organized a group known as the Citizens for the Republic. Several other Republican candidates soon followed suit. Ostensibly, the purpose of this committee was to raise money that would be used to support Republican candidates running in 1978. By the end of 1978 the committee had spent $4.5 million but, interestingly enough, only $615,385 went to financing the candidacies of approximately 400 Republicans. Most of the remainder went to pay for Reagan's travels to twenty-six states, where he campaigned for Republican candidates. Needless to say, these travels also provided Reagan with an excellent opportunity to promote his own upcoming Presidential candidacy. Moreover, since the $1,000 individual contribution limit applies only to money given directly to a Presidential candidate's campaign committee, the establishment of a separate candidate PAC enabled Reagan forces to solicit *individual* contributions of up to $5,000.[39] Nor should it come as any surprise that several 1984 Presidential hopefuls availed themselves of the candidate PAC opportunity.

The "draft committee" constitutes another vehicle for advancing Presidential candidacies outside of contribution restrictions. First employed in the 1980 election, nine of these committees were organized for the purpose of encouraging Senator Edward Kennedy to seek the Presidential nomination. The political arm of the International Association of Machinists gave a total of $30,000 toward the draft Kennedy effort, thereby precipitating a complaint from the Carter forces that the union's PAC had violated the $5,000 contribution limit. After failing to persuade the union to hand over its records for inspection, the Federal Election Commission took the PAC to court. Unfortunately for the FEC, the judge for the U. S. Circuit Court of Appeals (District of Columbia) ruled that since the campaign finance regulations made no mention of "draft committees," the FEC had no jurisdiction over them. Although the case was appealed to the Supreme Court, the judges decided not to review it. Thus, it appears that draft committees will be free to raise as much as they want, without their contributors being subject to either the $1,000 individual contribution limit or the $5,000 PAC limit.[40]

In summary, the criticisms outlined above are not meant to argue that there should be no limit on individual contributions. Such a course of action would only serve to reintroduce the problem of influence-buying into the Presidential selection process. Rather, they are to suggest that the current $1,000 ceiling ought to be raised. In 1980 a contribution of $1,000 constituted only 0.0005 percent of Carter's campaign treasury, 0.004 percent of Reagan's, and less than one-tenth of 1 percent of the modest $1.6 million raised by Dole in his brief foray into the Presidential sweepstakes.[41] Thus, the ceiling could realistically be tripled or even quadrupled without fear that candidates would become beholden to donors. Indeed, one can plausibly argue that since PACs are currently free to give up to $5,000 to a candidate, an individual citizen should not be subjected to a more stringent limitation.

Spending Limits

Those who choose to finance their nomination and general election campaigns solely from *private* contributions face no spending limits at either stage in the Presidential selection process. On the other hand, those who opt for public funding at the nominating stage must abide by state spending limits and also may spend no more than $14,720,000 (in 1980) on their nominating campaign (plus an additional 20 percent of this sum for fund raising and an unlimited amount on compliance costs). At the general election stage, each major party's nominee can spend no more than the $29.4 million (in 1980) flat sum given him in public funds. (No private individual or group contributions are allowed.) Although intended to prevent one candidate from overwhelming another, our experience with these limits suggests that they have been a mixed blessing.

Let us look first at the *state spending limits* imposed at the nominating stage. Each state's limit is 16 cents multiplied by its voting age population, with adjustments for inflation. Unfortunately, these limits overlook the fact that not all states are created equal in the nominating process. Some state contests may prove to be of greater strategic importance than others because of who is entered, as well as when and where they occur. Nor do the limits differentiate between caucus-convention and primary states, even though candidates typically spend more in the latter than the former by a margin of five to one. The failure to take these factors into account led to some ludicrous equalities in 1980. New Hampshire's state spending limit, for example, was $264,000, the same as that for the United States territory of Guam, with its caucus-convention system.[42] This despite the fact that New Hampshire was a primary state and an enormously important one at that. To avoid exceeding the low spending limit in the granite state, candidates were forced to spend the night across the border in Massachusetts and purchase television time from Boston channels also airing in New Hampshire.

There are also grounds for believing that the Presidential selection process has not been well served by the overall *prenomination spending limit*. While the law does provide for adjusting this ceiling to inflation, many campaign activities have risen at a more rapid rate than the average increase in cost of living. To be specific, although the latter rose by some 40 percent between 1976 and 1980, such big ticket items as mass mailings, television commercials, and air travel jumped 50, 100, and 300 percent, respectively.[43] Nor does the overall spending ceiling take into account the increase in the number of primaries or the 7.3 percent growth in the voting age population during this period. Indeed, given the impact of all these considerations on the costs of campaigning, a Harvard study group concluded that the spending limit in 1980 ought to have been 45 percent higher than it was.[44] The absence of a more realistic (that is, higher) ceiling in 1980 caused some candidates to approach the spending limit so early that they did not have sufficient funds to campaign effectively in the later primaries. Consider the case of Ronald Reagan. By December 1975 he had spent only 6 percent of the limit, whereas by this time in 1979 he had already spent one-third. Likewise, as of the end of March 1976 he had reached 40 percent of the allowable ceiling. On the other hand, by this point in 1980, with only one-third of the delegates chosen, he had already spent up to three-fourths of the limit. Nor was Reagan unique in this regard, for by the end of March 1980 Carter had reached 62 percent of the limit and Bush 66 percent. These figures contrast sharply with the 1976 nominating race, when no candidate had even reached the 50 percent mark until the end of April.[45]

The current low spending ceiling at the nominating stage has had two negative consequences for the Presidential selection process. First, during the May and June contests, which account for 49 percent of the delegates and 53 percent of the primary electorate, candidates cannot campaign as effectively as they can in the earlier contests. Second, with so much money being spent at the front of the primary season, these early contests, which are already too important, become even more so. For candidates must now generate enough early momentum to carry them through the later primaries, when they no longer have the money to spend.

We come finally to the *general election spending limit* consisting of the lump sum of public funds given to each major party nominee. In 1976 this amount came to $21.8 million. That neither the Carter nor Ford campaigns viewed this as an overly generous sum was indicated by their determination to keep tight control over the money. Most was spent where they thought it would have the greatest impact, namely, on media. Fearing that it might be squandered, almost no funds were channeled into state and local campaign organizations for purposes of generating voter enthusiasm at the grass roots level. As a result, scarcely in evidence were the posters, bumper stickers, buttons, and the like, all of which had been so much a part of previous Presidential elections. Nor could state and local parties take up the slack, for the 1974 FECA amendments limited them to spending $1,000 each. Although the national committee of each major party was allowed to spend up to $3.2 million on behalf of its nominee, as it turned out neither party reached the allowable amount. The Republican party, a bit gun-shy in the aftermath of Watergate, spent approximately $1 million and the Democrats $2.8 million. Concerned about the lack of grass roots activity in the Ford/Carter contest, Congress in 1979 amended the FECA to allow state and local party groups to spend unlimited amounts of money for registration drives, get out the vote campaign, bumper stickers, buttons, and the like.[46]

Reflecting the rise in the consumer price index, the sum of public funds awarded to each nominee in 1980 rose to $29.4 million. As already noted in discussing other spending limits, however, this increase did not take into account the greater than average rise in campaign-related activities, nor the 7.3 percent growth in the voting age population between 1976 and 1980. Based on this latter factor alone, one study concluded that the flat sum for each candidate ought to have been increased by an additional 10 percent.[47] Fortunately, the parties were able to provide greater assistance in 1980 than in 1976. Each national party committee raised and spent up to its allowable limit of $4.6 million. Moreover, if one adds to this figure the money spent by state and local party organizations on grass roots activities, the Democratic and Republican parties' total expenditures came to $6.4 and $13.5 million, respectively. While these figures reveal a two-to-one advantage for the Republican party, we should bear in mind that the Democratic party benefits from substantial sums spent by organized labor in registration and get-out-the-vote drives. In 1980, this sum was estimated at $15 million.[48]

In sum, the evidence presented here suggests that spending limits for both the nomination and general election periods should, at the very least, be significantly increased. Beyond this, Congress might also consider whether it might be desirable to abolish these ceilings altogether. At the general election stage, this would mean continuing the lump sum of public funds granted to each candidate, but also allowing it to be supplemented with individual contributions of up to $1,000 or $2,000. Removing these limits deserves serious consideration for several reasons. For one thing, most students of campaign financing agree that it is impossible to determine how much money is enough to wage an effective campaign. Second, spending limits may serve to curb freedom of expression in a process that ought to be encouraging it. Should a candidate reach his spending limit, his ability to communicate with the voters is inhibited, as is their ability to express their support to him through a direct contribution.

Finally, eliminating spending limits might serve to reduce the growing amount of money now being spent *on behalf of* candidates, money that has not always been spent in the most responsible manner and over which the candidates and their parties have no control.

Public Financing

The campaign finance reforms provide Presidential candidates with the option of drawing on public funds at both the nominating and general election stage. We have already discussed the flat sum given Presidential nominees for the general election campaign. Thus far, all nominees have accepted these funds. The awarding of matching public funds at the nominating stage is a bit more complicated. To qualify, a candidate must raise $5,000 in each of twenty states, in contributions no larger than $250. After qualifying, the federal government will then match the first $250 of any *individual* contribution (PAC donations are not matchable), but the total amount of matching funds received by a candidate cannot exceed one-half of the overall spending limit at the nominating stage ($14,720,000 in 1980). The public funds awarded at both stages of the Presidential selection process are raised through a tax checkoff plan (Revenue Act, 1971) whereby taxpayers may designate one dollar of their taxes for a general fund. Although only 7 percent of the taxpayers used the checkoff in 1972, over the last five years anywhere from 25 to 28 percent have done so.[49] This rate of participation has generated more than enough funds to implement public financing in the last two Presidential elections.

As one might expect, public financing of elections has not escaped criticism. Some, for example, object to the fact that a dollar contributed by a taxpayer may go to finance the candidacy of someone he or she may not support.[50] This problem is scarcely unique to the public financing of elections, however. One can safely assume that most taxpayers have at one time or another seen their taxes used for purposes they opposed, be it wars, social programs, foreign aid, weapons, or salary increases. Moreover, tax-paying citizens are well aware that their dollar will be used to finance all candidates opting for public funds. If such a prospect offends them, they are free to withhold their dollar. That more than one-fourth of the taxpayers have used the checkoff suggests their willingness to support a process as opposed to a preferred candidate.

It is also argued that matching funds at the nominating stage, far from alleviating the disparities in funds among competing candidates, actually accentuates them.[51] Candidate *A*, for example, may raise $20,000 in matchable funds during a given period, whereas candidate *B* raises $40,000. Once both sums are matched, candidate *A* has $40,000 and candidate *B*, $80,000. Thus, the matching principle serves to double the money gap between them. Although this criticism is not without merit, we should bear in mind that the matching provision was not intended to equalize money among competing candidates. Rather, its purpose was to bolster the candidate with limited funds to the point at which he could get his views heard—a point that might not even be reached in the absence of matching funds.

Others regard the matching provision as pernicious on the ground that it enables the moneyed to allocate more public funds than the unmoneyed.[52] Although only the first $250 of a contribution is matchable, the fact of the matter is that most people cannot afford to give even this much to a campaign. Those who can, however, have their $250 contribution doubled to $500, while small givers of $5 have their donation doubled to only $10. Furthermore, under the current system, a candidate with a substantially greater number of contributors than his opponent may nevertheless end up receiving considerably less in matching funds. In 1976, for example, 97,764 people gave to Morris Udall's nomination campaign, whereas only 94,419 donated to Carter's. However, since Carter's average contribution was $41.09 and Udall's only $21.84, the Georgian ended up receiving $3,465,584 in matching funds, and Udall received the considerably smaller sum of $1,898,686.[53]

In responding to these apparent inequities, several points are worth noting. First, even though the more well off are able to allocate a greater amount of public funds, the disparities that occur between a large ($250) and a small ($10) matchable contribution are far less than the gaps between large and small contributions which existed prior to the reforms. Second, with the current $1,000 limit on individual donations, candidates must be able to secure funds from some other source. If the current matching ceiling of $250 were dramatically reduced so as to minimize disparities in contributors' matching power, candidates would be hard pressed to raise enough funds. Third, the most commonly discussed alternative to matching funds, the voucher system, is not free of drawbacks either. Under this system, proposed by the late Senator Lee Metcalf, taxpayers who so indicated on their tax forms would receive one dollar of their taxes in the form of a voucher. They could then mail this voucher to the candidate of their choice, who in turn would redeem it at the federal treasury. Unlike the matching funds system, this proposal would ensure that each individual's contribution would be equal. Moreover, a candidate's financial support would probably be a more accurate reflection of his current support in the population. On the other hand, this plan would make a candidate's finances even more dependent on taxpayer initiative. The taxpayer, after all, would then be responsible for holding onto the voucher and mailing it. Under the existing matching funds system, however, the taxpayer need do no more than place a check in a box on the tax form. The government takes over from there. We may also anticipate that large organizations would attempt to pool the vouchers of their membership in order to exert leverage over the candidates. Finally, and most important, since money would go to the candidate who had the most support, the little known candidate in all likelihood would not generate enough money to secure a hearing. Indeed, under this plan, the gaps in funding among competing candidates would be even more pronounced than they are now.[54]

Major and Minor Parties

Under the campaign finance reforms, the lump sum of public funds ($29.4 million in 1980) for the general election campaign is given directly to each nominee and not to his party. Some feel this arrangement reduces party leverage over the candidates and encourages them to set up their own campaign organizations, thereby largely ignoring party structures.[55] The net result of all this is a further weakening of our parties.

Few would challenge the claim that our political parties are weaker today than they were fifteen or twenty years ago. At the same time, however, one suspects that bypassing parties as the distribution agency for public funds has had only a marginal impact on this erosion. Far more significant have been such factors as mass education, television, rule changes in the nominating process, and public cynicism. Moreover, apart from having no role in allocating public funds, our major parties otherwise enjoy a rather privileged position in the campaign finance reforms: (1) only the nominees of the two major parties are guaranteed public funding at the general election stage; (2) whereas individuals may give no more than $1,000 to a candidate and $5,000 to a PAC, they are entitled to contribute up to $20,000 to the national committee of a political party; (3) each major party is given $3 million in public funds to finance its nominating convention; (4) local party organizations may spend unlimited amounts of money on grass roots activity such as registration and get-out-the-vote drives; (5) and political parties are granted a postal subsidy.

The treatment of minor parties and independent candidates (not affiliated with any party) is quite another matter, however. Indeed, here it may be argued that the campaign finance reforms are at once both too harsh and too generous toward candidates not affiliated with one of the two major parties. Let us first consider the excessive burden imposed on them.

Although nonmajor party candidates are required to comply with contribution limits and disclosure requirements, they are not necessarily assured of public funding during the general election campaign. Rather, the law stipulates that minor party candidates may receive public funding (in proportion to their percentage of the popular vote) if they were on the ballot in at least *ten states* in the *preceding* Presidential election and managed to garner at least *5 percent* of the vote. If a third-party candidate is on the ballot for the *first* time, however, he cannot receive public funds until *after* the election, and only if he polled at least 5 percent of the vote. Although the 5 percent threshold does not seem unreasonable—since 1832 ten third-party candidates have exceeded this minimum[56]—the time at which a *new* third-party candidate receives public funding clearly is. Quite obviously, public funds provide little help to a new third-party candidate if he cannot secure them until after the election is over. John Anderson's Presidential candidacy may serve to illustrate the problem.

The only nonmajor party candidate to qualify for public funding subsequent to the reforms, Anderson ran as an independent candidate in 1980 and managed to receive 6.6 percent of the popular vote. This percentage converted to $4,242,304 million in public funds, which he did not receive until *after* the election. During the election campaign itself, Anderson succeeded in raising $9.6 million and an additional $2 million in loans from contributors.[57] While this total of $11.6 million represented more money than had ever been raised by a nonmajor party candidate, it must be viewed in the context of several considerations. In the first place his success in raising this much is explainable primarily by the fact that his views were well within the political mainstream. More extreme independent candidates would probably be hard pressed even to approach this amount. Second, as an independent candidate, he encountered obstacles that drained off a large portion of this money. Unlike Carter and Reagan who did not have to spend any money or energy on fund raising, Anderson had to commit $3 million and much of his time to this task. Moreover, he had to expend an additional $2 million in his drive to get on the ballot in all fifty states. Most of what was left went into operating costs (for example, headquarters, travel, staff salaries), leaving him about $2 million for media advertising. In contrast with this modest sum, Reagan and Carter each spent approximately $20 million of his $29.4 million in public funds on television advertising.[58] Clearly, Anderson needed his $4.2 million public grant during the campaign, not after.

If the campaign finance reforms are in some ways unduly harsh on third-party candidates, it may also be said that in other respects they are not demanding enough. Note that the law says these candidates are eligible for public funding if they received at least 5 percent of the vote in the previous Presidential election. Let us suppose that a third-party candidate running for President in 1980 received 10 percent of the vote. This means that in 1984 his party would be entitled to approximately $6.5 million in public money. This despite the fact that support for the candidate and his party might have completely dissipated during the intervening four years, a fate not uncommon to third parties. The current law, then, could well serve to sustain third parties beyond their natural life-span and thus promote candidacies which are essentially frivolous.

One may also question whether the standards for determining third-party status are sufficiently rigorous. In 1980, for example, the FEC ruled that John Anderson was eligible for public funding because he constituted the "functional equivalent of a party."[59] But no convention of any kind nominated him. Nor were there candidates running for other positions at the national, state, or local level under the Anderson banner. Moreover, if he was truly the "functional equivalent of a party," he should have been eligible to receive contributions of up to $20,000 from individuals and up to $15,000 from political committees (see Appendix, IA, IB). As a matter of fact, Anderson made precisely this argument before the FEC and was turned down.

Third parties may function as a constructive force in American politics by drawing attention to issues overlooked by the two major parties. Indeed, some third parties have set forth platforms that proved to be well ahead of their time. In 1912, for example, the Bull Moose party called for a minimum wage, women's suffrage, and occupational health and safety standards. Likewise, in 1948 the Progressive party advocated negotiations with the Soviet Union, repeal of the draft, national health insurance, and the right to vote at eighteen. In order that *new* minor parties may have a fair chance to make their case to the electorate, Congress should provide them the opportunity to secure public funding *during* the general election campaign. One way of accomplishing this might be to apply the matching funds approach currently being employed at the nominating state. In addition, it would seem only prudent for Congress to develop viability criteria for third parties so that we may avoid having to fund a third party which has become a dead letter between one election and the next.

Independent Expenditures

We now consider one final point of controversy surrounding campaign financing; one stemming not from the original legislation itself but rather from how the Supreme Court construed it. The 1974 amendments to the FECA not only limited how much individuals could give *directly* to candidates, but also stipulated that no person could spend more than $1,000 *on behalf of* a candidate. Although the Supreme Court upheld the restriction on direct contributions, it concluded that the limit on independent expenditures constituted an infringement on freedom of expression: "A restriction on the amount of money a person or group can spend on political communication during a campaign necessarily reduces the quantity of expression by restricting the number of issues discussed, the depth of their exploration, and the size of the audience reached." Thus, this ruling enabled citizens to spend as much as they wished on behalf of a candidate so long as it was undertaken in the absence of any collaboration with the candidate or his organization.

Since individuals and groups face stringent limits on how much they can give directly to candidates, it is hardly surprising that financial support for candidates would express itself through independent expenditures. Thus, although money falling into this category came to only $1.6 million in the 1976 election, it jumped to $13.7 million in 1980. This amount represented one-fourth of all the money spent on Presidential candidates that year. Of this sum, $12.9 million was used to *promote* candidates and the remaining $800,000 to campaign *against* them. By far the largest portion of these funds was spent in the general election, with Ronald Reagan the beneficiary of nearly all of it. More precisely, $12.2 million was spent on his behalf, whereas only a modest $45,869 was used to promote the election of Jimmy Carter.[60]

Who was spending this money? Some of it was done by individuals, with the single largest individual expenditure totaling $599,333.[61] Most of the spending in this area, however, came for ideological PACs organized around one or more issues and located to the right on the political spectrum (See Table 3-1).

The growth in independent expenditures is a legitimate source of concern. Certainly one of the purposes behind the campaign finance reforms was to reduce the wide disparities in financial resources among competing candidates. Public financing of general election campaigns perhaps achieved this goal best, since each nominee was given a flat sum of money with which to wage his campaign. This goal is compromised, however, when one of the nominees is the beneficiary of disporportionate sums of money spent on his behalf. Independent expenditures in substantial amounts also raise the specter of influence-buying. To be sure, the Supreme Court ruled that there can be no collaboration between the independent spender and the candidate, but this requirement can be easily circumvented. Moreover, even in the absence of collaboration, candidates will inevitably learn which individuals and groups are expending great sums on their behalf. And while the indirect nature of this spending may diminish a candidate's sense of obligation to these supporters, one suspects that it is not eliminated altogether. Finally, there is the issue of accountability to consider. In 1980 we faced a situation in which fully one-fourth of all the money spent on Presidential candidates was beyond the control of either the candidates or their parties. Independent spenders were free to run campaign advertisements for a candidate and against his opponent—advertisements whose style and content did not necessarily have the endorsement of the can-

TABLE 3-1
TOP TEN PAC INDEPENDENT SPENDERS IN 1980 CAMPAIGN

Congressional Club	$ 4,601,069
National Conservative Political Action Committee	3,307,962
Fund for a Conservative Majority	2,062,456
Americans for an Effective Presidency	1,270,208
Americans for Change	711,856
NRA Political Victory Fund	441,891
Christian Voice Moral Government Fund	406,199
1980 Republican Presidential Campaign Committee	314,740
American Medical Political Action Committee	172,397
Gun Owners of America Campaign Committee	119,891

Source: Congressional Quarterly Inc., *Dollar Politics,* 3d ed. (Washington, D. C.: Congressional Quarterly Press, 1982), p. 83.

didate or his party. This problem, it should be noted, is of major concern to officials in both parties, even though nearly all of the independent expenditures in 1980 were on behalf of the Republican Presidential nominee. Testifying before Congress in November 1980, the Chairman of the Republican National Committee observed: "I think it is obnoxious to the whole scheme of things; people coming into a campaign and saying things 'for' you or 'against' you without any accountability to the candidate."[62]

The infusion of independent expenditures into the 1980 campaign did not go unchallenged, however. The Federal Election Commission and Common Cause filed suit, charging that such expenditures by PACs were illegal. In support of their charge they pointed to a little noticed provision in the Revenue Act (1971) which stated that no group could spend more than $1,000 on behalf of a nominee if he accepted public funding in the general election. Their challenge proved unsuccessful, however, for a three-judge federal court struck down this provision as an unconstitutional intrusion into the area of free expression. The case was then appealed to the Supreme Court, which split on the issue (4–4, with Justice O'Connor abstaining), thereby letting stand the decision of the lower court.[63]

Clearly, to the extent that independent spending by PACs involves political expression, it would be inappropriate to bar it completely. As Archibald Cox points out, however, the nature of the expression in this instance also argues against granting it total immunity from regulation:

> Organized fundraising, purchase of television time, and other political advertising by a political committee are clearly types of conduct affecting speech and entitled to some degree of first amendment protection. It can be argued, however, that these activities are not speech itself, and therefore do not merit the full shelter of the first amendment. The argument is given point by asking whose right of speech is abridged by the restriction. Those who give the money are not engaging in communication. As in the case of a contribution directly to a candidate, there is "only a marginal restriction upon the contributor's ability to engage in free communication" because "the transformation of contributions into political debate involves speech by someone other than the contributor" [424 U. S. at 20–21]. Those who constitute the committee to raise and spend the money do not engage in speech; their concern is to provide the money. Having combined contributions into a pool, the committee will simply turn it over to one or more advertising agencies to conduct an advertising campaign through the mass media. . . . In short, the committee's activities are much more like the contributions held subject to regulation in *Buckley* than like the individual expenditures held immune.[64]

Barring a change of heart by the courts, the only way that independent expenditure might be reduced is by providing other outlets for this money. Toward this end, it might be desirable to allow limited individual and group contributions at the general election stage, in addition to the flat sum of public funds awarded each nominee. Congress might also consider raising the limit on individual and group contributions to the national committees of each political party.

CONCLUSION

The campaign finance reforms of the 1970s have had several salutary effects on the Presidential selection process. First, they have substantially curbed the ability of fat cats to use money as a means of obligating Presidential candidates. Second, they have narrowed the disparities in financial resources among competing candidates, particularly at the general election stage. Third, through a system of full and timely disclosure, the public may ascertain where candidates get their money and how they spend it.

It is equally clear that the reforms have affected Presidential selection in other ways that are equally significant and decidedly less beneficial. Candidates must now spend more time and money in order to raise campaign funds. They, along with the President, are forced to begin their campaigns sooner, thereby further extending an already lengthy nominating process. Candidates find it difficult to wage a vigorous campaign throughout the nominating period. Consequently, those whose opportunity to vote comes later rather than earlier in the primary season are denied the benefit of a robust political dialogue. Candidates feel compelled to search for circumventions of the law (for example, candidate PACs, draft committees), and prospective donors are obliged to funnel their money into channels which lie beyond the control of candidates and their parties. Meanwhile, new third parties are denied public funding when they need it most, and old third parties may be able to feed at the public trough even after they have ceased to be a viable political force.

That most of these consequences were not anticipated is hardly surprising. Our electoral process is, after all, highly complex and so too is the issue of campaign financing. Fortunately, these problems are subject to correction without at the same time doing serious damage to the goals of campaign finance reform. It now remains for Congress to act.

APPENDIX: Major Provisions of the Federal Election Campaign Act Amendments of 1974, 1976, 1979*

I CONTRIBUTION LIMITS

A An individual may give no more than $1,000 per election (nomination and general election campaign are treated as separate elections) to a Presidential candidate; no more than $5,000 a year to a political action committee; no more than $20,000 a

---

*Note: We have included only those provisions of the law that apply to the Presidential selection process.

year to the national committee of a political party. An individual's aggregate contributions in one year to candidates, committees, and parties cannot exceed $25,000.

B Organizations are limited to no more than $5,000 per election to a Presidential candidate; no more than $15,000 per year to the national committee of a political party. There is no aggregate limit on their annual contributions.

C Candidates who accept public funding are limited to giving no more than $50,000 of their own money to their campaign.

D Candidates financing their nomination and general election campaign exclusively from private sources may spend as much of their *own* money as they wish.

II SPENDING LIMITS

Prenomination Stage

A Candidates accepting public matching funds at the nominating stage may spend no more than $14,720,000 (in 1980) on their nomination campaigns. They may also spend 20 percent of this total ($2.9 million 1980) for fund raising and unlimited amounts on legal and accounting services necessary to comply with campaign finance laws. Neither of these expenses count toward the overall spending limit ($14,720,000).

B Candidates accepting public matching funds are also subject to spending limits in each state. These limits are based on voting age population times 16 cents, with adjustments for inflation.

C Candidates financing their nomination campaigns exclusively from private contributions are subject neither to state limits nor to the overall spending limit.

D Spending limits will be increased in proportion to annual increases in consumer price index.

General Election Stage

A Media spending limits contained in FECA of 1971 are repealed.

B Should a major party nominee decide to finance his campaign with public funds, he will be given the sum of $29.4 million (in 1980). This constitutes the total amount he is allowed to spend. This sum, however, will be adjusted to rises in the consumer price index.

C Major party nominees who decide to finance their campaigns exclusively from private sources are not subject to any overall spending limit.

D State and local party groups may spend unlimited amounts on voter registration drives, get-out-the-vote campaigns, buttons, posters, bumper stickers, handbills, brochures, and yard signs.

E The national committee of a political party may spend up to 2 cents times the voting age population ($4.6 million in 1980) in support of its nominee.

III PUBLIC FINANCING

Prenomination Stage

A To qualify for public matching funds a candidate must raise $5,000 in each of twenty states and in contributions no greater than $250.

B After qualifying, the first $250 of an individual contribution will be matched with public funds (contributions from political committees are not matchable). The total amount of matching funds for a candidate cannot exceed one-half of the total spending limit for the prenomination stage ($14,720,000 in 1980).

C Matching funds will be cut off to candidates receiving less than 10 percent of the vote in two consecutive primaries. They requalify if they win 20 percent of the vote in a subsequent primary.

D Each major party will be given $3 million in public funds to spend on its nominating convention.

General Election

A Major party nominees accepting public funding will be given $29.4 million (in 1980) in public funds. This figure will be adjusted to increases in consumer price index. They may accept no private contributions.

B Third-party candidates can qualify for public funds if their party appeared on the ballot in at least ten states in the previous Presidential election and polled at least 5 percent of the vote.

IV DISCLOSURE

A Each Presidential candidate must establish a committee to which all contributions and expenditures must be reported.

B Any candidate receiving or spending more than $5,000 must file a campaign finance report with the FEC.

C Any Presidential committee with contributions or expenditures in excess of $100,000 must file monthly reports with the FEC during an election year, as well as a pre- and postgeneral election report.

D Names of contributors must be reported if they give $200 or more.

E The FEC must be notified within 48 hours of contributions of $1,000 or more that were made between 20 days and 48 hours before an election.

F Political committees not affiliated with a candidate must file either monthly reports in all years or nine reports during a two-year election cycle.

G Individuals and political committees spending $250 or more *on behalf of* a candidate must report such expenditures and state that they were not made in collaboration with the candidate.

H Unions and corporations are permitted to maintain separate segregated funds.

V ENFORCEMENT

A The six-member FEC, nominated by the President and confirmed by the Senate, has sole authority to prosecute violations of the election laws. It may refer criminal violations to the Justice Department.

B Regulations made by the FEC may be voided by Congress.

C Individuals who knowingly violate the campaign finance laws in connection with a contribution of more than $1,000 are subject to a one-year jail sentence and a fine of up to $25,000 or three times the contribution involved in the violation, whichever is greater.

D Civil penalty fines are $5,000 or a sum equal to the contribution involved in the violation, whichever is greater. For an intentional violation, the fine is $10,000 or double the amount involved in the violation, whichever is greater.

NOTES

1 Cited in Congressional Quarterly Inc., *Dollar Politics,* 3d ed. (Washington, D. C.: Congressional Quarterly Press, 1982), p. 6.

2 Ibid., p. 4.

3 Ibid., p. 5.

4 Ibid.

5 Herbert E. Alexander, *Financing Politics: Money, Elections and Political Reform,* 2d ed. (Washington, D. C.: Congressional Quarterly Press, 1980), p. 68.

6 *Ibid.,* p. 68.

7 David W. Adamany and George E. Agree, *Political Money* (Baltimore: John Hopkins University Press, 1975), p. 38; Alexander, *Financing Politics,* p. 72.

8 Congressional Quarterly Inc., *Dollar Politics,* p. 6.

9 Herbert E. Alexander, *Money in Politics* (Washington, D. C.: Public Affairs Press, 1972), p. 140; Alexander, *Financing Politics,* p. 51.

10 Herbert E. Alexander, *Political Financing* (Minneapolis: Burgess Publishing Co., 1972), p. 8.

11 Arthur Miller et al., "A Majority Party in Disarray: Policy Polarization in the 1972 Election." (Paper delivered at the 1973 Annual Meeting of the American Political Science Association, New Orleans), pp. 17, 54.

12 Kenneth Prewitt and Alan Stone, *The Ruling Elites* (New York: Harper and Row, 1973), pp. 131–158.

13 Alexander, *Money in Politics,* pp. 55, 72, 74; Adamany and Agree, *Political Money,* p. 30; Alexander, *Financing Politics: Money, Elections and Political Reform,* 1st ed. (Washington, D. C.: Congressional Quarterly Press, 1976), pp. 90, 91.

14 Alexander, *Money in Politics,* pp. 61, 62, 64.

15 Alexander, *Financing Politics,* 2d ed., p. 49.

16 Alexander, *Financing Politics,* 2d ed., pp. 78, 79, 88, 89; Archibald Cox, *Freedom of Expression* (Cambridge, Mass.: Harvard University Press, 1980), p. 70; Adamany and Agree, *Political Money,* pp. 39, 40.

17 Alexander, *Financing Politics,* 2d ed., pp. 73, 77, 78.

18 Cited in Cox, *Freedom of Expression,* p. 69.

19 Congressional Quarterly Inc., *Dollar Politics,* pp. 6–8.

20 Ibid., p. 11.

21 Adamany and Agree, *Political Money,* p. 76.

22 Ibid., p. 32.

23 *Buckley v. Valeo,* 424 U. S. I, pp. 20, 21.

24 Ibid., pp. 16–19.

25 Campaign Finance Study Group, *Financing Presidential Campaigns,* A Research Report to the Committee on Rules and Administration of the United States Senate (Cambridge, Mass.: Institute of Politics, John F. Kennedy School of Government, January 1982), chap. 1, p. 2.

26 American Enterprise Institute, *Regulation of Political Campaigns— How Successful?* (Washington, D. C.: American Enterprise Institute, 1977), p. 18.

27 Jewel Bellush and William J. D. Boyd, "Subsidies for Campaign Time: Some Caveats," in Louis Maisel (ed.), *Changing Campaign Techniques* (Beverly Hills: Sage Publications, 1976), p. 61.

28 Cited in Congressional Quarterly Inc., *Dollar Politics,* p. 126.

28a *The Washington Post,* December 9, 1982, p. A2.

29 Cited in Samuel J. Eldersveld, *Political Parties in American Society* (New York: Basic Books, 1982), p. 322.

30 Campaign Finance Study Group, *Financing Presidential Campaigns,* chap. 2, p. 8.

31 Congressional Quarterly Inc., *Dollar Politics,* p. 94.

32 See, for example, Theodore S. Arrington, "Some Paradoxes of Campaign Finance Reform," *Common Sense,* 2 (Fall 1979), p. 61.

33 *The New York Times,* November 23, 1980, p. E3; Campaign Finance Study Group, *Financing Presidential Campaigns,* chap. 2., p. 42.

34 Congressional Quarterly Inc., *Dollar Politics,* p. 96.

35 Bruce F. Freed, "Political Money and Campaign Finance Reform, 1971–1976," in Jeff Fishel (ed.), *Parties and Elections in an Anti-Party Age* (Bloomington, Ind.: Indiana University Press, 1978), pp. 248, 249.

36 Ibid., p. 247.

37 *The New York Times,* November 7, 1982, p. E3.

38 Campaign Finance Study Group, *Financing Presidential Campaigns,* chap. 5, p. 22.

39 Alexander, *Financing Politics,* 2d ed., p. 89.

40 *The Washington Post,* October 14, 1981, p. 5; Congressional Quarterly Inc., *Dollar Politics,* pp. 27, 84.

41 Campaign Finance Study Group, *Financing Presidential Campaigns,* chap. 2., p. 43.

42 Richard B. Cheney, "The Law's Impact on Presidential and Congressional Campaigns," in Michael J. Malbin (ed.), *Parties, Interest Groups and Campaign Finance Laws* (Washington, D. C.: American Enterprise Institute, 1980), p. 242.

43 Congressional Quarterly Inc., *Dollar Politics,* p. 95.

44 Campaign Finance Study Group, *Financing Presidential Campaigns,* chap. 3, pp. 27, 28.

45 Congressional Quarterly Inc., *Dollar Politics,* p. 97; Campaign Finance Study Group, *Financing Presidential Campaigns,* chap. 3, pp. 22, 23.

46 Congressional Quarterly Inc., *Dollar Politics,* pp. 73, 79.

47 Campaign Finance Study Group, *Financing Presidential Campaigns,* chap. 1, p. 32.

48 Campaign Finance Study Group, *Financing Presidential Campaigns,* chap. 3, p. 45; Congressional Quarterly, Inc., *Dollar Politics,* p. 100.

49 Campaign Finance Study Group, *Financing Presidential Campaigns,* chap. 4, p. 2.

50 See, for example, American Enterprise Institute, *Regulation of Political Campaigns—How Successful?,* p. 8; Bellush and Boyd, "Subsidies for Campaign Time: Some Caveats," p. 58.

51 Bellush and Boyd, "Subsidies for Campaign Time: Some Caveats," pp. 67, 68; Nelson W. Polsby and Aaron Wildavsky, *Presidential Elections,* 5th ed. (New York: Charles Scribner's Sons, 1980), p. 51.

52 Joel L. Fleishman, "Private Money and Public Elections: Another American Dilemma," in Maisel (ed.), *Changing Campaign Techniques,* p. 50.

53 *The Washington Post,* July 11, 1977, p. A23.

54 Adamany and Agree, *Political Money,* pp. 189, 190.

55 See, for example, Jeane Kirkpatrick, *Dismantling the Parties* (Washington, D. C.: American Enterprise Institute, 1978), p. 14.

56 *Congressional Quarterly Weekly Report,* October 18, 1980, p. 3147.

57 Campaign Finance Study Group, *Financing Presidential Campaigns,* chap. 5, pp. 55, 56; Congressional Quarterly Inc., *Dollar Politics,* p. 100.

58 Congressional Quarterly Inc., *Dollar Politics,* p. 101.

59 Cited in Campaign Finance Study Group, *Financing Presidential Campaigns,* chap. 1, p. 38.

60 Ibid., chap. 3, p. 8; chap. 7, pp. 1–3.

61 Congressional Quarterly Inc., *Dollar Politics,* p. 83.

62 *The Washington Post,* November 21, 1981, p. A3.

63 *Congressional Quarterly Weekly Report,* January 28, 1982, p. 134; *The Washington Post,* January 20, 1982, p. A5.

64 Cox, *Freedom of Expression,* pp. 76, 77.

THE TURNOUT PUZZLE

Not even the three candidates on the ballot Tuesday bothered to vote in the county wide election for the Pinellas County Soil Conservation District board of supervisors.

In fact, nobody seemed to know anything about the election except the man who put it on, said Art Day, district conservationist for the U.S. Soil Conservation Service.

"Everybody's up in arms about conserving the resources of Pinellas County, but nobody bothers to vote," he lamented Wednesday. . . .

The only polling places were in Day's office and the County argicultural agent's office. . . . Day placed legal advertisements about the election in both the Times and the Clearwater Sun, but even the board's chairman, Wendell Salls, didn't know the election was being held. . . . Day said he will have to write the state office to find out what to do next. In the last election two years ago three people turned out.

St. Petersburg (Florida) *Times,* October 18, 1973, p. B1.[1]

Turnout in Presidential elections, to be sure, is much less of a problem. But this local contest occurred during the period of a great decline in voter participation even in Presidential races. In 1964, 69.3 percent of those eligible to vote cast ballots for President compared with just 59.2 percent in 1980. Indeed, the sharpest drop in turnout occurred in the period 1972–1976. Many Americans are worried that when people fail to vote they are expressing their frustration with a political system that they find difficult to understand. Perhaps our leaders are not discussing the key issues that are on the minds of the citizens; perhaps our leaders cannot even be trusted. The most prominent student of American voting behavior has recently argued, "if increases in nonvoting are the result of active rejection of the political system, then an increase in an already high rate of nonvoting may indeed indicate or foretell systemic crisis."[2]

Just how much of a problem is nonvoting and, what, if anything, can be done about it? We shall consider in this chapter: (1) the reasons for voting; (2) who votes and who doesn't vote; (3) who votes much less, and who more, than they used to do; (4) what proposals have been made for increasing turnout and how effective they are likely to be; (5) what might happen if we succeed in increasing turnout; (6) what might happen if we don't succeed; and (7) after all is said and done, should we be worried about whether people vote. These are large and complex questions. Perhaps no field of political science has been studied as extensively as voting. But for this very reason there are many different perspectives on turnout, so there is no possibility of having the "last word" on the debate over why people do or do not vote as much as they used to. There are disagreements on whether people ought to vote often or not, over why some people turn out more frequently than others, and even over whether there really are fewer voters today than in the recent past.[3]

We shall try to push most of the controversies among academic specialists to the side and focus on the most prominent findings. What we see in Table 4-1, which reports turnout rates for the entire country and for various population groups from 1964 to 1980, is that: (1) national turnout has declined sharply from the Presidential election of 1964 to the 1980 contest; (2) voting levels in Presidential races are higher than they are for Congressional elections in 1966, 1970, 1974, and 1978; (3) participation in Congressional elections has also declined sharply, from 55.4 percent in 1966 to 45.9 percent in 1978, paralleling the Presidential contests; and, (4) turnout has declined for every group we have

TABLE 4-1
VOTING PARTICIPATION IN THE UNITED STATES: 1964–1980

	1964	1966	1968	1970	1972	1974	1976	1978	1980
U.S.	69.3	55.4	67.8	54.6	63.0	44.7	59.2	45.9	59.2
White	70.7	57.0	69.1	56.0	64.5	46.3	60.9	47.3	60.9
Black	58.5	41.7	57.6	43.5	52.1	33.8	48.7	37.2	50.5
Spanish origin	(NA)	(NA)	(NA)	(NA)	37.5	22.9	31.8	23.5	29.9
North and West	74.6	60.9	71.0	59.0	66.4	48.8	61.2	48.9	61.0
South	56.7	43.0	60.1	44.7	55.4	36.0	54.9	39.6	55.6
South white	59.5	45.1	61.9	46.4	57.0	37.4	57.1	41.1	57.4
South black	44.0	32.9	51.6	36.8	47.8	30.0	45.7	33.5	48.2

Sources: U.S. Department of Commerce, Bureau of Census, *Current Population Reports,* Series P-20, no. 359, "Voting and Registration in the Election of 1980," January 1981 *(Advance Reports)* and earlier biennial series P-20 *Advance Reports.*

examined for both Presidential and Congressional elections with the sole exception of Southern blacks. It certainly appears that there is a turnout problem, especially since these figures are derived from surveys. More people claim to have cast ballots when they respond to pollsters than actually vote.[4]

WHY SHOULD ANYONE VOTE?

Many people view declining turnout with alarm because of the comparatively low voting rate in the United States and also because winning candidates can, and often do, claim mandates based on the support of only a small minority of the eligible population. In Japan more than 90 percent of those of voting age regularly vote and more than 85 percent in Austria and the Netherlands, compared with approximately 60 percent in the United States. Slightly smaller percentages regularly cast ballots in Nigeria and Spain, but not everyone in Spain is entitled to vote. Even though women are not permitted to vote in many parts of Switzerland, the Swiss have a slightly higher turnout rate. In Yugoslavia, where elections are less critical because of the domination of the Communist party in that country, 82 percent of the population regularly cast ballots.[5]

Furthermore, low turnout means that a minority might gain control of the political process in the United States. In the close 1976 Presidential race, for example, Carter won 57 percent of the popular vote, but (according to Table 4-1) only 59.2 percent of those eligible cast ballots. This means that just under 28 percent of the potential electorate supported Carter for President.[6] Does this constitute a mandate to govern? More importantly, does the support of approximately 30 percent of the eligible electorate mean that Reagan correctly interpreted the 1980 results as an indication of widespread support for a whole new direction for American politics? The answers to these questions depend on whether we believe that people have an obligation to vote.

Why should anyone vote? There are four reasons: (1) voting is what democracy is all about; (2) the entire system would collapse if no one voted; (3) voting is the only way that you can be sure that your voice will be heard; and (4) voting is simply important in itself. Let us examine each of these arguments. First, we have the claim that voting and democracy are essentially the same thing,[7] or at least that casting a ballot is the least you can do in a free society. To be sure, certain people are prohibited from voting. Aliens, prisoners, those with insufficient mental capacity, and people who have not lived in their states for at least thirty days before the election are prohibited from casting ballots. In earlier periods 18-year-olds were not permitted to vote in most states; residents of the District of Columbia were first allowed to ballot for President in 1964 and still have no representation in the United States Senate (although, they have a nonvoting delegate in the House of Representatives). Many blacks were prohibited from voting in the South prior to 1965 by a variety of devices.

And Jehovah's Witnesses choose not to vote for religious reasons. Also people who are away from home on election day and did not obtain absentee ballots cannot participate.[8] But, compared with other political activities, more people vote than do anything else. Only 22 percent of Americans take no part in any form of political activity; an additional 21 percent do not campaign for candidates or work on either local or national problems, but do vote. Just 11 percent take part in the full range of political life.[9] If democracy does not mean political participation, just what does it mean?

A more compelling argument is the claim that if no one participated the entire system would fall apart. The dilemma is this: Each citizen might argue that "since so many others are going to vote, [my] ballot is not worth casting."[10] Thus, "[w]hen no one votes, democracy collapses,"[11] since each person can confidently believe that he or she can leave the responsibility to someone else. This is clearly what happened in our Florida example. Nobody felt an obligation to vote in that contest or worried what would happen if no one voted. The system hardly collapsed as a result of that single contest. Such elections are to most citizens little more than curiosities. They do not fear that we will see a Presidential contest in which no one votes or even an election decided by just one vote. In either situation it would be very important for a citizen to vote, because he or she could control the whole nature of politics for the next four years. But we shall discuss this below. For the moment just argue that there are very few reasons why the average citizen should feel pressured into participating because of this threat. Everyone knows that most people do in fact believe voting is more than just a right; it is virtually an obligation in a democratic society.

However, increasing levels of nonvoting remain cause for alarm. One observer has written:[12]

> The will to vote is essentially religious. It rests on the belief that despite the overwhelming majority of elections that are not decided by one vote, each individual's vote will contribute to a general will that will yield honorable leadership, wise policy and sufficient checks on the excesses of power. It is precisely this faith that has been shattered.

Furthermore, some people fear that the habit of nonvoting will lead to apathy and a lack of concern for public life throughout the country. More precisely, such apathy may lead to a permanent class of citizens with no experience in the business of choosing a government. The larger this class becomes, the greater is the worry that people might lose effective control of their government. In good times there may be few problems that arise from widespread nonvoting. Most people do not think twice about the problems that might develop from abstention. But in periods of great upheaval there exists the possibility that many citizens who have not participated often might suddenly become activated and also give their votes to extremist candidates. Since they have not taken much interest in politics before, they do not have the sophistication to make informed choices among the competing candidates. A demagogue may appear on the political scene and exploit the ignorance of the traditionally uninvolved, as happened in Germany in the 1930s with Adolf Hitler and the Nazis.[13] America is not Germany, one might argue, but novelist Sinclair Lewis provided in *It Can't Happen Here*[14] a portrait of how such a movement might succeed in the United States. Thus, "[the] growing number of refrainers hang over the democratic process like a time bomb, ready to explode and change the course of our history."[15]

Even if people aren't worried about such massive disruptions in our democratic way of life, there is still the prospect of less dire changes that might not be desirable. At the simplest level, it may be argued: If you don't vote, you forfeit the right to complain should you decide that you don't like the policies of the new government. During the Watergate crisis, many residents of Massachusetts, the only state that gave majority support to Senator George McGovern in his race against President Nixon, put bumper stickers on their cars that stated: "Don't blame me. I'm from Massachusetts." But those who abstained in 1972 could not quite so easily claim, "Don't blame me. I didn't vote." If they had voted—voted for Nixon's opponent—they could perhaps have changed the outcome.

The lower the turnout, the easier is it for "organized minorities, special interests, and single-issue zealots" to dominate political life.[16] Thus, although public opinion polls show consistent support for freedom of choice on abortion and for gun control, issue activists take these questions much more seriously than do the rank-and-file voters.[17] The fewer the people who do vote, the easier it is for these interest groups to win in the Congress. Our legislators and, indeed, our Presidents listen to the people who can most help their reelection chances.

Finally, the act of voting is also necessary for the development of the citizen as a human being and a moral creature. This is not a view shared by everyone, but it is important in our understanding of the political theory underlying democratic government. According to this view, democracy is desirable not solely because it provides a method of reaching decisions and protects the rights of the minority but also because the very act of participating in public life makes every person a more complete human.[18] You develop responsibility toward your fellow citizens and you learn about your own thinking and your own personality.

However, just as we have arguments as to why people should vote, there are also claims that it is *not* necessary to increase participation. These are not arguments that you or anyone else shouldn't vote at all. Rather they focus on whether a high participation rate is either necessary or even desirable to a democratic government. Two such positions center around the individual, and a third on the impact of nonvoting for a democracy. The first dismisses the claim that nonvoters are mostly alienated from politics. They are not "turned off" misfits who have dropped out of participatory society. Instead, they are what Arthur T. Hadley has called "positive apathetics." Not only are they satisfied with the government, but also "things are going so well that voting seems irrelevant." They are educated, well-off, and happy. Furthermore, they are quite numerous, comprising 35 percent of the nonvoters who were interviewed in a poll.[19] This is not the traditional picture of nonvoters. Nor is it the one we shall see in our own examination below. Even if many nonvoters are happy and well-educated, their consistent failure to participate in our political life may still make them a target of extremist or special-interest groups. Even people with a college education may be politically naive. Although they may be well educated, they may choose not to follow politics avidly, or even at all. Or they may even be well-informed on some issues but be basically content with their lives and the direction of the government, so they may decide that there is little need to take a more active role in selecting a government. Voting, like riding a bicycle or playing tennis, must be "practiced" often if it is to be done well or intelligently.

Another argument against voting by all people maintains that many people are really not very interested in politics. Would it be right to insist that these citizens cast ballots? What would you say to someone who insisted that he or she shouldn't vote because a ballot cast by an apathetic person would not be based on an intelligent analysis of the issues and candidates? This nonvoter is not likely to be persuaded by appeals that he or she really ought to participate, that studying the issues is an obligation of every good citizen. The interested voter can peruse the stories about politics in the newspaper, the activist can examine in great detail all the election returns and the detailed analyses, but this nonvoter is likely to head straight for the sports and the comic pages, and perhaps go no further. Although many others who do vote don't know much about politics, few people would think that we ought to encourage voting on the basis of ignorance. We should deplore rather than extoll those who voted for Carter because he was a Southerner, for Reagan because they like his movies, or for any of the Kennedys because they are attractive.

The final argument is an extension of the second. It maintains that societies need indifference among some citizens to provide political leaders with the opportunity to respond to changing conditions. Suppose that everyone really was interested in politics and that on each issue there were highly committed citizens both pro and con. Consider the energy issue. In 1979–1980 attempts to impose a larger energy tax met with considerable resistance because political leaders were afraid to impose the costs of the tax on an unwilling public at a time of high energy prices. But in 1981–1982, as petroleum prices eased and many governments, particularly at the state level, were pressed for revenue sources in the recession, many places quietly raised energy taxes. Had everyone been mobilized on the issue, there would not have been this room for maneuvering by the political leaders. Since more people opposed the taxes than favored them, a heated debate would have forced politicians to do exactly what the public wanted. Thus, "some people are and should be highly interested in politics, but not everyone is or needs to be. Only the doctrinaire would depreciate the moderate indifference that facilitates compromise."[20]

This line of argument is not free of difficulties, however. What if everyone took this advice and abstained? Even if we agreed that apathetic people should not take an active part in politics, should we concur in the argument that it is desirable that some people are uninterested in politics? Are the nonvoters represented in our political system? What do we do about the nonvoters who are not satisfied with political life? Might their silenced voices contain a message to which our leaders ought to pay attention? We shall investigate the question of nonvoters' attitudes below. Even if they are not different, is there strong reason to believe that a higher voting rate would actually lead to such increased tension in the country? Are our voters so likely to be divided into warring camps that we need fear for the future of the republic? And is there necessarily anything wrong with insisting that our political leaders pay heed to the voices of the public? How much room for maneuvering do they need? When does maneuvering become manipulating?

Ironically, the defenders of both high and moderate levels of turnout—no one that we know has maintained that low turnout is desirable—both fear that there is the potential for instability. Too few voters may lead to a crisis of confidence in the political system; too many to an intense ideological conflict between opposing camps. The arguments on behalf of each thesis thus appear bewildering. The best way to get a clearer picture is to move to an examination of who votes and who doesn't.

WHO ARE THE VOTERS AND NONVOTERS?

We probably know more about voting and nonvoting than about many other events in our social and political lives. In the next several sections we examine who are the voters and nonvoters in Presidential elections. The results we present also hold, for the most part, for Congressional, state, and local contests. But our focus here is on the Presidential selection process and, as stated, we know that turnout is highest for these contests.

Because turnout has been extensively studied, there is evidence linking a wide variety of personal traits, attitudes. and contexts to nonvoting. This makes our task somewhat more complex. There are many sources of nonvoting to examine and we must try to make some sense of the pattern of more than three dozen traits associated with turnout. We can make the job somewhat simpler by dividing these factors into four broad categories: (1) socioeconomic traits; (2) citizen interest and involvement in politics; (3) partisan political factors; and (4) legal restrictions on voting eligibility.

Socioeconomic factors have played key roles in our understanding of who votes. For example, we know (consider again Table 4-1) that blacks vote less frequently than whites, that Hispanics vote less often than either blacks or whites. But there are many other socioeconomic factors associated with turnout. What are they and why are they important? Why do blacks vote less often than whites? It is evident why interest and involvement would be related to participation rates, but not all indicators of either relate very strongly to turnout. Partisan political factors include whether one identifies with a political party, how strong that identification is, whether the potential voter prefers one candidate to another, whether the election is preceived as close or a landslide, and whether the citizen has been contacted by a political party or candidate organization. Finally, many people may not vote simply because there are legal barriers to easy ballot access. Prior to 1964 and 1965 many Southern blacks had to pass difficult literacy tests and pay poll taxes. Furthermore, citizens throughout the fifty states and Washington D.C. have to fulfill some minimum requirements for voting: there are residency requirements and in most areas a voter must first register before casting a ballot. Some cities and states make it much easier for people to register than others, ranging from keeping evening and Saturday hours to eliminating the need to register before election day at all. Do these "legal" factors affect turnout? We shall consider each of these sets of determinants of participation in turn.

We know most about the relationship of socioeconomic factors to voting rates. Since not all studies are in agreement, we shall summarize the most prominent findings and indicate significant alternative positions. As we have seen in Table 4-1, blacks vote less than whites and Hispancis less frequently than either; turnout is lower in the South than in other regions. Our data, drawn from surveys taken by the United States Census Bureau, go back to 1964 and clearly indicate that these relationships hold for every election in this sequence. But racial differences in turnout were also found in earlier studies of voting behavior.[21] Furthermore, many studies have also found that blacks participate less in politics than whites.[22] Why? We know that Southerners vote less frequently than residents of the North and the West, a finding also well documented by others,[23] and also that Southern blacks vote less frequently even than Southern whites.[24] Is there something about living in the South that leads to both regional and racial differences in voting rates?

We know that the South has, until recently, been a poorer and less educated region of the country than the North and the West.[25] Furthermore. blacks are still less affluent and have less education than whites.[26] We are thus not surprised to find that high levels of education are associated with greater participation. Indeed, two studies have shown that for each additional year of school that a person has, he or she is 3 percent more likely to vote.[27] Put another way, only 38 percent of citizens with fewer than five years of school voted in 1972 compared with 69 percent with a high school diploma, 86 percent of college graduates, and 91 percent of people who had one or more years of graduate education.[28] Education is widely held to be the most important determinant of voting turnout among the socioeconomic factors.

The more educated citizen is more aware of how government affects the individual. Furthermore, he or she is more likely to be interested in politics and to follow campaigns, thus gaining more information about the stakes in the race. From this follows a greater sense of political sophistication and a willingness, even eagerness in many, to talk about politics with friends and neighbors. Also, the more educated person is likely to feel that he or she is capable of influencing the government.[29] Certainly this feeling of efficacy is reinforced by the civics education in our schools and by reinforcing features of home life; people who have gone to college quite often have parents who are also well educated.[30] The sense of competence obtained from the schools and the home is also reflected in the high-status, white-collar job that a college graduate is more likely to obtain. We also know that these occupations are associated with higher voting rates.[31]

Professionals, managers, and administrators have jobs that often bring them into contact with government officials, or at least they have to face issues in the job that are the subject of government action. They must, therefore, keep up with politics and become informed about the arguments that will affect their firms. We are not surprised to find that they vote more often. Indeed, government workers vote at a rate of 83 percent, considerably higher than the national average and even higher than one would expect given their level of education.[32] Of all occupation groups, they are the most directly exposed to political discussions day in and day out.

Farmers also participate more than most other groups. Their high voting rate can be explained by their relationship to politics as well. First, farmers have many contacts with the government because there are a large number of federal programs that affect agriculture; and, second, farmers are very susceptible to wide variations in income and they are more likely to be politically conscious.[33] One important agricultural issue, the grain embargo against the Soviet Union, was a prominent election issue in 1980, and President Reagan canceled his predecessor's ban on sales on his first day in office. Price supports are critical to many farmers, and it was not surprising that many of the key battles over Reagan's budget cuts involved agriculture supports. Farmers are indeed mobilized and vote frequently. As V. O. Key, Jr., argued as early as 1947, "Instead of a slumbering, rustic giant roused only by depression and adversity, farmers have become a well-organized and competently led group, with interest in public policy as keen and continuous as that of any business or labor group."[34] But since farmers are more volatile in their voting behavior,[35] they play an even greater role in American politics than their numbers would warrant. When one further adds their high rate of voting, their political impact becomes very potent indeed.

Yet farmers are not highly educated compared with other groups, nor are they particularly well-off economically.[36] Government workers, in contrast, may not be relatively affluent, but they are well educated.[37] For these occupations, the nature of the work itself demands that people pay attention to politics. But in a wide variety of other jobs there is a direct linkage from education to occupation to salary. Thus we find that the most well-off people have the highest turnout rates. Turnout is highest among those with incomes of $25,000 and more, and lowest among those with incomes of $5,000 or less.[38] In addition to the reasons for low turnout that are associated with little education (lack of interest in politics, not keeping up with current affairs. not reading about politics), low-income people cannot afford the luxury of a strong interest in politics as well as more affluent citizens can. Much of their time and effort is spent just coping. They do not read the newspaper for their job, if they have one, nor are they likely to discuss the election with their neighbors.[39] Not only does unemployment put a citizen at the lower end of the economic spectrum, but it also independently reduces turnout. That is, a poor person working full-time will still be between 1 and 3 percent more likely to vote than a person with the same "income" but without a job.[40]

The "socioeconomic" or demographic factors that we have examined so far indicate that people who can understand politics well and who have a "stake in the system" are the ones who are most likely to vote. It is not just the fact that one is black or white or rich or poor that is important, but what these factors tell us about one's position in the social structure. Thus, it is not surprising that younger people, women, and particularly married women traditionally have voted less frequently than the average citizen. Younger voters are less likely to have climbed the seniority ladder to well-paid, higher status jobs. Like the poor, they are more preoccupied with earning a living and getting started in life than with the political issues of our time. To be sure, their situation is not quite the same and many college-aged young people do participate in politics. But turnout is substantially lower for younger people. In every election since the Census Bureau started compiling figures on registration and turnout figures, 18-to-24-year-old voters had lower participation rates than the average. These figures are presented in Table 4-2.[41] In the 1950s older people also tended to vote less frequently than the middle-aged. Retired citizens did not see government as affecting their lives as immediately as those who were employed.[42] But more recent studies show that older people are voting even more often than the middle-aged.[43] Perhaps the greater mobilization of senior citizens over such issues as "gray power" and Social Security has played a key role in enhancing turnout.

Similarly women in the 1950s participated at a rate that was 10 percent below that of the turnout for men.[44] But the gap had narrowed to only 2 percent by 1972 and, if we compare men and women of similar social and economic status, participation rates are equal.[45] By 1976 and 1980 overall participation rates were almost identical.[46] As women have entered the work force and

TABLE 4-2
TURNOUT RATES BY AGE: 1964–1980

	1964	1966	1968	1970	1972	1974	1976	1978	1980
U.S.	69.3	55.4	67.8	54.6	63.0	44.7	59.2	45.9	59.2
Age: 18–20	39.2	21.9	33.6	25.6	48.3	20.8	38.0	20.1	35.7
Age: 21–24	51.3	31.7	51.1	30.4	50.7	26.4	45.6	26.2	43.1

Source: U.S. Department of Commerce, Bureau of Census, *Current Population Reports,* Series P-20, no. 359, "Voting and Registration in the Election of 1980," January 1981 *(Advance Reports)* and earlier biennial series P-20 *Advance Reports.*

become more politically conscious, their participation rates have sharply increased. Contrast these results with the findings for Chicago in 1923: almost 8 percent of all nonvoters in the municipal elections that year cited a belief that women should not cast ballots as their reason for abstention. In addition, many political leaders said that many women did not even register because they did not want to reveal their age![47] As women more clearly developed a "stake in the system," their turnout increased. In the 1950s, married women with young children voted less frequently than either single women or married women with children.[48] Yet by the 1970s, being married increased turnout levels for men and women.[49]

Finally, people living in rural areas tend to vote less frequently than urban dwellers.[50] The latter are exposed to more media carrying stories about politics—not just television, which is universal, but also newspapers; they are also more likely to discuss politics with their neighbors. Similarly, people who are new to their communities, wherever they live, are less likely to vote.[51] Many, of course, may not have met residence requirements. But still others are not fully settled in their new towns and do not know much about local or even state politics. They must register to vote again and this takes at least some effort, as we shall see below. They are much less likely to discuss politics with their neighbors than are longer-term residents. They simply haven't developed sufficient interest and may decide to skip the Presidential election as well since that may not be enough to get them to the polls.

We have seen that there are a variety of socioeconomic factors that lead to different rates of turnout. Many of them are related to each other. Almost all seem related to citizen interest and involvement in the political process as well. We turn now to these factors.

RATES OF INTEREST

At the core of the issue of interest and involvement is the question of "simple interest": Does the citizen care about politics at all? Is he or she informed about political issues? Then come the questions that we might label here as "compound interest" because they reflect both a person's involvement in political life and his or her belief that this interest really matters. Does the citizen trust politicians? Can the citizen do anything about political decisions that are felt to be wrong? Is there really a duty to vote?

It is hardly surprising that those who are most interested in politics vote more often than those who are not.[52] Furthermore, people who have a sense of involvement in political life, who care about the outcome of an election very much, and who perceive the result as having a direct impact on their personal lives are very likely to cast ballots.[53] But involvement is itself determined by some of the socioeconomic factors we have already examined. The well-off, the well educated, and the well situated are all more interested and involved in politics. Indeed, "[a]nything which increases psychological involvement in the election suffices to increase the likelihood of voting."[54] Thus, someone who is exposed to a lot of information about politics should be more likely to become involved and therefore to vote. This is indeed the case for media attention.[55] Since people are exposed to far more information about Presidential than Congressional elections, we can easily understand why turnout is so much higher in the former contests. The national media cover Presidential campaigns in depth, but simply could not cover every House and Senate election even if they wanted to do so. Since the President is the only nationally elected political leader, our attention is riveted on the race for the White House in a way that it isn't for lesser offices. Many people believe that their vote is more effective in influencing national policy at the Presidential level than in voting for local offices. The lower the office, the less well known the candidates are in general and, thus, the lower the turnout.

Moving beyond simple interest, we find that there is even a more pronounced relationship between "compound interest" and turnout. Nonvoters are substantially more cynical, or less trusting, toward government than are voters.[56] Yet there is also evidence that many people who are satisfied also may abstain. One study of nonvoting between 1952 and 1972 found that more people didn't vote because they were satisfied than because they felt estranged from the political system.[57] Thus, both the upset and the happy abstain. On the other hand, there is a clear relationship between participation and what has been called a sense of efficacy in politics. Citizens have a high sense of efficacy if they believe that: (1) government officials really do care about what ordinary people think; and (2) ordinary people really do have a say in what the government does.[58] People who feel efficacious do have higher turnout rates.[59] They feel more "at home" with politics and also tend to be more highly educated and well-off. They are the citizens who feel that their vote does matter. It might not decide the outcome of the election, but the politicians are listening to what they have to say; and should they choose to try to influence their elected leaders, the politicians would at least listen.

Perhaps the strongest determinant of participation, aside from education levels, is the straightforward belief that one has an obligation to vote.[60] Of course it makes sense that people who would say they have a duty to vote would in fact cast ballots, and those who don't think there is an obligation would be the ones who abstain. But there is probably more to the relationship than this. We learn in school that there is an obligation to vote in a democracy. But the more we learn about politics, the more interested we become, the more likely we are to believe that people really ought to vote. People who vote all the time, in every local election as well as the more widely publicized national contests, sometimes find it difficult to understand why others are not as deeply involved or, at least, why they don't fulfill their "civic duty" of casting a ballot. We thus must look toward other motivational factors, and we proceed next to what we have called "political factors."

PARTISAN POLITICAL FACTORS

The socioeconomic and interest/involvement factors we have considered so far tell us a lot about psychological orientations toward participation in general, but little about practical politics. Virtually everything we have discussed so far could be applied to almost any sort of participation, from joining church groups to participating in a protest movement. Where does politics fit in? We now consider two types of political factors, what have been called "long-term" and "short-term" factors.[61] The former refer to long-standing orientations that do not change quickly; specifically, whether one identifies with a political party. "Short-term" factors, in contrast, are specific to each election. Does the voter prefer one candidate to another, or is there a specific issue that might motivate someone to get out and vote? Has the party organization made contact with the citizen? Is the election close or not?

Many citizens consider themselves to be either Democrats, Republicans, or Independents (i.e., people without any formal attachment to either of the major parties). Independents have the lowest turnout rate of any partisan group and, as is widely known, Republicans the highest.[62] Furthermore, the more strongly people identify with a party, the more likely it is that they will vote.[63] As with other attachments and involvements, people who are strongly attached to a party tend to be well educated, well-off, and well situated. They also follow politics closely in discussions with friends and in the media. We shall have more to say about this turnout differential later. Specifically, we shall pose the question: If Republicans vote more frequently than Democrats, could we change the electoral balance by getting more Democrats to the polls?

There is considerable evidence that the long-term factors of both simple identification with a party and the strength of that attachment are very important factors in the decision to vote or not to vote. They reflect the same basic interest in politics that voting does. But short-term factors are also important. Indeed, they are critical in understanding variations in turnout from one election to another. One student of voting has argued that there is a cyclical pattern of "ups" and "downs" in turnout, what he called "surge and decline."[64] Politics gets heated and exciting in one contest, then cools off four years later. Think about the sequence: 1972, 1976, 1980. In the first contest a very liberal Democratic Senator challenged an incumbent President, who was a moderate conservative. In the second another moderate who had succeeded Nixon when he was forced to resign was challenged by a moderate Democrat in what was a decidedly low-key race. In 1980, by contrast, the Democratic incumbent lost in a heated race to a decidedly ideological conservative Republican.

The first short-term factor we consider is whether the voter prefers one candidate to another. Voters may have several reasons to select one candidate over another, including issue stands, a candidate's background, or personality. On the other hand, if a voter is indifferent to the choice of candidates, there is substantially less reason to vote. There is considerable evidence to support the thesis that if the citizen does indeed care who wins the election, the probability of voting is raised significantly.[65] But issues do not seem to be as great a stimulus to greater participation. There was some evidence that white voters who were concerned with the Vietnam war voted less frequently than did others, but this effect had vanished by the time the war ended in the Presidential election of 1976. Opposition to the war thus did not mobilize a new group of voters in 1968 or 1972; if anything, it disenchanted many with the political process. On the other hand, the Watergate issue had no appreciable impact on turnout in 1972 or 1976.[66]

People who are contacted by a campaign organization are also more likely to vote.[67] Apparently there is indeed a payoff from campaigning in turning out the vote. Also, people living in areas in which the two parties are more closely matched have higher voting rates.[68] This is indirect evidence for the argument that citizens who see the race for President as close will be more likely to go to the polls. Those people who believe the election result is a foregone conclusion may be less likely to believe that one vote makes a difference. Their calculation as to whether the effort of voting is worth the trouble might not be that different from that of our Florida example described at the beginning of this chapter. Since the probability that any one vote will change the outcome of the election is miniscule, the calculating citizen will never have an incentive to go to the polls on that basis alone.[69] But note that any voter in the Florida contest could have cast the deciding ballot! The real situation is likely to be somewhere in between, and it seems quite reasonable to assume that the closer the election is perceived to be, the more likely an individual will believe that his or her vote is meaningful. There is evidence for this view as well.[70]

Even though we have found that these factors, which are specific to each election, do have an impact on turnout, recent participation figures cast doubt on the applicability of the "surge and decline" thesis. Turnout was nearly the same in the "surge" election of 1980 and the "decline" election of 1976: both had rates of 59.2 percent (see Table 4-1 on page 108). It seems that voting is more of a long-term commitment and that fluctuations from one contest to another are not nearly as important as the overall attitude that it is one's duty to vote.[71] The sense of obligation does not tell us the whole story, however. Before one votes, one must register. And although the vast majority of those who register do vote, many people never register. Why don't they? We turn now to this question.

REGISTRATION AND VOTING

One recent study posed the familiar question "Why do people vote?" and responded: "Because they are registered."[72] This is clearly an oversimplification, but the turnout rate among registered voters is usually 90 percent or more.[73] But who are the people who are most likely to register? They are the same sort of people who have the highest rates of voting! There are some differences in how well political efficacy, party identification, political interest, race, sex, and similar factors predict voting behavior on the one hand and registration on the other hand.[74] These are not the really interesting questions, however. What we are most concerned with is how electoral laws affect registration and voting rates. By "electoral laws" we mean the full range of statutes and regulations that may restrict suffrage. Prior to the mid-1960s, these laws included poll taxes and literacy tests, both of which were used predominantly in the South. The poll tax was outlawed in federal elections by the ratification of the Twenty-fourth Amendment to the United States Constitution in January 1964, and further court cases struck down state poll taxes. The Voting Rights Act of 1965 prohibited the use of literacy tests for voting in those areas of the South covered by the Act; further amendments to the Act in 1970 eliminated the tests in other jurisdictions. Both the poll tax and literacy tests widely discriminated against blacks and greatly restricted black voting. The tax posed a particular burden on poor persons, as most Southern blacks were, and literacy tests often were administered quite differently for blacks and whites. Blacks had to take tests that would prove difficult even for political science professors, and many whites were exempted from the examinations altogether since their grandfathers had the right to vote. Prior to 1972, 18-to-20-year-old citizens were allowed to register only in Georgia, Kentucky, Alaska, and Hawaii.[75] Throughout the country there are residence requirements for voting in local elections that may also reduce turnout in national contests. However, the Supreme Court ruled in 1972 in *Dunn v. Blumstein* that the year-long residency requirement in Tennessee for local elections was too long and the amendments to the Voting Rights Act passed in 1970 established a maximum thirty-day residence requirement for Presidential elections.

We know that the Voting Rights Act did indeed mobilize black voters. Its suspension of the literacy tests, together with the effects of the abolition of the poll taxes, increased black turnout by 10 percent.[76] Also more lengthy residence requirements in a town or a county reduce the level of voting participation by its citizens.[77] These are only the most obvious of the electoral laws that vary from state to state and even town to town. We do not think very often about other factors, such as how easy it is to register and whether one has to register anew periodically. In some places one has to take time off from work to register; in others all one has to do is telephone to obtain a postcard and return it in the mail; in yet others, people will come to your door to register you; and in three states and several counties you don't have to register at all. Do more flexible electoral laws lead to increased rates of registration and do these new registrants actually vote?

In both cases the answer is a qualified "yes." There is a clear relationship between electoral laws and rates of registration and voting, but not all aspects of the registration process do in fact deter or encourage participation. First, it is important to realize that registration procedures do vary considerably throughout the nation, indeed even within states. Of the various aspects of registration, ranging from the availability of week-night and Saturday hours to the location of offices, the factor that has most consistently emerged as having the greatest impact on rates of registration *and* voting is the closing date. The closer the last day to register is to election day, the greater the probability that people will register in large numbers. Regarding turnout, closing registration a month before the election results in a decline in the likelihood that a person will vote of as much as 9 percent. We first consider all the other factors that we have associated with voting and nonvoting. Once we have taken these into account (such as education and occupation), we can estimate how likely a given person is to vote. If he or she must register thirty days in advance, the likelihood that the citizen will vote declines by as much as 9 percent. If, on the other hand, the closing date were fifty days before the election, the probability that a person would vote would decline by as much as .17.[78]

Registration offices that are open fewer than forty hours a week make it difficult for people to get to the office without taking time off from work. Such irregular hours reduce the probability of voting by as much as 4 percent. Turnout will decline by as much as 6 percent if offices are closed on Saturdays and by up to 4 percent in states that do not permit citizens to register by mail if they are sick, disabled or out of the state. On the other hand, if an office stays open for fourteen instead of twelve hours, the probability that an individual will vote increases by as much as 3 percent.[79] If the closing date were eliminated throughout the United States and if provisions were enacted calling for opening registration offices for the entire forty-hour week, opening registration in the evening and/or on Saturday, and permitting absentee registration, turnout would increase approximately 9 percent.[80] Clearly registration procedures do affect turnout, in some instances quite dramatically. There is also evidence that the requirement that people register anew periodically also depresses turnout. Many localities "purge" their voting rolls periodically so that people who have moved or died no longer remain eligible voters. When rolls are not purged, there is always the possibility of vote fraud if someone attempts to vote in the name of the citizen who is no longer eligible. But when rolls are purged, there are always some voters who do not take the trouble to register again.

In summary, we have seen that all sets of factors, including socioeconomic traits, levels of information and involvement, short-term and particularly long-term political forces, and electoral laws, play a role in determing turnout. The various studies generally point to a sense of duty to vote and a person's level of education as the most important factors in determining whether a person goes to the polls. But so far none of these studies tells us much about why participation has been *declining*. We have a pretty good idea of who votes and who doesn't vote, yet we know little about why people no longer vote. We turn now to this question.

CHANGES IN TURNOUT

The single most important change in turnout is the gradual decline from 69.3 percent of the eligible electorate voting in 1964 to 67.8 percent in 1968, to 63.0 percent in 1972, and to 59.2 percent in both 1976 and 1980 (see Table 4-1). Some see positive signs in the halt to the decline in 1980, but the participation rate remains very low in comparison with most other democracies. That turnout is no longer falling is hardly reassuring when we would expect it to increase. We have seen that registration laws, income, and particularly education are strongly associated with voting. We also know that levels of income and education have risen sharply over the past several decades in the United States and that registration laws have generally been made more lenient. Thus "the puzzle of political participation" in America: If some of the key factors leading to more participation show increases, why is turnout itself declining, or at best holding steady?[81]

Increasing levels of education should have led to an increase in voting rates of between 4 and 6.5 percent rather than the decrease we have observed over the last two decades.[82] Yet one study concluded that turnout since 1960 *among the college educated* has declined by almost 20 percent.[83] But the less educated and poorer, at least among whites, have been dropping out of the electorate faster.[84] Southern blacks, on the other hand, constitute the only major group with sizeable increases in participation during this period.[85] This trend can also be found in Table 4-2. It is clear that this increase is attributable to the constitutional amendment repealing the poll tax, the Voting Rights Act of 1965, and the intensive efforts at political mobilization among Southern blacks that occurred during the 1960s.[86] But black turnout began to decline after the election of 1968; in that contest, together with the election of 1964, the racial issue was very prominent. Since 1972, however, the Presidential contests have not involved issues of race very much and black turnout in the South has returned to slightly more than its post-Voting Rights Act level. National black turnout, mirroring that of whites, has declined sharply.[87] Since there was little association between electoral provisions and black turnout in the North in the 1950s,[88] there is little reason to believe that the same dynamics have affected blacks in both regions. The decline in Northern black turnout seems to be very similar to that for whites in both regions. But what factors led to this decline?

The decline in turnout becomes more puzzling when we note that women's rates of participation have *not* declined and that the sole source of decreasing sex differences in participation has been lower voting rates among men.[89] Men and women now vote at the same rates. We can understand why turnout has not declined for women, since the social and political movements of the last decade have heightened the consciousness of many women. But the education and income levels of men have also been increasing, even while turnout has been declining.

So far socioeconomic factors have not helped us in our search for sources of lower turnout. But we have a more promising candidate: age. Several studies point to a decline in voting among the young. The age groups 18–20 and 21–24 (see Table 4-2) have participation rates far below the national average. When looking at data over time for these voters, it is important to remember that unlike the black/white or male/female distinction, the age classification changes for voters. Someone who was 18 years old in 1976 was 22 in 1980 and in a different age group in our voting tables. Thus, it is important to make comparisons across what we call "cohorts." The people who are in the youngest group in, say, 1976 will be in the next category (21-to-24 years old) four years later. Each group such as this is a cohort. What we see across cohorts is that the youngest people in each election had very low participation rates until 1972, when the 18-year-old vote was made nationwide. There was a surge in participation for the new voters in that contest, induced by the opportunity to vote and also probably by the nature of the 1972 campaign. That election pitted a youth-oriented liberal Democratic Senator who opposed the war in Vietnam against the incumbent Republican President. The 18-to-20-year-old cohort in 1972 did vote somewhat less in 1976, but not significantly more so than the rest of the population did. But the next 18-to-20-year-old cohort voted at a much lower rate, and, even though national turnout did not decline from 1976 to 1980, the newest young cohort voted less frequently than did the youngest voters four years earlier.[90]

Why are people voting less frequently than in previous years? One answer to the total turnout decline is that a larger percentage of the eligible voters is in the youngest age cohort than ever before. But this doesn't tell us everything we need to know. The change in the age composition of the electorate doesn't account for the entire decline in turnout. Thus we must look to other factors. Two studies help us in this regard. They focus specifically on the decline in turnout in the Unites States and attempt to determine which attitudes and behavior can best account for this lowered participation. One study examines only the years 1960 to 1976 and the other is more comprehensive, examining trends from 1952 to 1980. The findings of each are quite similar, however, so it will be useful to consider their results together. Both take the total decline and attempt to break it down as follows: Of the full range of decreased participation, what percentage of that decline can be attributed to each attidudinal and behavioral factor?

The changing age distribution of the population—the larger number of younger people who are eligible to vote, the longer life-spans that have increased the numbers of potential older voters, and the *relatively* smaller size of the middle-aged cohorts—does have a major role in the decline in participation from 1960 to 1976. Taken by itself—that is, not considering other changes that have occurred during that period—this change in age distribution can account for slightly more than 25 percent of the decrease in turnout.[91] Is this a lot or a little? Clearly the change is substantial, even when we realize that other factors clearly are associated with age. For we saw that younger voters are also less informed, less well-off, less committed to political parties. But even though the change in the age distribution is clearly important, it cannot account for most of the lower turnout that we have observed.

Perhaps turnout has declined because people have simply become less interested in politics than they used to be. This is a plausible thesis, but surveys fail to show a lessening of interest by Americans in politics generally or the campaigns in particular. Furthermore, levels of information obtained through the media have also not declined. People are using the media at about the same levels as two decades ago. What has changed is reliance on newspapers. By itself, and again not considering other factors, the decline in newspaper readership corresponds to as much as 40 percent of the total decrease in turnout.[92]

But the medium is not the same as the message. It is not plausible to presume that people have stopped voting just because they watch more television than in the past or read fewer newspapers. What other factors are related to the lower participation rates? Somewhat surprisingly, in the era of Vietnam and Watergate, the decline in political trust has not had a strong impact on voting rates. One analysis shows very little impact on turnout for changes in trust,[93] whereas another attributes no more than 28 percent of the decrease in participation to different perceptions of the trustworthiness of public officials.[94] We know that citizen duty is one of the strongest determinants of voting. But it has little relationship to changes in participation since the sense of obligation to vote has not changed very much since the 1950s.[95]

There is one interest/involvement item that does have a major impact on the changing rate of voting: personal efficacy. An increasing number of citizens who maintain that "people like me don't have any say about what the government does" and that public officials don't care what ordinary people think also tends to be the same people who are voting less frequently. Between one-third[96] and one-half[97] of the decline in voting rates can be attributed to this increasing cynicism on the part of Americans toward their government. People drop out not because they don't trust government broadly but rather because they feel that political leaders are not being responsive to them. This is a more immediate concern to many people than the abstract question of whether government can be trusted at all. It is also not surprising that citizen duty is still a prevalent feeling among most people. We learn about it in school and come to believe it very strongly. Probably many nonvoters strongly believe that they ought to vote, but refrain from doing so because they are not sure that their efforts will be rewarded.

Like most of the interest/involvement attitudes, short-term forces among the political factors also do not explain changes in turnout well. Voting rates have declined consistently over time, but concern for which candidate wins has not fluctuated in the same way.[98] Similarly, there is no clear-cut relationship between citizens' perceptions of the closeness of elections and participation rates.[99] On the other hand, the long-term party identification factor *has* weakened among citizens in much the same way that turnout has. Over the past three decades people are becoming far less attached to political parties. In 1952 36 percent of the potential electorate strongly identified with either the Democratic or Republican party, a figure that remained steady until 1966. In that year only 28 percent were strongly attached to a party, and 12 percent considered themselves independents who did not even "lean" toward favoring one of the major parties. By 1978 just 23 percent of the electorate was strongly identified, compared with 14 percent "pure" independents.[100] During this period, turnout, of course, also dropped dramatically. Interestingly, participation rates for strong as well as weak party identifiers, as well as independents who lean toward one of the major parties, remained steady or actually rose since 1952! Only pure independents, of all partisan groups, are voting less frequently. Their turnout dropped from 74 percent in 1952 to just over 55 percent in 1976 and 1980.[101]

What are we to make of this decline in voting among only a small portion of the citizens? To be sure, the lower participation by independents only accounts for approximately a quarter of the overall decrease in turnout.[102] But there are two elements of this decrease: (1) lower voting rates among independents; and (2) the fact that more people are refusing to identify with the two major parties than ever before. We can understand the smaller turnout of younger voters as well. The largest increase in the pure independent category has come from this group. In 1976 there were more pure independents than strong party identifiers among people who were under 33 years old. The 18-to-20-year-old group was the most "anti-party."[103] On the other hand, older voters continued to maintain strong ties to the parties and to turn out in relatively large numbers. This "generational scar on the polity" has been traced to the "antipolitics, antiparty era" of the 1960s and 1970s in which the younger potential voters grew up.[104] Even though there were few direct relationships between attitudes on Vietnam and the Watergate scandal on participation and even though the decline in political trust did not correspond directly to decreases in turnout, it is evident that the entire political complexion of the past generation did indeed lead to lower participation. Even more important than the decline in partisan identification has been the lessened sense of political efficacy, the belief that politicians care what people are thinking and that the ordinary citizen can do something about the policies of the government.[105] This reflects the antipolitics sentiment of the youth quite strongly.

What we have seen so far is that the major reason for the lower rates of voting is a "behavioral" change, a different way of looking at politics and parties. It is thus not terribly surprising that many of the suggested reforms leading to more lenient electoral laws have not had the intended effects of raising turnout. More uniform national residency requirements in *national* elections did lead to a decrease, from 1968 to 1976 in the frequency of cases in which people said that they didn't register because of residency requirements.[106] But this hardly stopped the decline in turnout nationally. The introduction of postcard registration in Maryland and New Jersey in 1974 failed to stop the decline in either registration or voting rates.[107] We have little evidence that the greater convenience of the postcard system, in which voters only have to telephone to obtain the card and put the filled-in card back in the mail, would be sufficient to bring unwilling participants to the polls. An elaborate campaign to increase registration in California does not seem to have been a great success; even door-to-door registration in Idaho, where public employees made "house calls" on potential registrants, did not prevent declining turnout.[108] Evidence from Great Britain and Canada also indicates that even automatic registration does not stop decreasing participation at the polls.[109] There is some evidence that election day registration in Wisconsin and Minnesota in 1976 did lead to some increased turnout, but it is unclear whether the Minnesota rise was to be attributed to the change in electoral laws or the presence of a native son, Senator Walter F. Mondale, on the Democratic party ticket as the candidate for Vice President.[110]

We should not dismiss the impact of registration reform too quickly, however, because we simply cannot know what it is. We know that there has been a long-term decline in electoral participation. But it is difficult to say that, just because turnout has been dropping, changes in registration procedures are ineffective. The question that we must ask is: Would turnout have dropped even further without such reform? But the answer cannot be found by comparing those states that have changed their procedures with states that have not done do.[111] Citizens in Maryland and New Jersey, both states that have adopted postcard registration, are more like each other than either is like Illinois, Georgia, or even New York.[112] We cannot make simple comparisons over time without very detailed information as to how specific campaigns affected voters in each state, what long-term participation rates were, how the candidates campaigned in the states, and the level of concern on the part of citizens about the elections. The attempt to disentangle the effects of changes in electoral laws and more fundamental shifts in the attitudes of the mass public has long divided, and frustrated, students of voting behavior.[113]

The problem of determining the effects of electoral laws is not fundamentally different from the "puzzle of political participation" that we discussed earlier. This puzzle asks why turnout has declined when levels of education and income, two strong determinants of voting rates, have increased. Registration has been made easier, and we should also expect higher turnout on the basis of those changes. It is almost undoubtedly the case that without increasing education and income there would be considerably less turnout than we do in fact observe. It is also probable that more lenient electoral laws have had some measurable effect on stoping the slide in registration and voting rates. How much we do not know. But what seems indisputable is that no conceivable electoral reform will be sufficient to raise participation dramatically. If people are disaffected, alienated from politics, simply uninterested, or even just plain satisfied, they would not be likely to vote in great numbers even if you brought the ballots to them at home.

Thus a whole range of reform proposals to increase turnout seems misplaced because it does not get to the heart of the matter. In addition to the changes in registration procedures we have mentioned, these suggestions include: (1) making absentee ballots easier to obtain, perhaps automatic for certain people, such as those receiving either Social Security or disability benefits;[114] (2) providing voters with paid time off from work when they are casting their ballots;[115] (3) holding elections on either a legal holiday or Sunday;[116] and (4) most radical of all, make voting compulsory, either by fining those who don't vote or by providing an incentive, perhaps in the form of a tax deduction, for those who do go to the polls.[117] The idea of compulsory voting would undoubtedly be repugnant to many people; it might even be a violation of key provisions in our Bill of Rights, specifically that of freedom of speech. Moreover, even if compulsory voting did bring everyone to the polls, there is little reason to believe that this "reform" would actually make people more interested in politics. It is the proverbial problem of leading a horse to water. Would we be better off with more participation by people who really would not feel comfortable in the voting booth?

It might make a lot of sense to make absentee ballots easier for people to obtain, but the older people who would be the target of the automatic ballots, as suggested, already have high turnout rates. Thus this proposal would not stem the decline in turnout of the past two decades. Objections to paying people for their time at work while voting and for holding elections on a national holiday tend to center on the costs that this would involve. Few employers would be excited about paying for time not on the job. much less for an entire paid holiday on election day. In an era of increasing concern for how government funds will be spent, there is much resistance to a paid holiday beyond those that already exist for any reason. Much of the opposition to declaring Martin Luther King. Jr.'s birthday a national holiday has cited this reason. But it would be conceivable to hold elections on a Sunday, as is done in most of Europe. Arthur T. Hadley has argued, "Making election day a holiday reinforces the vote's importance, just as the holiday on Sunday for years reinforced the importance of the Sabbath."[118] But would turnout really increase if the election were shifted from Tuesday to Sunday? Might people be either too glued to their television sets during the professional football season, out for a drive in the country, or, among Sabbath observers, spending the entire day at church to bother voting? Aren't people who are really interested in the election just as likely to get to the polls regardless of the day the election is held? Even if there would be a small increase in turnout, this would still not resolve the more general problem of a lessening interest in politics and a weakened attachment to the parties.

WHO DOESN'T VOTE?

Let us put our doubts aside for a moment and assume that somehow we have found a magic formula for increasing turnout. What sort of a difference would the entrance of nonvoters into the electorate mean? Would our government and our policies look much different from the way they do today? Would we be better off with full participation than we were in the days of low-participation elections, say four years ago?

It would seem that things would be very different. One analysis of turnout rates for the period 1952–1976 concluded that in every national election, turnout among Republican identifiers has been at least 10 percent higher than for Democratic partisans.[119] Democratic party leaders thus have long believed that if they could find a way to increase turnout they would also have found a way to ensure that they would win national elections, since throughout this period they have held large leads in party identification over the Republicans.[120] Yet, counterintuitively, "the joke's on the Democrats,"[121] as one uncharitable observer commented. Virtually every study of the partisan and ideological composition of the full potential electorate has found striking similarities in both issue positions and candidate preferences between voters and nonvoters. How can this be so?

Let us start by recalling that whereas more Republicans vote than Democrats, most nonvoters are not terribly strongly attached to either party. The major reason why people don't vote or don't register is that they are simply not interested. Remember that the pure independents have the lowest turnout rate of anyone. These are people who are not strongly concerned with politics.

When these people do get sufficiently motivated to go to the polls, they will be responding to the same stimuli that the rest of the country will be: strong candidates in a close election.[122] Historically high turnouts have not benefited either the Democrats or the Republicans exclusively.[123] There is a tendency since 1938 for the minority party (the Republicans) to profit from boosts in participation.[124] This does not mean that Democrats never gain from increased voting nor that they might do even better if some nonvoters had made it to the polls. To see why they have not gained much in the past, let us think about what happens in high turnout elections. Since such contests are likely to be close, people will pay more attention to them than they might otherwise. But what makes an election close is a series of defections from the majority party in particular.[125] If every voter made his or her decision strictly on the basis of party identification and the independents split down the middle, the Democrats would always win. We thus have a paradox for the majority party. When the election looks as if it will be a landslide, the party's supporters among people who are not likely to vote will look at the situation and conclude that their votes are not going to have much of an effect on the contest; they will thus abstain, making the landslide somewhat less impressive. On the other hand, these same people may decide that they really ought to go to the polls in an exciting, closely contested election. But then they are likely to respond to the minority party's candidate in the same positive manner as others!

The evidence we have suggests that this is precisely what happens. A study of voters and nonvoters in 1972 found that changes in electoral laws would probably produce a larger electorate, but one with identical policy views on such diverse issues as federal government guarantees of jobs, federal government ensuring that all schools would be integrated, legalization of marijuana, an equal role for women in society, and self-identification as a liberal or conservative.[126] The partisan composition of the electorate was marginally more Republican and considerably less independent than that of the entire population, but the Democrats had the same percentage in both.[127] Furthermore, the differences were quite small and did not translate into changes on policy questions. In 1976 most voters and nonvoters had similar perceptions of the candidates seeking the Democratic and Republican nominations.[128]

When we examine specific elections for which the preferences of nonvoters have been compared with those of voters, we find no clear-cut pattern of partisan bias either. One study of the 1960 election argued that nonvoters were more likely to prefer John F. Kennedy, but another gave the edge to Richard M. Nixon.[129] In 1968 third-party candidate George C. Wallace would have performed best among nonvoters; in 1976 the advantage clearly went to Jimmy Carter.[130] In the landslides of 1956, 1964, and 1972 the nonvoters would not only have supported the winner each time, two Republicans and one Democrat, but would have given the victor considerably higher margins than did their counterparts who made it to the polls![131] People with lower rates of participation are thus simply more likely to "follow the crowd," especially if the crowd already is large.

IMPLICATIONS FOR PRESIDENTIAL SELECTION

If nonvoters are generally very much like voters and if there is no simple "quick fix" to the turnout problem, must we really care that turnout rates are declining? Yes, we must because the low participation level suggests that something is very wrong in our politics whenever people come to feel estranged from our parties and when they no longer believe that their leaders are listening to them. We should also be concerned that certain groups in our society—blacks, the poor, the young, the less educated—vote at significantly lower rates than the rest of us. Even though nonvoters may follow the crowd in their voting intentions and policy preferences, one cannot help but feel that some very different perceptions about the way the world works are not being fully represented in our electoral system.[132]

Lower turnout rates for certain groups, say blacks and Hispanics, probably work against the nomination of Presidential candidates from these groups. We know from the 1960 Presidential election that turnout among Catholics was very high and that most Catholics voted for their fellow Catholic John F. Kennedy for President. Even a large share of Catholic Republicans voted for Kennedy.[133] But it is unlikely that even increased participation by blacks and Hispanics, not to mention the lower-income citizens, would lead to any realistic chance that these voters might nominate a candidate from their own ranks. However, the larger a group's participation, the more leverage it will have over the selection of candidates who might be responsive to its demands, as we will see in the following chapter. There is no guarantee that higher turnout will translate into more political clout, but the cases of Kennedy and others show that the two factors may well be connected. Failure to vote, then, is not only an individual problem, but one that affects people as members of groups as well.

Aside from the question of any advantage that might accrue to specific groups within the potential electorate, decreasing levels of turnout also pose a threat to the larger political system. We have seen that lower voting rates are associated with larger numbers of people believing that they don't have any control over their elected officials. This lower sense of political efficacy can easily translate into a lack of confidence in, first, elected leaders and, second, the entire system of government. We learned in Chapter 3 that recent Presidents have been considerably less popular than their predecessors. To be sure, we can raise many legitimate questions about performance in office. But we also appear to have entered an age of far greater skepticism toward our chief executives, just as the nation's problems have become more complex and seemingly more intractable than ever before. Our economy is intertwined with those of other countries to an unprecedented extent. It is thus virtually impossible for any single leader to effect the necessary changes without international cooperation. Yet the demands for immediate action keep increasing, not only in the United States but in other democracies as well.

A President is expected to find a "quick fix" to our problems. When this proves difficult, the people who feel powerless become even more frustrated. They might be even less likely to vote—or if they do vote, to cast ballots for candidates who appeal to voters' cynicism. The Carter campaign of 1976 and the Reagan race of 1980, as we shall see in Chapter 6, were based precisely on these sorts of appeals. Since 1964, there has been an increasing number of "outsider" candidates for President, either directly challenging the two major parties (George C. Wallace in 1968 and John Anderson in 1980) or emerging "from nowhere" to capture the nominations of those parties (Goldwater in 1964, McGovern in 1972, and Carter in 1976). The "anti-Washington" appeals of these candidates are directed not just at the voters attached to the two major parties, but also to a large extent at the "alienated" corps of nonvoters. The immediate threat is that some candidate can succeed (although Wallace failed in 1968) in garnering a sufficient number of electoral votes so as to broker the election of a President, thereby gaining substantial control over the public agenda even with only, say, the 15 percent vote that Wallace received. The longer term threat is that such outsider assaults on the party system might so weaken the two major parties that the people who do cast ballots for Democrats or Republicans might not be sure what they would get for their efforts. If both major parties consistently sought to capture the ballots of alienated nonvoters, they might no longer be able to bargain with each other to put together the sort of coalitions between Congress and the President that are generally needed to govern the country. And the paradox is that turnout continues to decline even as candidates try to court the disaffected.

SHOULD WE CARE?

The ultimate irony is that, for all we must worry, there is little any of us individually can do about the problem. And because none of us has any incentive to act as an individual. certainly nothing will get done. What needs to be done? It is clear that we need to have more faith in our political leaders and political parties and in our own ability to get things changed. Yet it is difficult for us to think of ways that we individually can make our political world different. To be sure, we can vote, but there is no guarantee that participation alone will make us more trusting of our parties and our leaders. We know that a lessened sense of efficacy and a detachment from our parties has lowered participation, but would the opposite relationship hold? Would more voting make us feel better about our politics? Much of the blame lies with our elected officials who don't bring home the excitement of a campaign to most voters. Yet, we don't know what they could or should do that would really attract people's interest. This is the very same problem that we confronted in the "puzzle of participation."

As a minimum, the citizen can try to keep an active interest in politics and certainly should vote if for no other immediate reward than helping to maintain the system. The citizen must take a fair measure of the responsibility for the zero turnout in our Florida example. But an even greater burden is put on our leaders, who must redirect political discourse to the issues that are on people's minds. This is the task of our party leadership. The only way to bring people back to the voting booth is to convince them that the trip is really worth the effort. Since the array of candidates facing the voter is too large for most citizens to develop an interest in each race according to the personalities involved, the only way that people will really feel that politics deals with important questions is for the parties to take clear, unequivocal, and distinguishable stands from each other. If we are worried about low turnout rates, if we disagree that a "moderate" amount of indifference is a good thing and even necessary for government to function, we must be concerned with how we can make our elected officials responsive to public opinion. For such popular control over public policy is critical to democratic government. We know that turnout does increase when politics is sharpened by such partisan cleavages.[134] But our parties are in a state of disarray. A recent *Washington Post*–ABC News poll showed that approximately half of the people wanted a third party to challenge our two major parties.[135] This is clearly a warning sign to our political leaders that they must do something to stem a further decline in trust among the citizenry.

It would be too facile, however, to put all the responsibility on our leaders. In this television age there are many distractions from political discourse. They range from situation comedies, to sports, to commercials. Democracy is ultimately a form of self-protection, a political system in which you have the best chance of preventing someone else from imposing his or her will on you.[136] If for no other reason than self-protection, citizens must be on the lookout for any clues from our political leaders that they are taking us seriously.

NOTES

1   Helen Huntley, "They Gave an Election, Nobody Came," *St. Petersburg* (Florida) *Times* (October 18, 1973), p. B1.

2   Warren Miller, "Disinterest, Disaffection, and Participation in Presidential Politics," *Political Behavior,* 2 (#1, 1980), p. 11.

3 Ronald C. Moe, "The Empty Voting Booth: Fact or Fiction?" *Commonsense,* 2 (Winter 1979), pp. 23–24.

4 The data are taken from U.S. Department of Commerce, Bureau of Census, *Current Population Reports,* Series P-20, no. 359, "Voting and Registration in the Election of 1980," January 1981 *(Advance Reports)* and earlier biennial series P-20 *Advance Reports.* The Census Bureau surveys, like all polls, tend to overestimate voting rates. The Census Bureau also compiles turnout figures based on state-level election returns, which show for 1980 a voting rate of 53.2 percent. Cf. Paul R. Abramson, John H. Aldrich, and David W. Rohde, *Change and Continuity in the 1980 Elections* (Washington: Congressional Quarterly, 1982), p. 78 for aggregate turnout figures since 1920. However, the aggregate figures do not provide turnout rates for subgroups in the electorate such as we report in Tables 4-1 and 4-2, so the Bureau surveys were used for comparability.

5 Lester W. Milbrath and M. L. Goel, *Political Participation,* 2d ed. (Chicago: Rand McNally, 1977). p. 22; Kevin P. Phillips and Paul H. Blackman, *Electoral Reform and Voter Participation* (Washington, D.C.: American Enterprise Institute, 1975), pp. 4–5.

6 Curtis Gans, "The Empty Ballot Box: Reflections on Nonvoters in America," *Public Opinion* (September/October 1978), p. 283.

7 Joseph Schumpeter, *Capitalism, Socialism, and Democracy* (New York: Harper Brothers, 1950), p. 283.

8 William G. Andrews, "American Voting Participation," *Western Political Quarterly,* 19 (December 1966), pp. 639–652.

9 Sidney Verba and Norman H. Nie, *Participation in America* (New York: Harper and Row, 1972), pp. 72–74.

10 Anthony Downs, *An Economic Theory of Democracy* (New York: Harper and Row, 1957), p. 267.

11 Ibid.

12 Gans, "The Empty Ballot Box," p. 55.

13 Miller, "Disinterest, Disaffection, and Participation in Presidential Politics," p. 11; Arthur T. Hadley, *The Empty Polling Booth* (Englewood Cliffs, N.J.: Prentice-Hall, 1978), p. 113.

14 Sinclair Lewis, *It Can't Happen Here* (New York: Dell, 1961).

15 Hadley, *The Empty Polling Booth,* p. 113.

16 Gans, "The Empty Ballot Box," p. 55.

17 See Howard Schuman and Stanley Presser, *Questions and Answers in Attitude Surveys* (New York: Academic Press, 1981); and Eric M. Uslaner and Ronald E. Weber, "Cognitive Consistency and the Politicization of the Abortion Issue among the Mass Public, 1972–1976." (Presented at the Annual Meeting of the Midwest Political Science Association, Cincinnati, Ohio, April 1981).

18 See especially John Stuart Mill, *Considerations on Representative Government* (Chicago: Henry Regnery, 1962), p. 154: "To learn to be human is to develop through the give and take of communication an effective sense of being, an individually distinctive member of a community; who understands and appreciates its beliefs, desires, and methods, and who contributes to a further conversion of organic powers into human resources and values."

19 Hadley, *The Empty Polling Booth,* p. 113.

20 Bernard R. Berelson, Paul F. Lazarsfeld, and William N. McPhee, *Voting* (Chicago: University of Chicago Press, 1954), pp. 314–315.

21 Angus Campbell, Philip E. Converse, Warren E. Miller, and Donald E. Stokes, *The American Voter* (New York: John Wiley and Sons, 1960), p. 282.

22 Ibid, pp. 278–279; Raymond E. Wolfinger and Steven J. Rosenstone, *Who Votes?* (New Haven: Yale University Press, 1980), p. 90.

23 Wolfinger and Rosenstone, *Who Votes?* pp. 93–94.

24 Campbell et al., *The American Voter,* pp. 278–279

25 For example, the median income of families in 1979 was $18,960 in the South compared with $21,234 in the North and $21,113 in the West. The lower family income for families in the South is also reflected in the percentage of families with less than $5,000 annual income: 6.7 percent in the South; 4.9 percent in the North; and 4.8 percent in the West.

In terms of education the percent of high school graduates in the Southern states as of 1976 was 59.6 percent compared with 74.3 percent in the West and 68.4 percent in the North. U.S. Department of Commerce, Bureau of the Census, *Statistical Abstract of the United States: 1981* (Washington, D.C.: Government Printing Office, 1981), table nos. 728 and 235. (Note: some of these figures were computed from data in each of the tables.)

26 The mean income of black households in 1979 was $13,088 compared with $19,620 for white households. Also, although the percent of the black population completing four years of high school or more rose from 31.4 percent in 1970 to 51.2 percent in 1980, 70.5 percent of the white population reached this level of educational attainment. U.S. Department of Commerce, Bureau of the Census, *Statistical Abstract of the United States: 1981,* table nos. 721 and 230.

27 Orley Ashenfelter and Stanley Kelley, Jr., "Determinants of Participation in Presidential Elections," *Journal of Law and Economics,* 12 (1975), p. 707; Michael Hout and David Knoke, "Change in Voting Turnout, 1952–1972," *Public Opinion Quarterly,* 39 (Spring 1975), p. 67.

28 Wolfinger and Rosenstone, *Who Votes?,* pp. 17–18.

29 Milbrath and Goel, *Political Participation,* p. 99.

30 Wolfinger and Rosenstone, *Who Votes?*, p. 20.
31 Ibid., pp. 22–23.
32 Ibid., p. 95.
33 Ibid., pp. 32–33.
34 V. O. Key, Jr., *Politics. Parties, and Pressure Groups,* 2d ed. (New York: Thomas Y. Crowell, 1947), p. 30.
35 Michael S. Lewis-Beck, "Agrarian Political Behavior in the United States," *American Journal of Political Science,* 21 (August 1977), pp. 543–565.
36 Wolfinger and Rosenstone, *Who Votes?*, p. 31.
37 Ibid., p. 95.
38 David B. Hill and Norman Luttbeg, *Trends in American Electoral Behavior* (Itasca, Illinois: E. Peacock, 1980), p. 91.
39 Wolfinger and Rosenstone, *Who Votes?*, pp. 20–22.
40 Ibid., p. 29.
41 These are also Census Bureau data; see note 4 for the data sources. Prior to 1972, figures for the 18-to-20-year-old potential electorate reflect only those states in which citizens below the age of twenty-one were eligible to vote: Georgia and Kentucky, where eighteen-year-olds could vote; Alaska, where nineteen-year-olds were eligible; and Hawaii, where twenty-year-olds could vote.
42 Campbell et al., *The American Voter,* p. 494.
43 Wolfinger and Rosenstone, *Who Votes?*, p. 47.
44 Campbell et al., *The American Voter,* pp. 485–487.
45 Wolfinger and Rosenstone, *Who Votes?*, pp. 41–42.
46 These are again Census Bureau figures drawn from the sources in note 4.
47 Charles E. Merriam and Harold F. Gosnell, *Non-Voting* (Chicago: University of Chicago Press, 1924), pp. 34, 103.
48 Campbell et al., *The American Voter,* pp. 487–488.
49 Wolfinger and Rosenstone, *Who Votes?*, p. 44.
50 Campbell et al., *The American Voter,* p. 464; Hadley, *The Empty Polling Booth,* p. 18.
51 Milbrath and Goel, *Political Participation,* p. 113; Wolfinger and Rosenstone, *Who Votes?*, pp. 52ff.
52 Campbell et al., *The American Voter,* p. 102; John R. Petrocik, "Voter Turnout and Electoral Oscillation," *American Politics Quarterly,* 9 (April 1981), pp. 163–164.
53 Richard A. Brody and Paul M. Sniderman, "From Life Space to Polling Place," *British Journal of Political Science,* 7 (1977), p. 3.
54 Richard A. Brody and Bernard Grofman, "Choice Vs. Involvement in Electoral Participation." (Paper presented at the National Science Foundation Conference on Turnout, San Diego, California, May 1976), p. 7.

55 Berelson et al., *Voting,* p. 31.

56 Hadley, *The Empty Polling Booth,* p. 20.

57 Herbert Weisberg, "Rational Abstention Due to Satisfaction." (Paper presented at the meeting of the Midwest Political Science Association, Chicago, April, 1977); cf. Herbert F. Weisberg and Bernard Grofman, "Candidate Evaluations and Turnout," *American Politics Quarterly,* 9 (April 1981), pp. 197–220.

58 Paul R. Abramson and John Aldrich, "The Decline of Electoral Participation in America," *American Political Science Review,* 76 (September 1982), p. 510. The authors term these "external efficacy" items as opposed to "internal efficacy" questions, which ask whether people feel that voting is the only way that they can have an impact and whether people believe that politics is too complicated to understand. Ibid, pp. 510–512.

59 Hadley, *The Empty Polling Booth,* pp. 34–35; Campbell et al., *The American Voter,* pp. 103–105.

60 Campbell et al., *The American Voter,* p. 106; Abramson and Aldrich, "The Decline of Electoral Participation in America"; Ashenfelter and Kelley, "Determinants of Participation in Presidential Elections."

61 Philip E. Converse, "The Concept of a Normal Vote," in Angus Campbell, Philip E. Converse, Warren E. Miller, and Donald E. Stokes, *Elections and the Political Order* (New York: John Wiley, 1967), pp. 9, 39.

62 Petrocik, "Voter Turnout and Electoral Oscillation," pp. 163–164; Hill and Luttbeg, *Trends in American Electoral Behavior,* p. 91.

63 Campbell et al., *The American Voter,* p. 97; Petrocik, "Voter Turnout and Electoral Oscillation," pp. 163–164.

64 Angus Campbell, "Surge and Decline: A Study of Electoral Change," in Campbell et al., *Elections and the Political Order,* pp. 40–62.

65 Merriam and Gosnell, *Non-Voting,* p. 140; Elizabeth Sanders, "On the Costs, Utilities, and Simple Joys of Voting," *Journal of Politics,* 42 (October 1980), pp. 854–863; John P. Katosh and Michael W. Traugott, "The Effects of Local Administration on Voter Turnout in 1976." (Paper presented at the meeting of the Midwest Political Science Association, Chicago, April 1978.)

66 Howard L. Reiter, "Why Is Turnout Down?," *Public Opinion Quarterly,* 43 (Fall 1979), pp. 299–301.

67 Ashenfelter and Kelley, "Determinants of Participation in Presidential Elections;" Merriam and Gosnell, *Non-Voting,* p. 132.

68 Jae-on Kim, John Petrocik, and Stephen Enokson, "Turnout Among the American States: Systemic and Independent Components," *American Political Science Review,* 69 (March 1975), pp. 107–123.

69 Downs, *An Economic Theory of Democracy,* p. 262.

70 Campbell et al., *The American Voter,* p. 99; Richard A. Brody and Benjamin I. Page, "Indifference, Alienation, and Rational Decisions," *Pub-*

lic Choice, 15 (Summer 1973). pp. 5–6. But for contrary evidence, see John Ferejohn and Morris Fiorina, "The Paradox of Not Voting: A Decision-Theoretic Analysis," *American Political Science Review,* 68 (May 1974), pp. 525–536.

71 Ashenfelter and Kelley, "Determinants of Participation in Presidential Elections," p. 724.

72 Robert Erikson, "Why Do People Vote? Because They Are Registered," *American Politics Quarterly,* 9 (April 1981), pp. 259–276.

73 Ibid., p. 261.

74 Ibid., pp. 63–264; Ashenfelter and Kelley, "Determinants of Participation in Presidential Elections," pp. 695–733.

75 See note 4 for the states in which voters under twenty-one could cast ballots prior to 1972.

76 Ashenfelter and Kelley, "Determinants of Participation in Presidential Elections," p. 722. For an analysis that indicates that mobilization in Mississippi occurred with the greatest force in those areas that already had a stronger democratic tradition, see Ronald J. Terchek, "Polyarchy and Participation," in John G. Grumm and Stephen L. Wasby (eds.), *The Analysis of Policy Impact* (Lexington, Mass.: Lexington Books, 1981), pp. 43–51.

77 Ashenfelter and Kelley, "Determinants of Participation in Presidential Elections."

78 Wolfinger and Rosenstone, *Who Votes?,* p. 71.

79 Ibid., pp. 71–72.

80 Ibid., p. 73.

81 Richard A. Brody. "The Puzzle of Political Participation in America," in Anthony King (ed.), *The New American Political System* (Washington, D.C.: American Enterprise Institute, 1978), pp. 287–324.

82 Stephen D. Shaffer, "A Multivariate Explanation of Decreasing Turnout in Presidential Elections, 1960–1976," *American Journal of Political Science,* 25 (February 1981), p. 79; Thomas Cavanagh, "Changes in American Voter Turnout, 1964–1976," *Political Science Quarterly,* 96 (Spring 1981), pp. 53–54.

83 Hadley, *The Empty Polling Booth,* p. 22.

84 Reiter, "Why Is Turnout Down?"

85 Ibid.; Carol A. Cassel, "Change in Electoral Participation in the South," *Journal of Politics,* 41 (August 1979), pp. 907–917.

86 Ashenfelter and Kelley, "Determinants of Participation in Presidential Elections," p. 722.

87 See also Hill and Luttbeg, *Trends in American Electoral Behavior,* p. 92.

88 Campbell et al., *The American Voter,* pp. 276–277.

89 Miller, "Disinterest, Disaffection, and Participation in Presidential Politics," p. 24.

90 Cf. Cavanagh, "Changes in American Voter Turnout, 1964–1976," pp. 56–58.

91 Shaffer, "A Multivariate Explanation of Decreasing Explanation of Decreasing Turnout in Presidential Elections, 1960–1976," p. 79.

92 Ibid., pp. 72–79.

93 Abramson and Aldrich, "The Decline of Electoral Participation in America," p. 504.

94 Shaffer, "A Multivariate Explanation of Decreasing Turnout in Presidential Elections, 1960–1976," pp. 84–85.

95 Miller, "Disinterest, Disaffection, and Participation in Presidential Politics," p. 13.

96 Shaffer, "A Multivariate Explanation of Decreasing Turnout in Presidential Elections, 1960–1976," pp. 89–90.

97 Abramson and Aldrich, "The Decline of Electoral Participation in America," pp. 512–513.

98 Ibid., pp. 6–7.

99 Ibid.; Shaffer, "A Multivariate Explanation of Decreasing Turnout in Presidential Elections, 1960–1976," pp. 72–74.

100 Miller, "Disinterest, Disaffection, and Participation in Presidential Politics," p. 21.

101 Ibid., pp. 22–23.

102 Abramson and Aldrich, "The Decline of Electoral Participation in America," p. 507; Shaffer, "A Multivariate Explanation of Decreasing Turnout in Presidential Elections. 1960–1976," p. 79.

103 Miller, "Disinterest, Disaffection, and Participation in Presidential Politics," pp. 22–23.

104 Ibid., p. 22.

105 Abramson and Aldrich, "The Decline of Electoral Participation in America," p. 42; Shaffer, "A Multivariate Explanation of Decreasing Turnout in Presidential Elections, 1960–1976," p. 519.

106 Hill and Luttbeg, *Trends in American Electoral Behavior*, pp. 96–98.

107 Richard G. Smolka, *Election Day Registration* (Washington, D.C.: American Enterprise Institute, 1977). See also Richard G. Smolka, *Voters by Mail* (Washington, D.C.: American Enterprise Institute, 1977).

108 Kevin P. Phillips and Paul H. Blackman, *Electoral Reform and Voter Participation* (Washington, D.C.: American Enterprise Institute, 1975), pp. 15–18.

109 Ibid., p. 28.

110 Smolka, *Election Day Registration,* pp. 45–53.

111 A large share of the literature makes this mistake. For an elaboration on the problem, see Eric M. Uslaner, "Comparative State Politics, Interparty Competition, and Malapportionment: A New Look at V. O. Key's 'Hypotheses'," *Journal of Politics,* 40 (May 1978), pp. 409–432.

112 Turnout in 1980 in Maryland was 58.6 percent, in New Jersey, 59.6

percent. In contrast, the figures for other states were: Illinois, 66.4 percent; Georgia, 53.5 percent; and New York, 54.8 percent. See U.S. Department of Commerce, Bureau of Census, Current Population Reports, Series P-20, no. 359, "Voting and Registration in the Election of 1980," January 1981 (Advance Report).

113   For this debate see Philip E. Converse, "Change in the American Electorate," in Angus Campbell and Philip E. Converse (eds.), *The Human Meaning of Social Change* (New York: Russell Sage Foundation, 1972), pp. 263–337; Jerrold G. Rusk, "The Effect of the Australian Ballot Reform on Split-Ticket Voting," *American Political Science Review,* 64 (December 1970), pp. 1220–1238; Walter Dean Burnham, "Theory and Voting Research," *American Political Science Review,* 68 (September 1974), pp. 1002–1023.

114   Hadley, *The Empty Polling Booth,* p. 119.

115   Merriam and Gosnell, *Non-Voting,* p. 95

116   Hadley, *The Empty Polling Booth,* pp. 123–124; Merriam and Gosnell, *Non-Voting,* p. 95.

117   Phillips and Blackman, *Electoral Reform and Voter Participation,* pp. 59ff; Henry Abraham, *Compulsory Voting* (Washington, D.C.: Public Affairs Press, 1955), p. 8.

118   Hadley, *The Empty Polling Booth,* p. 123.

119   Petrocik, "Voter Turnout and Electoral Oscillation," pp. 161–162.

120   Miller, "Disinterest, Disaffection, and Participation in Presidential Politics," p. 21.

121   James DeNardo, "Turnout and the Vote: The Joke's on the Democrats," *American Political Science Review,* 74 (June 1980), pp. 406–420.

122   John H. Fenton, "Turnout and the Two-Party Vote," *Journal of Politics,* 39 (February 1979), pp. 231–232.

123   Ibid.

124   DeNardo, "Turnout and the Vote: The Joke's on the Democrats," pp. 417–418.

125   Ibid.

126   Wolfinger and Rosenstone, *Who Votes?,* pp. 86–87.

127   Ibid., p. 109.

128   William S. Maddox, "Candidate Images Among Voters and Nonvoters in 1976," *American Politics Quarterly,* 9 (April 1981), pp. 209–220.

129   Petrocik, "Voter Turnout and Electoral Oscillation," pp. 168–169; Reiter, "Why Is Turnout Down?," pp. 308–309.

130   Reiter, "Why Is Turnout Down?," pp. 308–309.

131   Petrocik, "Voter Turnout and Electoral Oscillation," pp. 169–171.

132   See Gerald M. Garvey, "The Theory of Party Equilibirum," *American Political Science Review,* 60 (March 1966), pp. 29–38, especially pp. 34–48.

133 See Ithiel de Sola Pool, Robert P. Abelson, and Samuel Popkin, *Candidates, Issues and Strategies* (Cambridge: MIT Press, 1964), pp. 116, 117.

134 Walter Dean Burnham, "Theory and Voting Research," *American Political Science Review,* 68 (September 1974), pp. 1002–1023.

135 Unpublished data from *The Washington Post*–ABC News national poll taken in September 1982.

136 Douglas W. Rae, "Political Democracy as a Property of Political Institutions," *American Political Science Review,* 65 (March 1971), pp. 111–119.

THE ELECTORAL COLLEGE

Americans do not vote directly for President. Instead, they cast ballots for people they are not likely to know at all, Presidential electors, who are charged with the responsibility of electing the chief executive. This system, the Electoral College, is a unique feature of the American political system. It has led on at least three occasions to situations in which the Presidential candidate who seemed to be "the people's choice" was not elected. It has also resulted in a seemingly endless controversy over the method of Presidential election, indeed perhaps one of the most prolonged debates over Constitutional procedures in American history.

After the Federal Convention drafting the Constitution was over, delegate James Wilson remarked to the ratifying convention of his state of Pennsylvania, "The Convention, sir, were perplexed with no part of this plan so much as with the method of choosing the President of the United States."[1] The ultimate compromise between reserving key powers to the states and representing the people as a whole provided for a Presidential election system that is complex indeed. The small states were concerned that the larger ones might dominate the new nation and they insisted on some guarantees, particularly the establishment of the United States Senate with its two members per state regardless of population. On the other hand, more populous states feared the possibility of veto powers by smaller ones, and thus a legislative body based on population size of each state, the House of Representatives, was also established.

The method of electing the President reflects this controversy. The people do not vote directly for President. Instead, each state is entitled to the number of electors equal to the number of seats it has in the House of Representatives (reflecting population size) and the number it has in the Senate (reflecting the equality of states, since each is guaranteed two seats regardless of population). In 1984 California, the most populous state, will have forty-seven such electoral votes, followed by New York with thirty-six. Six states—Alaska, Delaware, North and South Dakota, Vermont, and Wyoming—have the minimum number of three electoral votes, as does the District of Columbia. The citizens of the Nation's capital did not participate in Presidential elections at all until the Twenty-third Amendment to the Constitution became effective in 1964.

When people go to the polls in November of every fourth year, they do not vote for President, but rather for a slate of electors who pledge themselves to support a particular candidate. In virtually every case the slate of electors pledged to a particular candidate who gets the most votes in a state is elected. Thus, a one-vote plurality for a candidate's slate in California will result in all forty-seven of that state's electoral votes being cast for that candidate.

The framers of the Constitution were torn over so many aspects of the Presidential election process that they did not specify how the Electoral College was to work. Specifically, they made no provision for how a state was to choose its electors. Currently, three states do not use a winner-take-all system: Maine awards its two statewide votes to the candidate who has a plurality in the state and its other two votes to the candidate who carries each Congressional district; in Mississippi and South Carolina electors run throughout the state as individual candidates pledged to Presidential candidates rather than on a slate that is elected as a whole. The electors meet in the capitals of their respective states in December and go through the ritual of formally casting their votes for the Presidential candidate they pledged to support. These ballots are sent to the Congress in January, where the House of Representatives tallies all the electoral votes for President and the Senate all the votes for Vice President. To be elected, a candidate must receive an absolute majority of all electoral votes cast in the nation. Since the House of Representatives has 435 members, the Senate has 100 members, and the Twenty-third Amendment allocated three electoral votes to the nation's capital, there are 538 electoral votes throughout the nation. A victorious candidate must gain at least 270 electoral votes. A simple plurality is not sufficient, so if there is a three candidate race and one candidate receives 238 electoral votes, another 200, and the third 100, the Electoral College will fail to select a President. Indeed, in 1968 American Independent candidate George C. Wallace had little chance of winning the Presidency but hoped to gain a large measure of influence by securing enough electoral votes to deny outright election to either Richard M. Nixon or Hubert H. Humphrey, the Republican and Democratic nominees.

If no candidate receives a majority in the Electoral College, there is a "contingent election" in which the House of Representives selects the President and the Senate the Vice President. But, in keeping with the basic idea underlying the Electoral College of representing the states, the method of election in the House is not a simple roll call among the legislators. Rather, the vote is by states. Each state delegation casts a single vote, so a candidate must receive a majority of all states' ballots rather than a simple majority of the House of Representatives. If no candidate receives the votes of twenty-six state delegations, the House must keep voting until a majority winner is achieved. If a delegation is evenly split between Democrats and Republicans, it is likely that the state will simply be unable to cast a ballot at all. In the 98th Congress, elected in 1982, nine states—Arkansas, Colorado, Indiana, Iowa, Montana, Nevada, New Hampshire, Rhode Island, and South Carolina—had House delegations with equal numbers of Democrats and Republicans. If the 1984 Presidential election did not yield a candidate with an Electoral College majority *and* the House delegations remained the same as in 1982, a candidate would have to obtain the votes of 63 percent of the states (twenty-six of the forty-one that could cast ballots) to be elected President. The Vice President, under a contingent election, would be chosen by the Senate, with each Senator casting a single vote. However, the Senate allows unlimited debate, which effectively prohibits a vote on any question about which some Senators decide to engage in what is called a "filibuster." It takes sixty Senators to end a filibuster and proceed to a vote, so the election of a Vice President thus might also require more than a simple majority. If the House deadlocked and could not choose a President, the Vice President would become acting President. However, if the Senate were unable to select a Vice President, the acting President would be the Speaker of the House. Neither Representatives nor Senators are under any obligation to vote for the Presidential candidate who carried their state.

The contingent election provision has only been used twice in American history, in 1800 and 1824. Under the original plan in the Constitution, the candidate with the greatest number of electoral votes (assuming a majority was reached) would be the President and the runner-up would be selected Vice President. But in 1800 the Republican electors cast an equal number of ballots for the party's ticket of Thomas Jefferson and Aaron Burr, with Federalist incumbent John Adams trailing with sixty-five electoral votes. The contest was thrown into the House in 1801; it took thirty-six ballots to untangle the mess and elect Jefferson, with Burr as his Vice President. This confusion led to the adoption of the Twelfth Amendment to the Constitution, which provided for separate ballots in the Electoral College for the President and Vice President; incidentally, it also changed the contingent election system by permitting the House to select from only the top three candidates in the Electoral College, rather than five as previously allowed. In 1824 none of the four major candidates—John Quincy Adams, Andrew Jackson, William H. Crawford, and Henry Clay—received an electoral majority. Jackson won the largest number of popular votes (42.2 percent) and electoral votes (ninety-nine) with Adams in second place (31.9 percent, eighty-four electoral votes). The election was thrown into the House and Clay, having finished fourth, was no longer considered. There were rumors of an Adams-Clay deal, whereby Clay would pledge his support to Adams in return for being named Secretary of State.[2] Adams did prevail on the first ballot when Representative Stephen Van Renssaelaer of New York cast the deciding ballot in his state's delegation; he had been leaning toward Jackson but bowed his head to pray for divine guidance and saw a piece of paper on the House floor with Adams' name on it. He cast his ballot for Adams and the election was decided.[3]

The importance of the 1824 election is that it was the first contest in which the candidate who received the largest number of popular votes did *not* become President. This is a critical aspect of the Electoral College's "winner-take-all" provision for each state's electoral votes, or the "general ticket system," as it is often called. There is no Constitutional requirement that the voters in any state be permitted to register their preferences for President. Until the 1830s, many state legislatures did not even recognize popular elections for Presidential electors; the last time state legislators acted without a popular vote was in Colorado in 1876.[4] Indeed, it was 1876 when the second "misfire" in the Electoral College, the selection as President of a candidate who did not finish first in the popular vote, occurred. The contest between Republican Rutherford B. Hayes and Democrat Samuel J. Tilden took place as the period of Reconstruction after the Civil War came to a close. The Southern vote was very much in doubt and four states submitted double sets of electoral votes to the Congress. Faced with the possibility of an armed insurrection, Congress passed a law establishing a supposedly independent electoral commission to determine how the electoral votes under challenge would be counted. The popular vote tallies of both parties showed Tilden to be the winner and all the Democrats needed was one electoral vote of the twenty that were contested. The commission of five Democrats, five Republicans, and four Supreme Court justices was to appoint an independent to the body. But, in one of the great ironies of American history, the Democratic-controlled Illinois legislature named the leading independent candidate for the commission to the United States Senate on the very day that Congress established the independent commission. The member chosen in his place voted down the line with the Republicans, and Hayes was elected President.

Finally, in 1888 President Grover Cleveland was challenged by Republican Benjamin Harrison of Indiana. Although Cleveland scored a popular vote plurality of almost 100,000 over Harrison, he failed to carry his native state. Harrison's concentration of support in the larger, more closely contested states enabled him to secure an Electoral College majority. Cleveland did gain revenge four years later, when he was elected President again. Some people maintain that 1888 is the only clear-cut case of an Electoral College misfire since: (1) six states in the election of 1824 did not use popular elections at all to determine how the electoral votes would be cast; and (2) the evidence of widespread vote fraud in 1876 made it difficult to determine who actually won the popular vote.[5] There is also the claim that the 1960 election might have been a misfire. All Republican electors in Alabama were pledged to Richard M. Nixon, but the Democratic electors were split between John F. Kennedy and an unpledged slate. The Democrats carried the state and the unpledged electors cast their ballots for Senator Harry F. Byrd (Democrat, Virginia). But the popular vote totals that showed Kennedy with a national lead of approximately 120,000 votes made no effort to disentangle any portion of the Alabama votes that perhaps should be attributed to the unpledged elector slate. Thus, according to one analysis, Kennedy benefited from counting both sets of votes and, when the appropriate adjustments are made, Nixon emerges with a national popular vote lead of slightly more than 58,000 votes even though Kennedy's Electoral College majority still holds![6] This is, of course, a numbers game and one can make an equally good case that Kennedy's victory in 1960 was quite real since most Alabamans voted for both Kennedy and the unpledged slate. We may not know who the people's choice would have been in 1824 and, even though both parties' tallies showed Tilden as the popular vote winner in 1876,[7] it is possible that there was massive vote fraud. But this is quite beside the point. Very few elections have instant replays available and it is only armchair politicians who take pleasure in handicapping races after the two dollar windows have paid off. What matters is that it is possible at all for the Electoral College to select as President a candidate who did not win the most popular votes.

How likely is a "misfire," an outcome in which the Electoral College victor does not receive a plurality of the popular votes, to occur? One study concluded that in a contest as close as that between Nixon and Kennedy in 1960, the probability of an Electoral College misfire is 0.50; projected to the election of 2008, with an estimated turnout of 140 million, a 1 million vote plurality would misfire in one election of three, a 2–3 million vote plurality a quarter of the time, and a 4 million vote victory in one election of eight.[8] These figures are not exact since they fail to consider changes in traditional voting patterns (such as the growth of Republican strength in the South), but they are instructive. Another study develops a model of Presidential elections employing data from state-level returns since 1900 and estimates that in an election as close as 1960 the prospects of a misfire approached one in four whereas in 1976 the likelihood of a reversal was 0.50 percent. Although Kennedy had a smaller popular vote margin than did Carter, he carried fewer states by very small margins than did the Georgian. Indeed, in contests in which the victor's percentage of the *two-party* popular vote falls below 51 (as in 1960, 1968, and 1976), the probability of a misfire approaches one-half.[8] Clearly, the prospects of a verdict that does not conform to the popular vote are quite real.

What criteria ought we to consider paramount in assessing the democratic character of a nation? In the context of the present argument just how disturbing are "runner-up" Presidents? One argument is that these results have occurred infrequently in our history and that we ought not to make too much of them.[10] Furthermore, the present system takes the breadth of voters' preferences into account more than direct election of the President would. A candidate with widespread support across *states,* according to this thesis, would have a deeper basis of support than one whose votes were clustered in states with a minority of electoral votes.

Does a mature nation, such as the United States, with a higher proportion of its citizenry college educated than any other nation in the world, still need protection against its own voting choices, whether that protection takes the form of a unique way of counting the votes or a "deliberative body" to reinterpret the votes? If all citizens are supposed to be equal, one vote should not count more heavily than another. What is the rationale for a voter in Arizona (or New York or Louisiana) to be either more *or* less favored than voters elsewhere? If democracy doesn't mean that the majority rules *at least in election outcomes,* what does it mean? If three reversals aren't too many, would four (1960), five (1968), or six (1976)—when we include misfires that *almost* occurred in close races—also be acceptable? Does the fact that both Jackson and Cleveland (although not Tilden) later won make their earlier defeats more acceptable? It seems difficult to accept positive answers to these questions as defenses of misfires.

FAITHLESS, HOPELESS, AND UNCHARITABLE ELECTORS

Following the 1976 election Robert L. Brewster of Albuquerque, New Mexico, wrote all of the members of the Electoral College and pleaded with them to elect him President lest the country be ravaged by earthquakes and tidal waves. He received no votes in the Electoral College although Washington state elector Mike Paddon decided that Ford was not sufficiently opposed to abortion and cast his ballot (four years early) for Ronald Reagan. Indeed, in six of the nine postwar elections. the exceptions being 1952, 1964, and 1980, at least one member of the Electoral College has defied public expectations and voted for the candidate of his choice who was generally not on the ballot at all.[11] A classic example of this problem occurred in 1960 when six unpledged Alabama electors and eight from Mississippi tried to engineer a bolt throughout the South in favor of conservative Democratic Senator Harry Byrd (Virginia) to throw the election into the House. They were only joined by one maverick Republican elector. The tradition goes back to 1796 when a Federalist elector defected to the Republican Jefferson.

There is no requirement in the Constitution that an elector follow the dictates of the popular vote. Indeed, the Founders of the nation expected the electors to exercise some independent judgment. Nevertheless, those who violate their original commitment are called "faithless electors." Some people defend the practice as adding flexibility to the electoral system, particularly in the event that a winning candidate dies.[12] But it is highly unlikely that party leaders would leave the selection of a new President to the members of the Electoral College, who are chosen for a specific purpose only once every four years and who are accountable to no one after they perform their one duty. Furthermore, the Constitution does prohibit anyone holding a public office in the United States from serving as an elector. The only instance in which the death of a candidate even arose was in 1872 when three Georgia Republican electors insisted on casting ballots for their party's deceased nominee, Horace Greeley. The Congress refused to certify those ballots. It strains the imagination to consider the Electoral College as a deliberative body capable of reaching a decision on a new President, since the electors meet only in their respective states.

In Alaska, Florida, Oklahoma, and Oregon, electors must make specific pledges that they will support the national nominees of their party in the Electoral College. Several other states permit parties to exact pledges from potential electors, including even the possibility of removal of suspicious electors by the state party. Fifteen states, among them California and New York, require by statute that electors remain faithful; following the defection of the Republican elector to Byrd in 1960, Oklahoma requires each elector to take an oath to support the party's nominees, which if violated constitutes a misdemeanor punishable by a fine of $1,000.[13] The Supreme Court in *Ray v. Blair* upheld Alabama parties' rights to exclude from the ballot candidates who refused to pledge support for the nominee, but it did not rule on the casting of such ballots *per se*.[14] In 1969 a North Carolina elector pledged to Nixon voted instead for Wallace. Democratic Representative James G. O'Hara (Michigan) and Senator Edmund Muskie (Maine) filed a motion that the Congress not count the unfaithful vote, but they were unsuccessful. The problem of dealing with faithless electors remains with the states but that of counting and certifying the electoral votes is a Congressional task. If an elector is willing to risk any penalties involved, he or she apparently can vote with relative impunity for any candidate. Indeed, if a movement toward an alternative candidate gained sufficient national momentum, one can envisage a situation in which convictions of the unfaithful would be difficult to obtain.

A stampede is hardly likely, however. From the founding of the nation to 1980, only eight of 18,124 electors have unambiguously miscast their ballots. But the issue remains a prominent one in debates about the Electoral College. We are fascinated by faithless electors in part because they are so unusual in our politics. They lead us to conjure up all sorts of ideas about what might happen and provide grist for the mill for arguments in opposition to the present system. Supporters of direct election, frustrated in their unsuccessful attempts to attain their own goal, sometimes argue that a constitutional amendment providing for the automatic plan, which would abolish the office of elector and have electoral votes tallied according to state electoral returns, would constitute a useful first step. Defenders of the general ticket system are often willing to lend at least reluctant support to the automatic plan to indicate that they are not opposed to change on all grounds.

ALLEGED BENEFITS OF THE ELECTORAL COLLEGE

Defenders of the Electoral College maintain that the system does have some important benefits. In this section we consider these arguments, including the claims that: (1) the general ticket system reinforces federalism; (2) nonvoters are better represented under this system; (3) abolition of the Electoral College would increase vote fraud; (4) the Electoral College maintains the two-party system; and (5) the Electoral College provides mandates to Presidents who may have only received small popular vote margins. Should the present system be changed to direct popular election of the President, these advantages, it is argued, would be lost.

The Electoral College Reinforces Federalism

Since the Electoral College was fashioned at the Constitutional convention and both its composition and its method of selection were compromises, some supporters have argued that it is an integral part of our federal system. Abolition of the Electoral College would deprive the states of their role in the Presidential election process, since: (1) the present system awards two electoral votes to each state regardless of size; and (2) the electors are chosen in accordance with state law and cast their ballots in the respective state capitals. Any assault on the Electoral College is held to be a challenge to the entire scope of the federal bargain. Indeed, some defenders of the system argue that direct election of the President would weaken state and local parties and permit candidates to ignore certain sections of the country, thereby taking power away from the states. State control over party nominating conventions, criteria for candidates getting on the ballot, and the requirements for voting by citizens might become subject to national control, thereby abrogating the federal bargain of 1787.[15]

To be sure, *any* change in the method of election will result in some reorientation of candidates' appeals, but, as we shall argue in discussing the biases of the Electoral College, the magnitude of the shifts would not necessarily be great. Do certain states have an inherent *right* to candidates' attention? If a candidate chooses to ignore certain sections of the country, it must be the case that he or she would not expect to garner very many votes there. The argument that the role of the states would be weakened in general may have some elements of truth in it, but we cannot help but notice that throughout the twentieth century our attention has been riveted on Washington as never before in our history and particularly on the President. The growth of the importance of the media has focused attention on the country's only nationally elected political leader. Reforms in national party conventions, which we have discussed in Chapter 1, have indeed taken power away from the states and placed them with the national committees of the political parties. Regarding the part of the federal bargain on qualifications for voting, amendments to the Constitutions have extended suffrage and thereby made state requirements for voting more uniform. The Supreme Court has sustained the right of Congress to set qualifications for voting in national elections in *Oregon v. Mitchell* (1970)[16] when it upheld the national statute establishing a voting age of eighteen.

All these national "intrusions" into the federal bargain occurred without any change in the way we elect our President. Thus, major changes in our federal system have occurred without any alteration in the Electoral College. Federal control over candidate access to the ballot has also progressed somewhat in the last two decades as American Independent George C. Wallace, Independent Eugene J. McCarthy in 1976, and National Unity candidate John B. Anderson all fought successful legal battles to obtain ballot access in all fifty states. The key elements of federalism in our elections have already been weakened; even if a change in the method of electing the President were to strengthen national control still further, the area for new federal intervention seems limited. Perhaps national legislation on ballot access for a national office might be a desirable outcome. The cause of federalism is hardly served by permitting state officials or statutes to frustrate the national candidacies even of people with little actual chance of serving as President. It is set back even further by a folly masquerading as a state's right under which Wallace ran in Alabama in 1968 as the official nominee of the *Democratic* party, while the national candidate Humphrey had to set up an independent line on which to contest the state's electoral votes. If the federal bargain on electoral laws and procedures has been abrogated, it is not because of the way we elect our President but rather because the country has simply become more homogeneous.

The Electoral College Represents Nonvoters

Electoral votes are awarded on the basis of a state's population, not on the number of registered voters or on the number of people who actually cast ballots. Supporters of the present system correctly maintain that voters in states with low turnout derive an advantage over those in states with high rates of voting.[17] The latter are more likely to be in the Mountain region and the West, although some Eastern states also have strong turnout rates. The low turnout states are largely concentrated in the South. Historically, low turnout in that region can be traced to restrictions on black voting and the lower economic status of many residents of that region. But Southern turnout has dramatically increased in the last two decades as a result of: (1) the Voting Rights Act of 1965, which greatly improved ballot access for blacks; and (2) the general increase in prosperity of the Sunbelt. Although regional turnout rates still vary considerably, there is little reason to presume that a change in the method of electing the President will itself have an impact on voting rates.

The important question thus becomes: Should a state's impact on a national election be based on the number of people living there or the number of people who turn out to vote? The original rationale for basing electoral votes, as well as House representation, on population figures was derived from the idea of the Constitutional convention as a meeting of then-sovereign states. But today the population basis for the Electoral College only perpetuates the fiction that there are clearly identifiable "state" interests in selecting the President. If failure to vote is a serious problem throughout the nation, as we argued in Chapter 4, there does not seem to be a compelling reason why some nonvoters should have their "interests" better protected than others.

The Electoral College Minimizes Voter Fraud

Would a change to direct election lead to an increase in vote fraud? In a close election there is always the potential for vote fraud. One hears stories about late votes coming in from the graveyards in Chicago, Philadelphia, and all over New Jersey. In a Tennessee Congressional election in the mid-1970s, a black candidate rescued a victory when one of his aides found several unopened ballot boxes accidentally misplaced in a city dump on election night. Supporters of the general ticket system worry that direct election of the President would lead to an increase in the potential for such fraud.

The rationale is that under the present method of electing the President candidates must carry particular states. In those states in which a nominee won handily there would be little rationale for any candidate to demand a recount. But, as one advocate of the present system argues, direct election of the President might be a different matter altogether: "If the defeated candidate called for recounts in isolated states where he had reason to believe irregularities worked to his detriment, the winning candidate would surely call for recounts in other states where he believed he could pick up some advantage." Under the present system, candidates must try to gain votes in specific states. "It may well be more difficult to pick up five thousand to ten thousand votes in Missouri or Nevada than to pick up a hundred thousand votes in the country as a whole."[18] Under direct election, every state would be fair game for recounts since it would not matter what a candidate's margin of victory in that state was as long as there might be still more votes to discover.

In elections such as those of 1960 and 1968 in which the electoral vote margin for the victor is much greater than the popular spread, this argument is quite correct. In the former contest the Electoral College margin for Kennedy was eighty-three votes compared with a popular margin of just over 100,000 votes; for 1968 the respective figures were 120 electoral votes and slightly more than 500,000 popular votes. But consider an election such as the 1976 contest in which the electoral vote margin was *not* significantly greater than the popular spread. Carter won fifty-seven more electoral votes than Ford with a 2 percent margin in the popular vote, translating into 1.7 million more popular votes for Carter than for Ford. But many states had very close contests in this race and it would have taken a shift of fewer than 9,300 votes in Ohio and Hawaii together (appropriately distributed) to have put Ford in the White House for a second term, whereas more than 850,000 popular votes would have had to be changed to result in a Ford plurality under direct election.[19]

The argument about where popular votes need to be picked up under alternative voting systems is thus not so straightforward. In some elections, in which there are a large number of very competitive states but also a fair number of quite "safe" states for the winning candidate, the current Electoral College might put a greater premium on vote fraud than direct election! Indeed, even in the 1968 contest, it would not be quite so easy to reverse the outcome by fraud since more than a quarter of a million ballots would have to be changed from Nixon to Humphrey—or, perhaps, some 520,000 new Humphrey votes discovered nationwide. Our guess is that, if an election can be stolen, it will be and the motivations underlying vote fraud have relatively little to do with Constitutional provisions; they are hardly constrained by any method of electing the President.

Direct Election and Multiple Candidacies

Advocates of the present system also maintain that it serves to preserve the two-party system in the United States by discouraging minor parties from making serious challenges for the Presidency. The thesis is that since only one candidate can get the electoral votes of a state under the winner-take-all system, only two parties can effectively compete.[20] The votes of all but the winning candidate in a state are effectively "wasted." In states in which the two main parties compete closely, there is at least a good chance that the Presidential candidate of your party will win all of the state's electoral votes. But, if you represent a small party that might get at best 10 to 20 percent of the vote in *any* state, you effectively have no chance of becoming President and this simple fact might well discourage you from running since you will gain no electoral votes at all.

On the other hand, under a direct election system, there are fewer reasons to refrain from running. Even if you don't carry any states, you still might have a big impact on the election if the system requires the winning candidate to obtain a majority of the popular votes. If you can get 10 percent of the national vote, a major party candidate needs more than 55 percent of the remaining ballots to gain a majority of the popular votes. Since 1940 only three candidates, all incumbents (Eisenhower in 1956, Johnson in 1964, and Nixon in 1972) running against exceptionally weak challengers, have received this high a percentage of the vote. Defenders of the present system also argue that once barriers to third-, fourth-, and fifth-party candidates are let down, party control over nominations would also break down.[21] But there is little evidence for this latter claim as can be seen from our arguments in earlier chapters on the nominating system. Compared with twenty to thirty years ago, there is scarcely much strong national control over our parties anymore. The "reformed" conventions have indeed encouraged multiple candidacies, but candidates have clustered where the action is—in contesting nominations for the two major parties. It would seem that abolition of the Electoral College would have little effect on multiple candidacies, since it would be difficult at best to get more aspirants for the White House than we already have in the party primaries (Democrats in 1976 and 1984, Republicans in 1980). The attachment to our parties on the part of both voters and activists has declined dramatically without any tampering with the Electoral College.

What about minor party challenges for the Presidency? When we look to statewide contests for Governor and Senator, virtually all of which are straightforward *plurality* elections, we find very few instances of multiple candidacies by minor parties. The various movements on the right and left in California, the Libertarians in Alaska (the only state in which this party has had any noticeable impact), former Independent Senator Harry F. Byrd, Jr., of Virginia, and the various small parties in New York (which usually endorse major party nominees in return for patronage) are exceptions. But they have had limited impact and there is little evidence that they presage a national movement.

Under the present system we have had three major national independent candidates in the last four Presidential elections. Both McCarthy and Anderson cost Carter some states in 1976 and 1980, respectively, but studies of the 1968 election indicate that Wallace did not have a greater impact on Humphrey than he had on Nixon.[22] There was also a third candidate in 1972, John G. Schmitz of Wallace's old American Independent movement, but he did not get on the ballot in every state. One can make a reasonable case that the present Electoral College system provides as great an opportunity for disrupting two-party domination as it does for restraining competition. More specifically, it encourages regional minor candidacies such as those of Wallace who divided the country into sectional disputes. Had the contest between Nixon and Humphrey been closer in several key states, Wallace might have indeed achieved his goal of an Electoral College stalemate, a target also established by J. Strom Thurmond in his Dixiecrat States' Rights party in 1948. Wallace obtained almost 10 million popular votes and forty-six electoral votes; Thurmond's 1.2 million popular votes translated into thirty-nine electoral votes. A nationally based fourth party in 1948, the Progressive movement of former Vice President Henry A. Wallace received 20,000 fewer votes than Thurmond, but no electoral votes because its popular support was spread throughout the states of the East, Midwest, and West.

There is more evidence to support the claim that the Electoral College fosters sectionalism than there is that plurality elections will yield multiple candidates. If the direct election of the President required an absolute majority of the popular votes, perhaps multiple parties would be fostered. But few Electoral College reform proposals envisage this situation; more typical is the requirement that the winner get at least 40 percent of the popular vote, with a provision for a runoff contest between the top two vote-getters otherwise. Only once in American history (1860) has a candidate failed to garner at least 40 percent of the popular vote. If we are to have multiple candidacies, it will not be because of the way in which we elect our Presidents.

The Electoral College Provides a Mandate to Govern

It was also in 1824 that a Presidential candidate last failed to win a majority of electoral votes. Even in the "misfires" of 1876 and 1888, the second-place popular vote candidate nevertheless obtained an absolute majority of electoral ballots. What is certain is that much of the time the present system magnifies the margin of victory of the electoral vote winner. Not since 1824 has a victor's percentage of the popular vote been equal to that he obtained in the Electoral College and in only seven elections since has the disparity been less than 10 percentage points. Thus, in 1976 Carter did "relatively poorly" when his electoral vote tally ran only five points ahead of his percentage of the popular ballots. In contrast, Reagan, like Lincoln, Woodrow Wilson, Franklin D. Roosevelt, Johnson, and Nixon before him, saw a comfortable popular margin turned into an Electoral College landslide. Reagan won 51 percent of the popular vote, but 91 percent of the electoral votes, a margin only matched by Wilson in 1912, although Roosevelt with a 37 percent spread in 1936 and Nixon with a 36 percent difference in 1972 came close. These Electoral College landslides turn, in many people's minds, into broad mandates for bold policy innovations. We remember not that Reagan got only 51 percent of the popular vote, but that he carried forty-four of the fifty states. Thus, the victory indicated widespread support *across the country*.[23] It does not matter much whether academic analysts or pollsters perceive a mandate from the people, but whether the press, politicians, and particularly the President see one. In Table 5-1, we present an updated version of Judith Best's comparisons of the two percentages, arrayed according to popular vote pluralities.[24] In general we see that the ranks of the two percentages are similar; when the popular and electoral tallies diverge markedly, this indicates that the winning candidate carried several states by small margins. In 1980, for example, Reagan won eleven states by margins of less than 5 percent over Carter.

We see from the table that only landslides have this potential "mandate" effect, although a President's latitude in interpreting such an effect depends on the size of the Electoral College victory. In 1968, in contrast to the 1972 land-

TABLE 5-1
DIRECTION OF DISTORTION IN THE RELATIONSHIP OF POPULAR TO
ELECTORAL VOTE
(Round Numbers)

	Winner percentage			Winner percentage	
Year	Popular vote	Electoral vote	Year	Popular vote	Electoral vote
1860	40	59	1908	52	66
1912	42	82	1840	53	80
1968	43	56	1868	53	73
1856	46	59	1944	53	81
1892	46	62	1924	54	71
1848	47	56	1832	55	77
1876	48	50	1864	55	91
1880	48	58	1940	55	85
1888	48	58	1952	55	83
1884	49	55	1872	56	82
1916	49	52	1904	56	71
1844	50	62	1932	57	89
1948	50	57	1956	57	86
1960	50	56	1928	58	84
1976	50	55	1920	60	76
1836	51	58	1936	61	98
1852	51	86	1964	61	90
1896	51	61	1972	61	97
1980	51	91			
1900	52	65			

Source: Judith Best, *The Case against Direct Election of the President* (Ithaca, New York: Cornell University Press, 1975), p. 56.

slide, Nixon won only 43 percent of the popular vote. Yet he still won a very comfortable 56 percent of the electoral ballots. In 1960 Kennedy's 50 percent of the vote translated into 56 percent of the electoral votes. Reagan's 40 percent advantage in 1980 seems dwarfed, however, by Wilson's similar margin in 1912. In that contest, a three-way race involving incumbent William Howard Taft and former President Theodore Roosevelt, the strong races run by all candidates transformed a strong Wilson plurality into an overwhelming victory in the Electoral College. The respective vote percentages were 42 and 82.

Is this mandate effect a good or a bad thing? To the extent that it provides the new President with public acceptance after a close contest, there are clearly benefits. But there might also be real danger in the President's claiming a mandate based on widespread support across the states but hiding some very close divisions in the popular vote. The popular vote total should serve as a reminder to the President as to the depth of his support and the limits of any proclaimed mandate. So should the inevitable tendency for a President's popularity to decline as tenure in office increases, as Reagan, Nixon, Johnson, and Wilson all learned. The lesson was not lost on chief executives who did not get large mandates, such as Harry S Truman and Jimmy Carter. Indeed, among land-slide winners only Franklin Roosevelt and Eisenhower seemed immune to a steady erosion of their popular support. Perhaps Presidents ought to be able to claim a mandate, but they should also be cautioned against making too many demands on their supporters. It seems that "mandated" leaders, such as John-son, Nixon, and Reagan, have fallen further and more quickly than others, and it is far from clear that these leaders have quite comprehended the reasons for their decline in popularity. But, to the extent that these mandates are "caused" by the Electoral College system, we must either accept the general idea of a mandate or admonish our leaders that political support after inauguration is something to be nurtured rather than assumed.

UPSTAIRS, DOWNSTAIRS/BIG STATES, SMALL STATES

One of the most astute observers of the American political scene, V. O. Key, Jr., wrote then Representative Estes Kefauver (Democrat, Tennessee) in 1948: "the electoral college as it stands is completely useless, but, on the other hand, it does no harm."[25] Key's analysis hardly stands unchallenged by other observ-ers. Virtually every conceivable type of bias has been attributed to the present method of electing the President. The general ticket system favors big states, small states, both big and small states, metropolitan areas, rural localities, lib-eral voters, conservative voters, nonvoters, blacks, Jews, and nonminorities. It is truly all things to all people, and this in no small measure explains its lon-gevity. Since so many people believe that the present arrangement favors their cause, the many attempts to amend the Constitutional provisions for the Elec-toral College have been doomed to failure. We shall examine these competing claims in an attempt to determine if the Electoral College really does no harm. For if Key is correct, much of the hue and cry over the way we elect our Pres-ident is little more than background noise. On the other hand, if we do uncover systematic biases, our position on the method of electing the President will be shaped by whether our own favored causes are helped or hurt and, whether we believe that an electoral system should provide additional access to some forces at the expense of others.

THE ALLEGED "SMALL STATE BIAS"

Let us begin with the most widely debated alleged bias of the Electoral College: big states versus small states. The latter are claimed to have an advantage because they are overrepresented in the Electoral College relative to their pop-ulation. Every state is entitled to at least one Representative regardless of population, so Alaska and South Dakota each have one member in the lower House although the latter state almost qualifies for a second member. More important, each state is awarded electoral votes equal to the number of Senators and Representatives it elects. Clearly the impact of the two "Senatorial" electoral votes to Alaska is greater than it is for California with its House delegation of forty-five. Hubert H. Humphrey, a liberal critic of the Electoral College, argued in 1955: "these bonus votes . . . give an unfair advantage to the voters who reside in the smaller States."[26] Twenty-two years later, the principal advocate of the direct election of the President in the Congress, Senator Birch Bayh (Democrat, Indiana), chairman of the Senate Judiciary Committee Subcommittee on Constitutional Amendments, responded: "residents of small to medium-sized states are the most disadvantaged group of voters under the electoral college system."[27] These comments reflect not changing times, but rather different perspectives on who is advantaged.

Power To The People?

One way of assessing these arguments is to determine how much "voting power" people in different states have. We consider two approaches to the study of voting power here. Each is based on the idea of selecting a voter at random in a state and considering how likely that person might be to change the outcome of the national election. The first approach is based simply on the comparison of a state's number of electoral votes to its population. Since small states are advantaged by their two "bonus votes" representing their Senators, their residents are said to have more power. Furthermore, Alaska is more advantaged than South Dakota even though both states have three electoral votes because, as noted above, Alaska has a smaller population, and thereby a larger ratio of electoral votes to population.

The second approach envisages a situation in which the popular vote is a tie, with our randomly selected person casting the deciding vote. How much power will that person have nationally? That is, what is the probability that he or she might change the national outcome based on how the voter's home state goes? If our voter is an Alaskan, he or she would swing only three electoral votes, thus making it unlikely that the national outcome would be changed. On the other hand, a Californian would decide forty-seven electoral votes and would be considerably more likely to change the national result. This suggests a large-state bias in the Electoral College[28], and there is an argument that indeed this ought to be the case. The Congress, it is argued, is weighted toward rural interests, particularly given the two seats each state has in the Senate, regardless of size; thus, the Presidency should reflect a national constituency.[29]

The arguments on both sides seem reasonable, so much so that Longley and Dana conclude that there is *both* a small-state and a large-state bias in the general ticket system.[30] The most disadvantaged states are those in the

TABLE 5-2

VOTING POWER UNDER THE ELECTORAL COLLEGE IN THE 1980s, ARRANGED
BY SIZE OF STATE

	1	2	3	4
State name[1]	Electoral vote: 1984, 1988	Population: 1980 census	Relative voting power[2]	Percent deviation from per citizen-voter average voting power[3]
Alaska	3	400,481	1.396	−7.6
Wyoming	3	470,816	1.287	−14.8
Vermont	3	511,456	1.235	−18.2
Delaware	3	595,225	1.145	−24.2
District of Columbia	3	637,651	1.106	−26.8
North Dakota	3	652,695	1.093	−27.6
South Dakota	3	690,178	1.063	−29.6
Montana	4	786,690	1.231	−18.5
Nevada	4	799,184	1.221	−19.1
New Hampshire	4	920,610	1.138	−24.7
Idaho	4	943,935	1.124	−25.6
Rhode Island	4	947,154	1.122	−25.7
Hawaii	4	965,000	1.111	−26.4
Maine	4	1,124,660	1.030	−31.8
New Mexico	5	1,129,968	1.149	−23.9
Utah	5	1,461,037	1.084	−28.2
Nebraska	5	1,570,006	1.046	−30.8
West Virginia	6	1,959,644	1.082	−28.3
Arkansas	6	2,285,513	1.000	−33.8
Kansas	7	2,363,208	1.131	−25.1
Mississippi	7	2,520,638	1.095	−27.5
Oregon	7	2,632,663	1.071	−29.1
Arizona	7	2,717,866	1.054	−30.2
Colorado	8	2,888,834	1.156	−23.5
Iowa	8	2,913,387	1.151	−23.8
Oklahoma	8	3,025,266	1.129	−25.2
Connecticut	8	3,107,576	1.114	−26.2
South Carolina	8	3,119,208	1.112	−26.4
Kentucky	9	3,661,433	1.142	−24.4
Alabama	9	3,890,061	1.107	−26.7
Minnesota	10	4,077,148	1.209	−19.9
Washington	10	4,130,163	1.201	−20.5
Louisiana	10	4,203,972	1.191	−21.2
Maryland	10	4,216,446	1.189	−21.3
Tennessee	11	4,590,750	1.228	−18.7
Wisconsin	11	4,705,335	1.213	−19.7
Missouri	11	4,917,444	1.187	−21.4
Virginia	12	5,346,279	1.240	−17.9
Georgia	12	5,464,265	1.227	−18.8
Indiana	12	5,490,179	1.224	−19.9
Massachusetts	13	5,737,037	1.288	−14.7

TABLE 5-2
(*Continued*)

	1	2	3	4
State name[1]	Electoral vote: 1984, 1988	Population: 1980 census	Relative voting power[2]	Percent deviation from per citizen-voter average voting power[3]
North Carolina	13	5,874,429	1.273	−15.7
New Jersey	16	7,364,158	1.401	−7.3
Michigan	20	9,258,344	1.522	0.6
Florida	21	9,739,992	1.562	3.3
Ohio	23	10,797,419	1.628	7.6
Illinois	24	11,418,461	1.643	8.7
Pennsylvania	25	11,866,728	1.701	12.5
Texas	29	14,228,383	1.773	17.3
New York	36	17,557,288	2.027	34.0
California	47	23,668,562	2.352	55.2

[1]Includes the District of Columbia.
[2]Ratio of voting power of citizens of state compared with voters of the most deprived state.
[3]Percent by which voting power deviated from the average *per citizen-voter* of the figures in Column 3. Minus signs indicate less than average voting power.
Source: Lawrence D. Longley and James D. Dana, "Minorities and the Electoral College in the 1980s," (paper presented at the Annual Meeting of the Southern Political Science Association, Memphis, November 1981) p. 26.

"medium-to-small" states. We present their findings in Table 5-2 for average voting power in the 1980s.[31] The third column provides an estimate of the relative voting power of a citizen of each state, compared with that of the most disadvantaged voters, those of Arkansas. Arkansas is disadvantaged because it has six electoral votes but almost qualifies for seven, based on its population. No other state "misses" an extra electoral vote by so little. The most disadvantaged voters are given relative voting powers of 1.000 each. The final column provides a measure of the deviation of voting power from the national average in each state. Thus, Alaska's voters have 7.6 percent less voting power than the average voter throughout the country; that is, they have a 7.6 percent lower chance of altering the outcome of an election than a voter picked at random throughout the nation. In the least powerful, Arkansas, the average voter has almost 34 percent less of a chance of affecting the outcome of the election than a random voter. Only voters in the eight most populous states have a greater than average chance of altering an election, with the two most populous states, California and New York, having extreme values. It seems that it pays to live in the big states.

The federal bargain that gives greater power in the Congress to rural interests also redresses this imbalance in Presidential elections. Not only are large-state voters supposed to be favored in the Electoral College, but so are, in particular, the residents of the big cities in those states. Minorities within those cities are also said to be advantaged, once more in contrast with their under-representation in the Congress. Peirce and Longley indicate that citizens in the East and Far West have above average voting power; those in the rural South and the Mountain states, also more sparsely populated, are the most disadvantaged.[32] Putting these factors altogether, we see the making of a potential Electoral College majority of big states based on the traditional Democratic party electoral coalition that lasted from the 1930s until the 1970s. Thus it is not surprising to find two students of the Electoral College arguing:[33]

> Campaigns have ... tended to concentrate on populous states and their metropolitan areas. Political strategists go where the most votes are to be won. Usually this means focusing on densely populated areas whose turnout rate and/or choice is doubtful. For Democrats this means giving prime attention to New York City, Philadelphia, Chicago, Los Angeles, and so on; in a close race these major cities may swing a state's entire bloc of electoral votes.

This same line of reasoning suggests that the ethnic minorities which have comprised the Democratic coalition would also benefit from the existing arrangement. Two prominent columnists argue that "Jewish voters, less than three percent of the electorate, must be given some attention now because they can tip the scales in New York or Illinois or California."[34] In Senate hearings on direct elections of the President in 1979 Howard Squadron, president of the American Jewish Congress, concurred with this analysis and urged retention of the Electoral College. Similarly, Vernon E. Jordan, Jr., then president of the Urban League, a major civil rights organization, argued that "Blacks can reasonably expect to build coalitions with other minorities and whites ... in the large states, especially the industrial states of the North and West. ... [T]hese coalitions ... would (no longer) exist because direct elections would change many of the political parameters which make such coalition-building possible."[35] The analysis of Peirce and Longley showed that although big city voters did have more voting power than their rural counterparts, black voters are actually *disadvantaged* by the Electoral College! Jews, on the other hand, are advantaged considerably.[36]

Who is correct, then? Are the political leaders among blacks who perceive the Electoral College as helping their groups right or are the voting power analysts who don't agree? Let us suggest that both may be using the wrong logic. What we need to consider is what we mean when we usually talk about "voting power." The second concept of voting power, which underlies the studies we have been discussing, assumes that we can pick a voter at random who might affect the national outcome. But the very claim that we have selected a voter *at random* seems to contradict the assumption that we pick out urban voters, blacks, or Jews. Let us consider a more realistic approach to voting power that does reflect real politics.

Consider the 1976 election. California cast forty-five electoral votes for President Gerald R. Ford, and New York's forty-one electoral votes went to the victorious Carter. Since California went for Ford and Carter won the election anyway, there is nothing that any Californian could have done to change the national outcome! On the other hand, had 150,000 New Yorkers who voted for Carter changed their ballots to Ford, the incumbent would have won a national victory. Thus, Californians had no power in 1976 and New Yorkers were quite powerful indeed, or at least those New Yorkers who voted Democratic. This is quite a different conclusion than we find in Table 5-2 in which Californians are the most powerful voters in the country.

To have voting power, there must be a threat that a citizen can withdraw support from one candidate and give it to another, as well as the possibility that such strategic behavior can change the outcome of the election. But blacks, Jews, and big-city voters in general have not compiled this sort of voting history. All have been very loyal to Democratic candidates year in and year out. Although there may be very good reasons for these groups to support Democratic candidates, their party regularity makes them unlikely candidates for the role of "swing voters." And the reason why the District of Columbia is the least powerful "state" is not because the capital is underrepresented in the Electoral College based on its population. Rather, the majority black District is even more heavily Democratic. Looking at voting history for states and various groups, we find little reason to believe that blacks and Jews are courted in the larger states because they are likely to defect from Democratic ranks. What makes states such as New York, California, Ohio, Illinois, and Pennsylvania political prizes is not their large blocs of electoral votes, but primarily their delicate political balance of power between the two major parties. Many smaller states have more homogeneous populations and also strong one-party traditions. Thus, the Democrats do not seriously expect much support in New Hampshire, Utah, and Alaska, and the Republicans have low expectations in Hawaii, Rhode Island, and West Virginia.

A study of voting power, based on this more realistic view, in the ten Presidential elections from 1876 to 1968 in which no candidate received more than 65 percent of the electoral vote, found a tendency for the swing states to be among the larger ones.[37] But there were also a substantial number of small states that were pivotal. The strength of large states under the Electoral College has thus probably been exaggerated by both its defenders and critics. Ohio, Delaware, and Hawaii, the states classified by Peirce and Longley[38] as having the potential to alter the outcome in 1976 further suggest that two-party competition in Presidential contests is not confined to the largest states. Urban influence has also been disputed in a study of voting patterns in Presidential contests from 1920 to 1948 in twelve major cities; large cities were not needed

to provide the margin of victory for a Presidential candidate in a state 63 percent of the time and in an additional 17 percent of the contests, the metropolitan centers supported a candidate who did not carry their states.[39] Members
of these groups who argue that the party has long taken their support for
granted may very well have a more convincing case than those who proudly
point to their clout. The voters in large states who are likely to have the most
power are those who are self-proclaimed independents, or perhaps weak party
identifiers, unabashedly willing to shift their vote from one party to another
depending on politicians' responses to the concerns of this part of the electorate.
But these voters are hardly the liberals who seemingly dominate the voting
power of the largest states.

Who Really Wins?

Who are the really advantaged voters under the Electoral College? The answer
is straightforward: Those in the closest states, the states that have the greatest
prospect of going either way in a Presidential contest. In 1976 Carter was
informed late in the campaign that Texas and Louisiana were extremely close,
but California seemed lost. He thus canceled a trip to the West Coast on the
last weekend of the campaign and visited these two states instead. The argument that large states are advantaged under the general ticket system can still
be made, however. Large states have an edge over small ones because they are
more heterogeneous.[40] Their populations include not only blacks, Jews, and city
dwellers, but also farmers, suburbanites, Protestants. There is little evidence
for the thesis of political dominance of metropolitan centers under the Electoral
College. In a study of ideological biases in the Electoral College, estimates of
statewide public opinion on seven issues were applied to an analysis of potential
bias in the Electoral College versus direct popular election of the President for
the 1960 contest.[41] Contrary to conventional mythology—one hesitates to call
it "wisdom"—on most issues, including self-identification as a liberal or a conservative, there was a small bias toward the *right* under the present
arrangement.

Earlier we posed the questions: (1) ought there to be any bias in the way we
select our President?; and (2) if so, are certain biases more acceptable than
others? Liberal defenders of the present arrangement reverse the order of our
two questions and maintain that they derive certain advantages in Presidential
elections to which they are entitled because of other features in the American
political system, particularly the grant of two Senators to every state. Because
the Electoral College is presumed to have biases favoring the liberal cause,
these supporters of the present system conclude that it is indeed acceptable to
have some bias in the method of selection. One can readily challenge this reversal of the order of the two questions, but since the alleged advantages of the
Electoral College to the liberal cause are more illusory than real, the issue of

whether *any* biases are legitimate must be addressed. This is not a question that is easily answered; each person must resolve it for himself or herself.

However, the case for such advantages does not appear strong to us. Wallace Sayre and Judith Parris contend that under the Electoral College "it has been quite reasonable to assume that New Yorkers would have a greater opportunity to see presidential candidates in person than would their fellow countrymen living in Velva, North Dakota."[42] But, if there is no clearly identifiable metropolitan bias in the current system, what reason is there to assume that things will change markedly under direct election of the President? Indeed, even if one could demonstrate such a metropolitan advantage, why would candidates reorient their strategies? In 1964 Republican nominee Barry Goldwater stated that the best strategy for duck-hunting is to go where the ducks are. His own campaign fell far short of attaining success, but there is little reason to assume that just because every individual vote is equal candidates will flock to the sparsely populated areas. The simple fact of greater population density in the large cities will continue to drive both candidates and the media that follow them to these locales. Indeed, there might be even greater concentration, at least among Democrats, on some urban areas since the emphasis of campaigning under direct election will be even more heavily focused on turnout among the most devoted party supporters. Whatever the method of election, the ducks will still be in the duck swamp. Candidates need not fear that they will be stuck in quicksand by a change in the method of election. What they and citizens have to decide is whether the prospect of a runner-up Presidency is acceptable on the basis of *any* criteria.

Put another way, to what extent should we design our electoral system to benefit certain groups? If a minority-vote President is chosen under our Electoral College, as has already happened at least three times, are we to defend that victory simply because we agree with the winning candidate's program? If so, we should realize that biases are not necessarily "eternal." A liberal bias today may be a conservative one in future years, at least in terms of policy agreement. This may be the most convincing argument for selecting a system with as few biases as possible.[43]

THE OPTIONS AVAILABLE

So many attempts have been made to change the current system that virtually every conceivable way of selecting a President has by now been proposed. None of them seems any closer to adoption than at any previous time. Of course, one key option is the retention of the present general ticket system or a minor modification of it by replacing independent electors by the mechanical casting of a state's electoral votes for the state plurality winner, the "automatic plan." The principal alternative today is the direct vote plan, generally proposed as a two-stage process in which a first election is held among however many candidates qualify for the ballot and, should none obtain 40 percent of the vote, a runoff would follow among the top two contenders. This modification of a simple plurality election is designed to guard against the prospect that direct election would in fact stimulate multiple candidacies and splinter our major parties. The reform efforts have met with little success, either early in our history, in the post-World War II burst of reform effort in Congress, or in the more intense drive for change from 1969 to 1979.[44] Although direct vote proposals have passed the House, filibusters prevented a Senate vote until July 10, 1979. The small-state Senators, including the vast majority of Southerners, and many Northeastern liberals seeking (in our view, misguidedly) to protect the interests of large states, metropolitan areas, liberals, blacks, and Jews joined forces as the proposed Constitutional amendment received 51–48 support, fifteen votes short of the two-thirds majority needed to pass such a motion. With direct vote at least in abeyance, attention has turned to some alternatives of the past and one new proposal. We shall mention the older proposals briefly because liberal opposition to them should affectively prevent their adoption.

The District System

The "district system," generally considered to be a "conservative" reform because it would destroy the winner-take-all system believed to advantage liberals, would award each state's two electoral votes to the plurality vote winner. The remaining electoral votes would be allocated to the plurality winner in a series of electoral districts equal in number, but not necessarily identical, to a state's Congressional delegation. Should a candidate fail to obtain a majority of electoral votes, the present House contingent election would be replaced by an election by a joint session of Congress. This plan was first proposed in 1800, but its most prominent advocates were Republican Senator Karl Mundt (South Dakota) and Representative Frederic R. Coudert, Jr. (New York), who first introduced it in 1949. A critical objection to this plan is that, because Republican districts in the House are more competitive than most Democratic seats, a district system based on Congressional lines would magnify the impact of the GOP popular vote for President.[45] But observers also worry that the Congressional districts would not be employed and that state legislatures would draw Presidential elector districts in clearly partisan ways so as to concentrate minority party supporters into as few electoral settings as possible.[46]

It is difficult to determine how often a "misfire," the election of a candidate who placed second in the popular vote, would occur because there are no reliable district-level Presidential returns for most of American history. But we do know that the district system would have elected Nixon in 1960 and would have left Carter and Ford tied with 269 electoral votes each in 1976.[47] The major argument for this system today is that Maine adopted it beginning with the 1972 election, with the electoral districts corresponding to those for the

House. Interestingly, the candidate who has carried the state has also won both districts in the three Presidential elections since the system was introduced. But there has been no rush to copy the Maine initiative by other states and there is even less interest in Congress in reforming the system in this way nationally.

The Proportional System

Another reform largely of historical interest is the "proportional system," proposed first in 1848 and in its modern incarnation by Senator Henry Cabot Lodge (Republican, Massachusetts) and Representative Ed Gossett (Democrat, Texas). This method would also abolish the winner-take-all general ticket system and replace it with allocation of each state's electoral votes according to the proportion of popular votes received by a candidate. A proportional plan passed the Senate in 1950, but was defeated in the House as members feared that Democratic strength in the South would be diluted by this measure.[48] This plan also envisaged a contingent election administered by a joint session of Congress. Aside from partisan considerations, critics have argued that the possibility of a misfire under both this and the district system are quite real, perhaps even greater than under the current method. Although the Lodge-Gossett proportional system would not have reversed the 1876 and 1888 elections, it would have done so in 1880, 1896, and possibly 1900.[49] What is most disturbing is the proportional system's seeming inability to reach definitive solutions in many recent contests. In three of the nine post-World War II elections (1948, 1960, and 1968) the proportional system would have thrown the contest into the House-Senate joint session. It would have selected Carter by the narrowest of margins with 269.7 electoral votes, which is 50.13 percent of the total 538 electoral votes.

The National Bonus Plan

The new proposal that has been circulating was proposed by a Task Force on the Reform of the Presidential Election Process of the Twentieth Century Fund in 1978. Members of the Task Force consisted of academics, journalists, and political activists. They proposed a system called the "national bonus plan," a hybrid of direct election and the Electoral College. This plan would retain the Electoral College, but provide a bonus 102 electors to the winner of the *national* popular vote plurality. The figure of 102 represents two votes for each state plus the District of Columbia. Under this system it is virtually inconceivable that the popular vote winner would fail to receive an Electoral College majority. Should the unlikely come to pass, a runoff between the two top candidates would be held.[50] This plan would also abolish the office of elector and provide for an automatic recount of all the votes in the nation to protect against fraud. No election in American history would have had an Electoral College misfire under this plan. The advocates of this plan agree that direct election would be preferable to the present system, but maintain that the extra mandate effect given to the winner under the bonus plan is desirable. The mandate would be greater than under the present Electoral College because the national popular vote victor would automatically get more than 100 additional electoral votes.[51]

As we have argued above, there are many dangers in overinterpreting mandates. What is a virtue to the Task Force may not be to others. Since the practical effect of the proposal would be to guarantee that the popular vote winner would be elected, the question arises as to why one needs the national bonus plan at all. A camel, it is said, is a horse designed by a committee (a task force?). One asks: What is that extra hump all about? The members of the Task Force must respond to the query: Why is their system preferable to direct election? The argument that is most likely to be offered is that, unlike direct election, the national bonus plan is a politically realistic alternative.[52] But the arguments advanced on behalf of this proposal seem so similar to those on behalf of direct election that it would take an act of some higher power to convince traditional proponents of the general ticket system that a reasonable compromise has indeed been found. The direct vote alternative is an all-natural substitute to a polyester national bonus plan. A new proposal might be in order were there not substantial public support for the direct vote plan, but Gallup poll data indicate that: (1) Substantial majorities supported direct election in both 1976 and 1977; and (2) Among every subgroup examined, as well as the entire population, approval of direct election increased substantially.[53] The February 1967 figures show 58 percent of the national sample favored this reform, 22 percent opposed, and 20 percent with no opinion. By February 1977 the figures were 75 percent approval, only 14 percent disapproval, and 11 percent with no opinion. Electoral College reform is favored by many, but it is pressing to very few. Thus political leaders pay an inordinate amount of attention to the claims of those who believe, correctly or not, that they would be adversely affected by a change in electoral method.

THE ELECTORAL COLLEGE AND DIRECT ELECTION: IMPLICATIONS FOR PRESIDENTIAL SELECTION

The general ticket system actually is based *against* blacks, Jews, and large-city residents and this has important implications for the types of candidates who are likely to be nominated and elected for the Presidency. Why does the Electoral College work against these groups? The reason is their constituency in voting patterns. Since these voters are overwhelmingly Democratic, they have little chance of swinging an election to the Republicans. Nor in a close election are they likely to be the "target groups" that just barely put the Democrats over the top. Thus, the Democratic party largely takes their votes for granted and its more likely to pay attention to the swing voters among the independents in selecting candidates. The need to gain support among independents makes both the Democratic and Republican parties more moderate than they might otherwise be.

To be sure, this would be true under any electoral system, but the Electoral College magnifies the tendency toward moderation by giving the most competitive states the greatest impact on the election. There is no incentive for a party to pick up votes in states that might not give it a plurality; so Democrats have a greater incentive to pay attention to independents in San Diego than to their own adherents in Omaha or Richmond. Similarly Republicans are better off hunting for independent votes in New York City than they would be looking for their partisans in Providence or Honolulu. The most devoted followers of each party are the ones who will be most overlooked under the Electoral College's strategies. This makes both parties seem very much alike; it reduces the number of new ideas in politics by restricting the ability of politicians who espouse them to appear to be viable candidates who could win a majority of electoral votes.

To be sure, there is no guarantee that direct election would produce a tremendous amount of diversity either. American politics *is* basically moderate. But it would permit candidates to build coalitions of supporters throughout the country, without having to worry whether a local campaign would be sufficient to carry an entire state. Even if a Democrat couldn't carry California in a particular election, it still might be worthwhile to campaign in San Francisco, a bastion of the party's support. The democratization of the nominating system, discussed in Chapter 1, has given some of these groups the opportunity to influence some primaries in states in which they are particularly numerous. Jewish participation in New York, Pennsylvania, Maryland, Illinois, and California has made an impact on the Democratic party, as has black voting in these same states and even many places in the South. But this impact is limited in comparison with the weakness of these groups under the Electoral College. The direct election plan is likely to let these various groups and others representing labor, farmers, large and small business, ideological groups, and other ethnic groups test their true influence in both political parties.

Similarly, many fine candidates might be at a disadvantage in seeking the Presidential nomination under the present system. Thus, leaders from small states have an immediate problem. Because they can deliver only a handful of electoral votes either as President or Vice President, campaign contributors might see a small payoff in, say, the candidacy of a Senator or a Governor from South Dakota. It is thus not surprising that only two Presidential and three Vice Presidential nominees since 1952 have come from states with fewer than ten electoral votes. Both Presidential nominees were not mainstream candidates, but ideologically oriented candidates who went down to crashing defeat (Goldwater for the Republicans in 1964, McGovern for the Democrats in 1972). The general tendency under the Electoral College is to select Presidential and Vice Presidential candidates from the very large states it overrepresents. California, Texas, and Minnesota have been good places to be from in recent years; New York and Massachusetts are not quite as good because they are more predominantly one party (Democratic). Virginia, in the early years of the nation the "state of Presidents," is now so predictably Republican that there is little incentive for either party to select a candidate from that state.

What is remarkable is that these tendencies seem to continue even after the nominating system itself has become so open. Theoretically, under the democratized nominating system, a candidate is free from such problems. These issues are of greater concern to the leaders of party organizations than to the average voter. Under direct election, in which every vote would count equally, no matter where or by whom it was cast, small-state Presidential candidates might be less disadvantaged. However, the major argument on behalf of direct election is that it gives no particular favor to any candidate or group of voters. It is not only neutral in terms of group advantage but also the only system that will guarantee that a misfire never occurs. It is the system we use for every elected office other than President, and the question remains: Why should we not use it for that office as well?

NOTES

1   Quoted in Lucius Wilmerding, Jr., *The Electoral College in America,* (New Brunswick N.J.: Rutgers University Press, 1958), p. 3.

2   Lawrence D. Longley and Alan G. Braun, *The Politics of Electoral College Reform,* 2d ed. (New Haven: Yale University Press, 1975), pp. 50–51.

3   Ibid., p. 51.

4   Neal R. Peirce and Lawrence D. Longley, *The People's President: The Electoral College in American History and the Direct Vote Alternative,* rev. ed. (New Haven: Yale University Press, 1981), pp. 50–51.

5   See Thomas E. Cronin, "The Direct Vote and the Electoral College: The Case for Meshing Things Up!," *Presidential Studies Quarterly,* 9 (Spring 1979), p. 149; Judith Best, *The Case against Direct Election of the President* (Ithaca, N.Y.: Cornell University Press, 1975), pp. 24–26.

6   Ibid., pp. 65–67.

7   Ibid., p. 53.

8   Peirce and Longley. *The People's President,* pp. 116–119.

9   Samuel Merrill, III, "Empirical Estimates for the Likelihood of a Divided Verdict in a Presidential Election," *Public Choice,* 33 (1978), pp. 127–133; Longley and Braun, *The Politics of Electoral College Reform,* p. 117n.

10 Best, *The Case against Direct Election of the President,* pp. 51–52.

11 Longley and Braun, *The Politics of Electoral College Reform,* p. 83.

12 Best, *The Case against Direct Election of the President,* p. 83.

13 Peirce and Longley, *The People's President,* pp. 99–100.

14 Best, *The Case against Direct Election of the President,* p. 177.

15 Wilmerding, *The Electoral College in America,* p. 105.

16 *Oregon v. Mitchell,* 400 U.S. 112 (1970).

17 Best, *The Case against Direct Election of the President,* p. 128.

18 Best, *The Case against Direct Election of the President,* p. 194.

19 Peirce and Longley, *The People's President,* p. 83.

20 Best, *The Case against Direct Election of the President,* p. 212.

21 Ibid.

22 Philip E. Converse, Warren E. Miller, Jerrold G. Rusk, and Arthur C. Wolfe, "Continuity and Change in American Politics: Parties and Issues in the 1968 Election," *American Political Science Review,* 63 (December 1969), pp. 1083–1105.

23 Cf. Cronin. "The Direct Vote and the Electoral College: The Case for Meshing Things Up!"

24 Best, *The Case against Direct Election of the President,* p. 56.

25 United States Senate, Committee on the Judiciary, *Nomination and Election of President and Vice President,* 84th Congress, First Session (Washington, D.C.: Government Printing Office, 1955), p. 190.

26 Ibid., p. 93.

27 Peirce and Longley, *The People's President,* p. 199.

28 John E. Banzhat III, "One Man, 3.312 Votes: A Mathematical Analysis of the Electoral College," *Villanova Law Review,* 13 (Winter 1968), pp. 304–322.

29 Nelson W. Polsby and Aaron Wildavsky, *Presidential Elections: Strategies of American Electoral Politics,* 4th ed. (New York: Charles Scribner's Sons, 1976), pp. 252–253; Cronin, "The Direct Vote and the Electoral College: The Case for Meshing Things Up!," p. 149.

30 Lawrence D. Longley and James D. Dana, "Minorities and the Electoral College in the 1980's." (Paper presented at the Annual Meeting of the Southern Political Science Association, Memphis, November 1981.)

31 Ibid., p. 26.

32 Peirce and Longley, *The People's President,* pp. 126–127.

33 Wallace S. Sayre and Judith H. Parris, *Voting for President* (Washington. D.C.: Brookings Institution, 1970), p. 53.

34 Jack Germond and Jules Witcover, quoted in Cronin, "The Direct Vote and the Electoral College: The Case for Meshing Things up!," p. 149.

35 Quoted in Lawrence D. Longley, "Minorities and the 1980 Electoral College." (Paper presented at the Annual Meeting of the American Political Science Association, Washington, D.C., August 1980), pp. 47–48.

36 Peirce and Longley, *The People's President,* pp. 126–130; Longley and Dana, "Minorities and the Electoral College in the 1980s," p. 17.

37 Eric M. Uslaner, "Pivotal States in the Electoral College: An Empirical Investigation," in L. Papayanopoulos (ed.), *Democratic Representation and Apportionment* (New York Annals of the New York Academy of Science, Vol. 219, November 1973), p. 73.

38 Peirce and Longley, *The People's President,* p. 259.

39 Samuel C. Eldersveld, "The Influence of Metropolitan Pluralities in Presidential Elections Since 1920: A Study of Twelve Key Cities," *American Political Science Review,* 43 (December 1949), pp. 1189–1206.

40 Peirce and Longley, *The People's President,* p. 245

41 Eric M. Uslaner, "Spatial Models of the Electoral College: Distribution Assumptions and Biases of the System," *Political Methodology,* 3 (1976), pp. 355–381.

42 Sayre and Parris, *Voting for President,* p. 245.

43 Testimony of Neal R. Pierce in U.S. Senate, Judiciary Committee, Supplemental Hearings on Electoral College Reform, 91st Cong., 2nd Sess. April 15–17, 1970, p. 230.

44 Longley and Braun, *The Politics of Electoral College Reform,* chaps. 6 and 7.

45 Ibid., pp. 59–61.

46 Ibid., pp. 62–63; Wilmerding, *The Electoral College in America,* p. 155.

47 Longley and Braun, *The Politics of Electoral College Reform,* pp. 51–53, 145.

48 Ibid., p. 50.

49 Ibid., pp. 51–53.

50 Twentieth Century Fund Task Force on Reform of the Presidential Election Process, *Winner Take All* (New York: Holmes and Meier, 1978), pp. 4–5.

51 Ibid., pp. 67–68.

52 Cronin, "The Direct Vote and the Electoral College: The Case for Meshing Things Up!," p. 155.

53 Ibid., p. 157.

THE PROBLEM OF
PRESIDENTIAL LEADERSHIP

In the past 147 years only four American Presidents have served two or more consecutive four-year terms to their conclusions: two who are generally recognized as "great" leaders, Woodrow Wilson and Franklin D. Roosevelt, and two immensely popular former war heroes, Ulysses S. Grant and Dwight D. Eisenhower. This is ironic since the office has come to be recognized as the most powerful in the world. The holder of the office is looked up to by people throughout the world, as well as by American citizens, as the preeminent leader of the free world. Yet the American public has been remarkably fickle in its support of Presidents. In the twentieth century alone, four sitting Presidents have been defeated for reelection (William Howard Taft, Herbert Hoover, Gerald R. Ford, and Jimmy Carter); a former President failed in his attempt to regain the office (Theodore Roosevelt in 1912); one (Richard M. Nixon) was forced to resign the office less than halfway through his second term; at least two others were scared off from running for a second term because of popular discontent (Harry S Truman and Lyndon B. Johnson); and one simply walked away from renomination (Calvin Coolidge). In the two most recent Presidential elections voters seemed dissatisfied with the choices before them and it is little surprise, then, that they became disenchanted with the men they elected before either had finished even two years of his term. In 1980, indeed, a majority of the electorate indicated for much of the year that it really would prefer a different set of choices altogether.[1]

Of course, the rise and fall of the many men who have held the Presidency

171

over the past century and a half varies from one person to another. But it is surely no accident that the political fortunes of our chief executives have waned so quickly. After Franklin D. Roosevelt served an unprecedented three full terms and a small portion of the fourth to which he was elected, the Congress passed and the states ratified in 1951 the Twenty-second Amendment to the Constitution prohibiting anyone from being elected more than twice to the Presidency. But the real problem seems to be finding someone who can secure the type of public and legislative support to last two full terms. One observer has said that the central question we must face is "why we have poor Presidents."[2] That is an uncharitable way to pose this question. Another student of the Presidency has argued that, given the immensity of the job, we are lucky indeed that so many really good people have occupied the White House.[3] We shall not pursue this argument here, but merely note that our chief executives have seemed beleaguered and that public tolerance for them has grown quite short in recent years.

We seek in this chapter to examine why this is so and what might be done about it. We consider three arguments in particular: (1) the changes in the nominating process described in Chapter 1 have led to the nomination of candidates who are better equipped to campaign for the highest office than to hold it and to make national and international policy; (2) the increasing distrust and lack of efficacy of American citizens discussed in Chapter 4 have led not only to declining rates of turnout but also to a "national malaise" in which it has become easier for "outsider" candidates such as Carter and Reagan to gain the nomination but virtually inevitable that they will face severe problems as President when confronted with the "insiders" Washington; and (3) the problem is not new, but has plagued our system for at least a century and must be traced to the criteria we have used to nominate our Presidential candidates. Then we consider several criteria by which we can judge Presidential leadership, even Presidential greatness, as well as the questions: Can we predict greatness, or at least failure, in advance? Is there a "Presidential leadership test" that we can apply to potential candidates so as to screen out a Nixon or a Carter or a Ford? Finally, is there a better way to nominate our Presidents that might make them more likely to win public support and legislative respect? We turn first to the causes of our present discontent.

PROFESSIONAL POLITICIANS AND PROFESSIONAL AMATEURS

If we look at other democratic nations, from Canada close by to Western Europe to faraway Australia, we are struck by at least one thing: The chiefs of government attained their position by long service within their parties in the legislature and attained office either by replacing a former leader of the same party after climbing the ranks, or by defeating the similarly entrenched head of the other major party.[4] In the United States, on the other hand, the chief occupation of our recent Presidents before attaining office has been "professional Presidential candidate." Jimmy Carter began his quest for the White House as a *full-time* candidate in 1974, two years before the 1976 election. It was a wise choice, since Carter was virtually unknown and the race for the 1976 nomination began with the Iowa caucuses held on January 19, 1976. Not only was it a long way to November, but the Carter candidacy, not just its official announcement, had actually begun just after the 1972 Democratic National Convention had ended![5] Ronald Reagan began his long quest for the White House while still Governor of California, planning out his abortive 1976 challenge to Ford. But from 1975, when he left the state house in California, until he was sworn in as President in January 1981, Reagan had no other full-time occupation than his status as Presidential candidate. Indeed, virtually everything he did was directed toward this end.

By 1976 there were thirty primaries; in 1980 there were thirty-five. But caucuses such as in Iowa were hardly less strenuous on candidates. Campaigning for President became a full-time job, as we have argued in Chapter 1, and it is very difficult for a leader of the legislative party to take off sufficient time to make a concerted campaign for the nomination. *Washington Post* columnist David S. Broder has attributed the "more widespread dissatisfaction being expressed (in 1980) with the choices for the general election than this reporter has heard in 25 years on the political beat" to the more open nominating process. Specifically, he argued:

> The selection system . . . largely determines the kind of candidates you get. With our present system, you get Carters and Reagans—men who are capable free-lance campaigners of somewhat idiosyncratic background and views, self-proclaimed outsiders, most remarkable for their relentless energy, prepared to spend years of their lives seeking the presidential prize, but not viewed by their political peers—or by much of the public—as unusually gifted in governmental leadership.[6]

On the other hand, the pre-1972 nominating system would produce "people with the characteristics of the (Howard) Bakers and (Walter F.) Mondales," the candidates Broder believed would have been nominated under different systems. Baker was then Senate Minority Leader (later Majority Leader), the leader of his legislative party in the upper chamber since 1977, a Senator since 1967, and in 1973 vice chairman of the Senate Watergate Committee. Baker came from an old-line political family in Tennessee and is the son-in-law of the late Everett McKinley Dirksen, Republican leader in the Senate for most of the 1960s. Mondale was Vice President under Carter and before that was a Senator from Minnesota and the chief protégé of former Vice President Hubert H. Humphrey. Both are legislative men primarily, indeed so much so that "many of (Baker's) colleagues think he is better suited by temperament to the majority leader's position" than to the White House.[7]

What are these characteristics that Broder values? They are "people of less consuming ambition but more experience, people of moderate views who had been tested in lesser leadership responsibilities, were familiar with the national governmental and political processes and were equipped with the alliance and friendships that would enable them to marshal the machinery of government at hand."[8] Yet, as we have argued in Chapter 1, there seems to be a compulsion to look back to the "good old days" and assume that the pre-reform conventions of party leaders were really wiser or at least had the good sense to protect us from "outsider" nominees or others who lacked vision. "Unreformed" conventions gave us the ultimate outsider, Dwight D. Eisenhower, and the eminently qualified but politically disastrous Herbert Hoover. We can easily extend this list to others. Furthermore, it is far from certain that we want a Presidential candidate who is *not* quite so ambitious. As we shall see below, a drive for power is generally associated with the qualities we often prize in the Presidency. Yet, as Meg Greenfield, editorial page editor of *The Washington Post,* commented: "I absolutely agree with those who point out that the 'reformed' system, with its marathon primaries and its nit-picking financing rules, is crazy. But I always thought the old system was pretty crazy too, as we have a crazy system, reformed or unregenerate."[9]

Greenfield believes that the causes of our discontent run deeper than nominating systems. She argues that the same underlying values that produced the reforms have also led to a plethora of lower quality candidates in recent years, what one might call the "bargain basement" theory of Presidential nominations. Specifically, there is a new political consciousness in the country. It has produced support for "loners, outsiders, men who came to political power at the edges of the life of their national parties and who had to overwhelm recalcitrant and fearful party mainstream regulars to succeed. They are . . . men who have risen to the pinnacle of politics on the strength of people's perception (encouraged by them) that they are different from, and better than, regular politicians."[10] They are part of the political process, but not of it. They run for President by running against Washington, capitalizing on the increasing distrust and lack of efficacy that people feel toward their political system. The trends in trust and feelings of efficacy are presented in Table 6-1.[11]

This decline has had profound implications for governing. The President and Congress are no longer a "team." There is no single focus of government, not even the President and his party in Congress, that will admit responsibility for the actions of the national administration.[12] Carter's difficulties with a Democratic Congress were well known and have been widely documented.[13] Part of the problem was that the vast majority of Democratic members of Congress carried their own districts by far more than Carter did in 1976.[14] Thus freed of Presidential coattails, individual members of Congress felt little obligation to support their chief executive even within their own party. But in 1980 the Republican landslide temporarily restored the fragile unity between Congress

TABLE 6-1
TRENDS IN TRUST AND EFFICACY: 1964 to 1978

Trust in Government (Question: How much of the time do you think you can trust the government in Washington to do what is right—just about always, most of the time, or only some of the time?)

	1964	1968	1972	1974	1976	1978
Always	14%	8%	7%	3%	3%	3%
Most of the time	62	53	45	33	29	26
Only some of the time/ None of the time	22	37	45	61	62	67
Don't know	2	2	3	3	1	4
	100%	100%	100%	100%	100%	100%

Efficacy (Question: People like me don't have any say about what the government does.)

	1964	1968	1972	1974	1976	1978
Agree	29%	41%	36%	40%	41%	45%
Disagree	69	58	63	57	56	52
Don't know	2	1	1	3	3	3
	100%	100%	100%	100%	100%	100%

Source: David B. Hill and Norman R. Luttbeg, *Trends in American Electoral Behavior* (Itasca, Illinois: F. E. Peacock, 1980), pp. 114–115.

and the White House; when the economy turned sour, however, many GOP legislators up for reelection in 1982 tried to dissociate themselves from Reagan as surely as Democrats did from Carter in 1978 and 1980.

There is a mad scramble in the Congressional race for popularity as well. Congress as an institution is even less popular than specific Presidents have been,[15] so members of Congress do everything within their power to dissociate themselves from the legislature as well as from unpopular Presidents. Members run *for* Congress by running *against* the *Congress*.[16] Just as Carter and Reagan, the outsiders, campaigned on the platform of cleaning up the mess in Washington, so members of the House and Senate pledge to upgrade the quality of the Congress. By telling the voters that their beliefs about corruption and waste in Washington are true, Presidential and Congressional candidates reinforce those very ideas. Members of Congress can always seek protection against the wrath of the electorate by blaming the *other* 534 Representatives and Senators, but there is no other President for the chief executive to blame. Carter tried to blame everyone but himself—Iran, the Russians, the special interests, the world economy, and in one case (high energy consumption) the unlikely target of the voters themselves—yet the tactic didn't work. Reagan, although refusing to play what he called "the blame game," nevertheless attributed most of the country's economic ills to the Democrats. Boxing a shadow is difficult at best.

This idea that nobody's at fault but phantoms is, according to Greenfield, the essence of an antipolitics attitude. People no longer are ready for a good, clean partisan political fight. Carter is a good case in point: "He is not transfixed by power. He does not seem intrigued by the challenge of using it forcefully and to good ends without abusing it. He doesn't even seem to enjoy it very much."[17] To be sure, Reagan did seem to enjoy power and to excel at its exercise for at least the first year of his administration; that is, while he was on a winning streak.[18] But, despite a far better sense of humor and a greater ability to laugh at himself, Reagan had great difficulties comprehending what was happening to him politically in 1982 as many previously loyal Republican legislators took shelter under some Democratic economic programs. Greenfield summed up the modern dilemma well:

> We have developed something new in our politics: the professional amateur. It is by now a trend, a habit, a cult. You succeed in this line of activity by declaring your aversion to and unfitness for it. That will bring you the cheers of the multitude. It will also bring in time . . . the kind of troubles the Carter presidency has sustained and seemed, almost perversely, to compound.[19]

Greenfield's argument is more persuasive than Broder's. There have been cycles of Presidential power and styles of politics throughout American history.[20] But there is strong evidence that the decline in collective responsibility among the branches of government, that is, a sense of cooperation between the President and at least his party in the Congress, has reached an all-time low.[21] Yet there are two countervailing arguments that must be taken into account and both are damaging to Greenfield's thesis: (1) after eight years of Carter and Reagan, not to mention other candidates outside the mainstream even when they did hold high public office (Goldwater, Wallace, McGovern), the two parties appear for 1984 at least to be focusing their attention on potential nominees closer to the center influence within each party; and (2) although outsiders may have played a more prominent role in our politics in recent years, they are hardly a new phenomenon, from Aaron Burr to Andrew Jackson to William Jennings Bryan to Theodore Roosevelt to Wendell Wilkie and even to John F. Kennedy. War heroes Ulysses S. Grant and Dwight D. Eisenhower were selected more for their electoral appeal than for either party regularity or a readily identifiable promise of greatness in office.

Not all of these candidates were the compulsive candidates that Carter and Reagan have been. But the critical factor is that the outsider strategy is not new. Nor are the dilemmas that we face in selecting the Presidential candidates new. Broder and Greenfield are probably both right *in part*. It seems only plausible that the nominating system would have an impact on the type of candidates who emerge and that the decline in trust and efficacy would affect not only turnout (see Chapter 4) but also the political appeals that candidates would make and the chances of candidates who make those appeals to gain the nominations. But neither explanation seems sufficient to account for all the problems in Presidential leadership we face.

Indeed, the very question of the quality of leadership is not at all new. Long before the changes in the nominating system and long before the levels of trust and efficacy had begun to decline (much less be measured), a young political scientist who had just finished his graduate training peered beyond the era of the weak President into another in which executive power would be more important. Woodrow Wilson, writing in 1885, worried:[22]

> We are too apt to think both the work of legislation and the work of administration easy enough to be done readily, with or without preparation, by any man of discretion and character. No one imagines that the drygoods or hardware trade, or even the cobbler's craft, can be successfully conducted except by those who have worked through a laborious and unremunerative apprenticeship, and who have devoted their lives to perfecting themselves as tradesmen or as menders of shoes. But ... administration is regarded as something which an old soldier, an ex-diplomatist, or a popular politician may be trusted to take to by instinct. No man of tolerable talents need despair of having been born a Presidential candidate.

This was not dangerous at the time that Wilson wrote because, in contrast to parliamentary systems in Europe, "the business of the President, occasionally great, is usually not much above routine."[23] Indeed, the President "is part of the official rather than of the political machinery of government" and Wilson suggested that in the states there should be "a lower grade of service in which men may be advantageously drilled for Presidential functions."[24] When he became President almost three decades later, the young scholar would move to expand the power of the Presidency following the lead of Theodore Roosevelt. But the lament of poor Presidential candidates hardly originated with the post-1968 reforms in the nominating process. In the era of a stronger Presidency the need for better selection may be more acute, but the basic problem remains.

Writing only thirty years after Wilson wrote, and, indeed during his Presidency, the English observer Lord James Bryce entitled a chapter of his famous *The American Commonwealth* "Why Great Men Are Not Chosen Presidents." Bryce issued a complaint that would hardly have surprised a contemporary observer:[25]

> In America, which is beyond all other countries the country of a "career open to talents," a country, moreover in which political life is unusually keen and political ambition widely diffused, it might be expected that the highest place would always be won by a man of brilliant gifts. But from the time that the heroes of the Revo-

lution died out with Jefferson and Adams and Madison, no person except General Grant, had, down till the end of the (nineteenth) century, reached the chair whose name would have been remembered had he not been President . . . Who knows or cares to know anything about the personality of James K. Polk or Franklin Pierce? The only thing remarkable about them is that being so commonplace they should have climbed so high.

Again, comparing the United States with Europe, he charged, not without reason, that "the ordinary American voter does not object to mediocrity."[26] The voter looks more for candidates with appealing personalities than for a keen intellect. Unlike Wilson or perhaps because of him and Roosevelt before him, Bryce maintained that intelligence and eloquence were at least useful traits for a chief executive, if a bit superfluous for most of his duties. These more routine tasks, not unlike those of "the chairman of a commercial company or the manager of a railway," require firmness, common sense, and, critically, honesty.[27]

The few great responsibilities, as well as the tolerance of the citizenry for candidates of modest abilities, are only part of the reason why Presidents have not been great. What was the great villain in the process of excluding the intelligent and the eloquent from the nation's highest office? Why, it was the nominating system, of course! Assembled in convention, the people who are responsible for choosing the nominees tend to give great consideration to issues such as what state a candidate comes from, his regional bases of support, and whether the candidate is a Protestant.[28] All in all, great men are not generally chosen President because: (1) there simply aren't many great men in politics; (2) the nominating system will rarely select them anyway; and (3) interestingly, "because they are not, in quiet times, absolutely needed."[29] Yet even in times when greatness is called for, the nominating system hardly helps out in the quest for the best. For "the merits of a President are one thing and those of a candidate another thing."[30] What is even more frustrating, however, is that the need for a great President cannot readily be predicted. Times of crisis do not necessarily follow the four-year Presidential term. Since World War II, Presidents have been called on to make many more important decisions. The international role of the United States has changed dramatically, and the number of "crises" has also skyrocketed. Indeed, in the 1980 contest for the Democratic nomination for President, Senator Edward Kennedy charged Carter with "lurching from crisis to crisis."

The arguments of Wilson and particularly Bryce indicate that the debate is not a new one. But there is one critical aspect of Bryce's comments that deserves further attention: his criticism of the nominating system. Is it likely that both Broder and Bryce are wrong? We think not. But the real problem may be not whether party leaders or the citizenry at large pick the nominees. Rather, the entire selection process is organized less around choosing a politician who might suffice at leadership than a leader who might be electable. As Bryce commented: "the previous career of the possible candidates has generally made it easier to say who will succeed as a candidate than who will succeed as a President."[31] Before we can deal with this problem, we must elucidate the criteria for Presidential leadership. It is to this task that we now turn.

CRITERIA FOR LEADERSHIP

It might be difficult to formulate a set of criteria for Presidential greatness in leadership that can be used as a predictive tool. We cannot always be sure, as we shall see in the next section, that our forecast will be accurate no matter how well formulated our criteria are. But we can set out some basic ideas as to what constitutes, based on performance in office, a strong leader. *First, we would require that a leader be popular with both the mass public and with the Congress.* The essence of leadership is having a followership. A President who does not have the public's confidence cannot press the legislature to adopt his program and a chief executive without the support of Congress has lost one of the most critical elements of his following. In Table 6-2 we present the maximum and minimum levels of public support for Presidents as measured in Gallup surveys from 1938, when the questions began to be asked systematically, to 1982; and the Presidential "box scores" of legislative success in the Congress from 1953, when *Congressional Quarterly* began to calculate them, until 1982.[32] The public surveys ask citizens whether they approve or disapprove of the President's performance. Here we report approval levels, but, recognizing that there may be wide fluctuations in the course of even a single year, employ both the high and the low for each year. The "boxscore" is the percentage of bills on which the President took a position and prevailed.

But, as several keen observers of the Presidency have noted, great Presidents are not merely those who are popular. To be a strong leader means provoking conflict.[33] As the old saying goes, you have to break some eggs to make an omelet. Or, more bluntly, "Leadership is dissensual."[34] This does not imply that the mark of a great leader is that he has turned the nation or the Congress against himself. We need only remember Richard M. Nixon during Watergate or Herbert Hoover at the end of his administration when the nation was in the Depression or to recall that antipathy does not mean greatness. But neither does it mean, as was the case with Eisenhower or Kennedy, that a high level of public approval would translate into either favorable treatment for a President's program by the Congress or even popularity with the members of the legislature. Among the key qualities of executive leadership are empathy with the public, an ability to communicate, credibility, and vision.[35] These are all elements involved in leading the public and the Congress, in convincing people that the President is indeed right. This is a function that is unique to the President, argued Woodrow Wilson in 1908, just five years before he assumed the office himself: "He is the only national voice in affairs. Let him once win the admiration and confidence of the country, and no other single force can with-

TABLE 6-2
LEVELS OF PUBLIC SUPPORT AND PRESIDENTIAL SUCCESS IN CONGRESS: 1938–1982

Year	Public approval High	Low	Presidential success ("box scores")
Roosevelt			
1938	60%	54%	—[1]
1939	65	57	—
1940	64	64[2]	—
1941	76	70	—
1942	84	70	—
1943	75	66	—
Truman			
1945	87	75	—
1946	63	32	—
1947	60	54	—
1948	39	36	—
1949	69	51	—
1950	46	39	—
1951	36	23	—
1952	32	25	—
Eisenhower			
1953	75	58	89.0%
1954	75	57	82.8
1955	77	66	75.0
1956	79	67	70.0
1957	73	57	68.0
1958	60	48	76.0
1959	76	57	52.0
1960	66	49	65.0
Kennedy			
1961	83	71	81.0
1962	79	61	85.4
1963	74	56	87.1
Johnson			
1963–1964	80%	69%	88.0%
1965	71	62	93.0
1966	61	44	79.0
1967	52	38	79.0
1968	48	35	75.0
Nixon			
1969	67	56	74.0
1970	64	51	77.0
1971	56	48	75.0
1972	62	49	66.0
1973	67	27	50.6
1974	28	24	59.6

TABLE 6-2
(*Continued*)

| Year | Public approval | | Presidential success ("box scores") |
	High	Low	
Ford			
1974	66	42	58.2
1975	52	37	61.0
1976	53	45	53.8
Carter			
1977	67	51	75.4
1978	55	39	78.3
1979	61	28	76.8
1980	58	21	75.1
Reagan			
1981	67	49	81.9
1982[3]	49	46	—

[1]Not available.
[2]In 1940 only two polls were taken in the months of January and February. The percentage approval was the same in both polls.
[3]As of March 1982.
Source: Congressional Quarterly Weekly Report, January 18, 1982, p. 18; *The Gallup Report* (April 1982), rept. no. 199, p. 22; *The Gallup Report* (November 1981), rept. no. 94, pp. 3, 23–31.

stand him."[36] A President who has no significant following cannot be a great leader.

Second, we would require that a leader be successful with his or her own program. To be a leader, in other words, a President must be more than a follower. He or she must not merely sway in the wind with public opinion and propose only that legislation that seems popular; nor can the President simply follow the Congress and let its leadership set the agenda. The chief executive must propose a program for action and press for its adoption vigorously. To do this requires a sense of timing, courage, decisiveness, flexibility, and power.[37] Furthermore, a successful President must not only press for a program, but must also win. Indeed, it was "Wilson's *failure* to bring the United States into the League of Nations, not his high-sounding moralistic platitudes, that has given him such a bad historical press."[38] The President had launched a national campaign to take his case to the people in an effort to get the United States to join an international peace-keeping agency following World War I. Facing a difficult fight against a Republican-controlled Senate in 1919, a battle he ultimately lost, Wilson stumped the country in the effort to win the battle. This judgment of Wilson's place in history may be too harsh. As we shall see, many observers rate Wilson much more highly based on the extensive social legislation enacted under his New Freedom program in his first administration (1913–1916). Thus, we must recognize that leadership is not simply an all-or-nothing phenomenon in a given Presidency. Wilson was a strong and forceful leader early in his Presidency, a much lesser figure in his second term. Lyndon B. Johnson similarly started off extremely strong, but, like Wilson, stumbled on foreign policy (Vietnam) and lost both popularity and credibility with his public and Congressional following. Even a President who is not very popular with the mass public can exert strong leadership. Harry S Truman did so when he fired the very popular General Douglas MacArthur after the general disobeyed Presidential orders regarding military strategy in the Korean war in 1950. There are many times when leadership may require bold actions that may not meet with public approval, but a great leader can build up confidence following such difficult decisions.

As a keen observer has noted, "Leadership is causal."[39] The President must make things happen with Congress, molding and shaping public and elite opinion. Eisenhower, who largely left the legislative agenda to the Democratic leaders in Congress during the six years that the Democrats controlled both houses of the legislature, was not therefore a causal leader. Neither was Kennedy, despite his tremendous popularity and his seeming success as measured by the "box scores." The problem with relying only on the "box scores" is that they do not give us an idea as to what was being attempted. Kennedy asked for little from a Congress that he thought he could not control; it is unclear whether he would have pushed much harder even if he believed that he could prevail.[40] On the other hand, Wilson, both Roosevelts, Johnson, Truman, and Reagan, among others, have pressed the Congress very hard indeed. On this basis, it would seem logical to conclude that Truman, who may not have prevailed as often as Kennedy did but at least put up many fights, was more of a leader than Kennedy was. We demand that a strong leader press for a program that is clearly identifiable as the President's agenda. Furthermore, the President must appear to be "in control" of the agenda, indeed to win most of the key battles to adopt the program. When a President must act decisively in the face of hostile opinion among the public and perhaps even the Congress, he must strive to rebuild the bases of support needed to reassert control.

Third, we would require that a great leader press for major changes in policy direction and content. James MacGregor Burns says that a great leader must propose and enact "real change."[41] Furthermore, such leadership must be morally purposeful, that is built on a vision of a just society.[42] What is "real change" or a "major change"? It is difficult to define, but let us give some examples: Lincoln's fight to save the Union in the Civil War and his ultimate decision to abolish slavery and proceed with Reconstruction; Wilson's broad range of labor and social welfare legislation in his New Freedom; and the tremendous range of governmental programs established under Franklin D. Roosevelt's New Deal and later under Johnson's Great Society. These are all major changes, or what is sometimes referred to as "sea change." The new policies must be perceived not just by historians but by the public and the Congress as having an important, perhaps even fundamental, impact on the direction of national public policy. One can argue endlessly about how extensive any President's program is. And this point should make clear the contention that one simply can't say that President A was a great leader and President B wasn't. There are variations in leadership capacity. We may not be able to agree on all aspects of measurement, but at least we can try to reach some accord as to what the crucial questions are.

This kind of leadership demands vision and a sense for power more than simple intelligence. Although Wilson clearly was brilliant, neither Franklin D. Roosevelt nor Lyndon B. Johnson was regarded as among the brightest intellects to have occupied the White House. On the other hand, John Quincy Adams and James Madison were said to have, perhaps, the two most gifted minds of any Presidents, yet neither achieved recognition for their leadership.[43] But the vision and sense for power must be tempered by a sense of flexibility, an ability to determine what is possible to achieve and how to get it. Taft, Hoover, and Eisenhower were accused of attempting too hard to impose a sense of rationality on all decision-making: "the lawyer, the engineer, and the soldier—all three shared, by virtue of their training and their careers, a stubborn sense of the Presidency as essentially a place for the reign of order and reason and system."[44] One can certainly add Carter, also an engineer, to this list. In contrast, Jefferson, Franklin D. Roosevelt, and Johnson were all master politicians and pragmatists.[45] Wilson was less flexible, but he had another advantage. So persuasive was he said to be that he could by the force of his arguments get most of what he wanted, at least on domestic policy during his first term.[46] But Wilson, like Roosevelt and Johnson, came into office without a clear idea as to the program he was to propose.[47] Indeed, all three were, at the outset of their administrations, regarded with suspicion by the liberal forces whose program they were to embrace. It has been argued that great leaders come from largely patrician backgrounds and Wilson and Roosevelt certainly did.[48] Johnson came from a poor family, but his political ties in the Senate were distinctly "establishment." Thus the major changes in social policy that occured under these three leaders were the products of "conservative turncoats."

What distinguishes all these leaders who clearly have produced "real change"—as well as other Presidents who have tried but were not quite as successful, including Truman (who succeeded in establishing the Marshall Plan to aid Europe after World War II and the North Atlantic Treaty Organization alliance, but failed in most of his innovative domestic program) and Reagan (who has been less successful in dismantling the Great Society than it initially appeared he would be)—is that they were also party leaders. The greatest Presidents "all were—with the exception of Washington—

unabashedly ambitious for the office they finally won. They all were—even Washington—zealous partisans."[49] The ambition gave them the drive to provoke conflict; the partisanship provided the mobilization of their most likely supporters to ensure victory and thus solidify their popular base among the mass public. As Wilson wrote earlier, so he acted in office. He was a devoted partisan, committed to government by political parties, and he saw the President as the only single source of both public opinion and party strength.[50]

Finally, we would require that a great leader be respected internationally. Too many Presidents are preoccupied with domestic policy and give short shrift to foreign policy issues. When they do become involved in international affairs, they may find themselves overwhelmed by the complexity of the events and the unwillingness of other nations to bargain with the President as the leaders of Congress do. But particularly in this complex world, a great President must act as a world leader and gain the confidence and respect of other chiefs of state. The problem is complicated by the fact that Presidential elections typically revolve around domestic issues and the candidates' personalities to a far greater extent than they do around foreign policy questions.[51] Indeed, for many years the office of Governor was considered the best training ground for future Presidents since it, in contrast with membership in the Congress, provided experience in administration.[52] With the dramatic growth in importance of world affairs since World War II, these attitudes have shifted. Now the Senate, the only body other than the Presidency to have foreign policy duties explicitly spelled out in the Constitution (the Senate must give its advice and consent to treaties and, with the House, must concur in a declaration of war), has become the main center of recruitment of Presidential nominees. Since the end of World War II, seven former Senators have been nominated for the White House by the two major parties, compared with only four ex-Governors; Vice Presidential nominees have been overwhelmingly drawn from the Senate, with ten Senators and only one Governor since 1948. Furthermore, there is a pronounced tendency for Senators who make it to the national ticket to have served on the major foreign policy committees in the chamber.[53]

The 1976 and 1980 elections were both marked by winning campaigns of former Governors, however. And it is scarcely surprising that much of the criticism of these administrations has centered on handling of foreign policy. Despite the notable achievements of the Camp David peace treaty between Israel and Egypt and the crusade for human rights, Carter was widely perceived as struggling with foreign policy. His advisers were constantly bickering among themselves about matters large (basic policy directions) and small (internal power struggles), culminating in the resignation of Secretary of State Cyrus Vance in June 1980 over differences in handling the Iranian hostage problem.[54] In the Presidential elections of that year, Reagan roundly criticized Carter's ineptness in foreign policy; yet, on taking office, the new President found himself engulfed in similar squabbles among his Vice President, his Secretary of State, his National Security Adviser, and others on the White House Staff.[55] Neither Carter nor Reagan was primarily interested in foreign policy, and, indeed, it would be fair to say that most American Presidents have been far more domestically oriented than concerned with international events. It was foreign policy issues that wreaked havoc with the historical reputations of Wilson (the League of Nations) and Johnson (Vietnam). Of recent Presidents, only Kennedy and Nixon could really be said to have had a burning interest in international politics, sometimes to the expense of their own domestic programs, whereas Franklin D. Roosevelt and Truman were among the only ones to be able to strike a healthy balance of interests. Unfortunately for Truman, his difficulties getting his domestic program through the Congress, despite a zeal for such conflict, tarnished somewhat his historical reputation as a potentially great chief executive.

Since so much depends on the specific historical circumstances, it is difficult to state precisely what a President has to do to maintain respect in the international community. But this problem itself suggests at least a broad answer: To be successful internationally, as domestically, a President must have a flexible approach to foreign policy. Chief executives who have had difficulties in foreign policy, Wilson, Johnson, Carter, and Reagan, have all approached this arena moralistically. Like Taft, Hoover, and Eisenhower in domestic policy, as discussed above, they sought to impose rationality, their own sense of rationality, on a disorderly world. Carter had many of the same problems with domestic policy, but the other three (Reagan primarily in the first year of his Presidency) were masters of pragmatism, tempered by a sense of vision, in dealing with the Congress on domestic legislation. Ford, and to a lesser extent Eisenhower, delegated much of the policy-making on foreign affairs to their chief aides. Perhaps the only President who mastered the arts of negotiating domestically and internationally was Franklin D. Roosevelt, first dubbing himself "Dr. New Deal" and later "Dr. Win-the-War." [56]

Here we are faced with a dilemma. It seems that inadequate background in foreign policy decision-making contributes to the difficulties that many recent Presidents have had internationally. The situation is compounded by the "outsider," anti-Washington election strategies of candidates such as Carter and Reagan. As President, they must deal decisively with the very "establishment" questions of foreign policy that they sought to dispel during the campaign. Citizens in other democracies marvel at how the most powerful nation on earth provides only "on-the-job training" in foreign policy for the supposed leader of the free world and are hardly surprised when neophytes to the national government have difficulties dealing with such veteran chiefs of government as Leonid Brezhnev of the Soviet Union, Deng Tsaio-Ping of China, François Mitterand of France, or Pierre Elliott Trudeau of Canada.

Yet the record of accomplishment both domestically and internationally of Franklin Roosevelt suggests that training may be important, but it is hardly necessary. Roosevelt came to the White House from the governorship of New York. His only prior national experience was as Assistant Secretary of the Navy in the Wilson administration. Although his tenure in that office was regarded as successful, perhaps even innovative,[57] and gave him experience in dealing with a world war, it did not involve any extensive dealings with major international figures. Did Roosevelt have sufficient background in international politics? Was the twelve-year period in between his tenure in that office and his inauguration as President "too long"? Or was the critical factor Roosevelt's personality and temperament more than his prior training? We simply don't know, but it is a lot to expect of future chief executives that they perform at Roosevelt's level. Thus, some prior background may be a useful criterion for judging potential candidates. We are seeking, to reiterate, a chief executive who: (1) can command the support of both Congress and the mass public; (2) must press for a program; (3) strives for major changes in policy direction and content; and (4) is respected internationally as well as domestically.

Who have been the best Presidents? In Table 6-3 we report the results of five polls of academics and one of the mass public.[58] The academic surveys were conducted largely among historians: (1) in 1948 Arthur Schlesinger, Sr., polled fifty-five prominent historians for *Life* magazine; (2) in 1962 he repeated the survey among seventy-five historians, political scientists, and journalists; (3) in 1970 Gary Maranell and Richard Dodder surveyed 571 historians; (4) in 1977 the United States Historical Society polled ninety-three historians; and (5) in late 1981 the Chicago *Tribune* surveyed forty-nine historians and other social scientists and asked them to rate the ten best and ten worst Presidents; the results were published in early 1982. Also the Gallup organization surveyed the mass public in 1975 in an attempt to determine which Presidents were the best. Although the questions varied slightly from one analysis to the next, the overall rankings are what is most important.

First we notice that the academic surveys reveal a strong degree of agreement as to which leaders were great. In contrast, the public showed a strong bias toward Kennedy, whose personal popularity and charisma were still remembered by a large number of citizens, although not quite so highly valued by historians. When we look at all six polls, however, we are hardly surprised by the results. The greatest consensus is found on Lincoln, Washington, and Franklin D. Roosevelt. A survey conducted in 1983 among 970 historians showed continued "support" for Lincoln, Franklin D. Roosevelt, Washington, and Jefferson as the nation's greatest Presidents.[59] When we consider these Presidents, it is not difficult to make the case that each: (1) had considerable popular support both among the mass public and within the Congress; (2) did indeed press for a legislative program; and (3) presided over major changes in national policy. Perhaps only Roosevelt had an important reputation on foreign policy as well, but that was because the United States had not yet emerged as a world power under Lincoln and was still struggling to get its internal politics

TABLE 6-3
EVALUATIONS OF PRESIDENTIAL PERFORMANCE

Schlesinger poll 1948	Schlesinger poll 1962	Maranell-Dodder poll 1970	Gallup poll 1975	(%)	U.S. Historical Society poll 1977	Votes	Chicago Tribune poll 1982
Great	**Great**	**Overall prestige**	What three U.S. presidents do you regard as the greatest?		**Ten greatest presidents**		**Ten greatest presidents**
(1) Lincoln	(1) Lincoln	(1) Lincoln	Kennedy	52	Lincoln	85	(1) Lincoln
(2) Washington	(2) Washington	(2) Washington	Lincoln	49	Washington	84	(2) Washington
(3) F. Roosevelt	(3) F. Roosevelt	(3) F. Roosevelt	F. Roosevelt	45	F. Roosevelt	81	(3) F. Roosevelt
(4) Wilson	(4) Wilson	(4) Jefferson	Truman	37	Jefferson	79	(4) T. Roosevelt
(5) Jefferson	(5) Jefferson	(5) T. Roosevelt	Washington	25	T. Roosevelt	79	(5) Jefferson
(6) Jackson	**Near Great**	(6) Wilson	Eisenhower	24	Wilson	74	(6) Wilson
Near Great	(6) Jackson	(7) Truman	T. Roosevelt	9	Jackson	74	(7) Jackson
(7) T. Roosevelt	(7) T. Roosevelt	(8) Jackson	L. Johnson	9	Truman	64	(8) Truman
(8) Cleveland	(8) Polk	(9) Kennedy	Jefferson	8	Polk	38	(9) Eisenhower
(9) J. Adams	(8) Truman	(10) J. Adams	Wilson	5	J. Adams	35	(10) Polk
(10) Polk	(9) J. Adams	(11) Polk	Nixon	9	L. Johnson	24	**Ten worst presidents**
Average	**Average**	(12) Cleveland	All others	9	Cleveland	21	**(with worst no. 1)**
(11) J. Q. Adams	(10) Cleveland	(13) Madison	Don't know	3	Kennedy	19	(1) Harding
(12) Monroe	(11) Madison	(14) Monroe			Madison	16	(2) Nixon
(13) Hayes	(12) J. Q. Adams	(15) J. Q. Adams			J. Q. Adams	14	(3) Buchanan
(14) Madison	(13) Hayes	(16) L. Johnson			Eisenhower	14	(4) Pierce
(15) Van Buren	(14) Mckinley	(17) Taft			Monroe	7	(5) Grant
(16) Taft	(15) Taft	(18) Hoover			Hoover	6	(6) Fillmore
(17) Arthur	(16) Van Buren	(19) Eisenhower			McKinley	4	(7) A. Johnson
(18) McKinley	(17) Monroe	(20) A. Johnson			Van Buren	2	

TABLE 6-3
(*Continued*)
EVALUATIONS OF PRESIDENTIAL PERFORMANCE

Schlesinger poll 1948	Schlesinger poll 1962	Maranell-Dodder poll 1970	Gallup poll 1975	U.S. Historical Society poll 1977		Chicago Tribune poll 1982
(19) A. Johnson	(18) Hoover	(21) Van Buren		Arthur	2	(8) Coolidge
(20) Hoover	(19) Harrison	(22) McKinley		Tyler	1	(9) Tyler
(21) Harrison	(20) Arthur	(23) Arthur		Buchanan	1	(10) Carter
Below average	(20) Eisenhower	(24) Hayes		Grant	1	
(22) Tyler	(21) A. Johnson	(25) Tyler		Hayes	1	
(23) Coolidge	**Below average**	(26) Harrison		Taft	1	
(24) Fillmore	(22) Taylor	(27) Taylor		Coolidge	1	
(25) Taylor	(23) Tyler	(28) Coolidge		Nixon	1	
(26) Buchanan	(24) Fillmore	(29) Fillmore		W. Harrison	0	
(27) Pierce	(25) Coolidge	(30) Buchanan		Taylor	0	
Failure	(26) Pierce	(31) Pierce		Fillmore	0	
(28) Grant	(27) Buchanan	(32) Grant		Pierce	0	
(29) Harding	**Failure**	(33) Harding		A. Johnson	0	
	(28) Grant	(Harrison and		Garfield	0	
	(29) Harding	Garfield not		B. Harrison	0	
		included due to		Harding	0	
		brevity of tenure)		Ford	0	

Source: Robert E. DiClerico, *The American President*, 2d ed., Englewood Cliffs, N.J.: Prentice-Hall, 1983, pp. 332–333.

in order under Washington. Jefferson is at the periphery of greatness, and, again, there is little doubt that he met at least the first three criteria. Wilson's case is particularly interesting. For all the attention given by historians to his failure to gain entrance for the United States into the League of Nations, Wilson's ranking as a great leader still stands, although less so among the mass public. This reinforces our argument that leadership is not an "all-or-nothing" phenomenon. As a dynamic domestic leader early in his Presidency and a strong force internationally during the beginning of his second administration (when the United States entered World War I), Wilson achieved greatness before losing the nation's affection. One could make the same argument about Johnson during the first three years of his Presidency, largely a domestic one, and it will be interesting to see how history (and historians) view him half a century from now.

What we see in these rankings, both of academics and historians, is that there is a clear preference for activist, even liberal, Presidents. Why should this be the case? Activist Presidents present an image to the public and to the Congress that they are "doing something," in contrast with more passive chief executives such as Eisenhower and Ford. Indeed, this may be the reason why Kennedy was regarded so highly, even in 1975, by the public. Furthermore, liberal activists who expand the scope of government are more likely to favor lasting changes in policy that will be recalled by future generations. Thus, the reputations of Roosevelt, Jefferson, Wilson, and Lincoln are attributable not only to their style of actions, but also to what they accomplished while in office.

We still face the difficulty of determining which candidates have the potential to achieve greatness, near-greatness, or even satisfactory performances. At the least, perhaps we could screen candidates who might be regarded as disastrous Presidents. Is there a mechanism, a test, that we could apply to candidates to determine future performance in office? We turn to such a proposal.

CAN WE PREDICT PERFORMANCE?

It is almost certainly impossible to predict greatness. To a certain extent such eminence depends on the objective situation in the nation and the world: Washington was leading a new nation; Jefferson presided over the first peaceful transition of power from one party to another; Lincoln struggled to reunite a nation; Wilson and Roosevelt both led the nation through world wars; and Roosevelt also took the country through its worst economic crisis. But we should strive at least to find competent chief executives. To this end, James David Barber, a political scientist, has proposed a method of examining potential Presidents by looking into their backgrounds. This tool, called psychohistory, has been widely used to interpret the careers of Presidents and other world leaders.[60] But it was Barber who first suggested in 1972 that it had predictive value as well and proceeded to do so by forecasting that the Nixon administration might end in dramatic failure.[61] The striking success of this prediction, as well as the very novelty of the thesis itself, brought a great deal of attention to this approach.

Barber starts with three basic elements of personality. First is *style,* how a President handles himself and deals with others. Does he work well with others? Is he a hard worker? Does he pour a lot of energy into his job? Does he communicate well to the nation and to other political leaders? Nixon, Johnson, and Wilson were compulsive workers; Eisenhower and Coolidge were quite relaxed; Ford, Kennedy, and Reagan probably rank in between these extremes. Carter's energy kept him up late at night and had him rising early in the morning to tend to the details of the Presidential office; Reagan, on the other, is well known for his longer vacations and his naps, even preferring not to be awakened for less than earth-shattering news. Second is *world view,* which is not just ideology but rather an outlook as to how the world works. Are people basically good or bad? Is the world basically controllable? Is the world divided into black and white, good and evil? Roosevelt's statement in his inaugural address in 1933 that "we have nothing to fear but fear itself" was an expression of an optimistic world view. The belief of Nixon, as well as Hoover and to a lesser extent Carter, that he was surrounded by hostile forces is a more pessimistic, even negative outlook. Finally, we have *character,* the President's view of life and his role in the world "not for the moment, but enduringly."[62] The fundamental question here is: Does a person enjoy being President? Roosevelt, Truman, Kennedy, and Reagan certainly could all give affirmative answers to this question. On the other hand, Hoover, Andrew Johnson, and to a lesser extent Eisenhower often found the demands of the job distracting, sometimes downright irritating. Greenfield's suggestion that Carter really didn't like exercising power, that he felt uncomfortable doing it (even though he was regarded as an excellent campaigner in elections), may imply that Carter had more in common with Hoover than with the more activist leaders.[63]

This method of analysis thus examines the personal background, going as far back as early childhood, to determine whether an individual has a positive psychological outlook. Can he or she relate well to others? Did he or she have a happy childhood with good relationships with parents and schoolmates? How well has the individual adjusted to new situations? Is he or she basically upbeat or pessimistic about life prospects? From questions of this type, Barber develops an overall typology of Presidential behavior. Style tells us about a potential chief executive's *activity* level: Will he or she be an energetic leader? World view and character tell us about the President's outlook on his job and his enjoyment of it. Merely putting a lot of energy into something doesn't guarantee that you will succeed, as happened to Wilson on the League of Nations, to Johnson on Vietnam, to Hoover on the Depression, to Nixon on extricating himself from Watergate.[64] Is the basic approach of the President, then, *positive or negative?*

Barber proposes a typology based on these two key elements. The ideal President is an "active-positive," someone who likes the job and puts a lot of effort into it. Such a person is well adjusted, rational but flexible, and has a well-articulated set of personal goals.[65] Among the Presidents who have been classified as active-positives are Franklin D. Roosevelt, Truman, Kennedy, Ford, and Carter.[66] The type most to be feared is the active-negative, the compulsive but aggressive leader who feels very insecure. Such a President recoils from the joy of politics and often fights a lonely inner battle against what he perceives as hostile forces from the outside. As time passes he becomes more and more a loner, withdrawing from the normal political bargaining and ultimately from much of the public. Such leaders are likely to have had unhappy childhoods, with a felt need to prevail against a world that was against them from the outset. Examples that Barber gives are Wilson, Johnson, Hoover, and Nixon.[67] Wilson and Johnson had lonely crusades in favor of unpopular foreign policies; Hoover had a similar difficulty with public opinion over the Depression; and Nixon faced the public over the Watergate scandal.

The passive-positive enjoys the job but does not believe that much is demanded of him either in terms of new programs or even as a bold leader. He is an amiable figure whose public stature depends less on his actions in office than on his personality. Examples include William Howard Taft, the immensely popular post-World War I President who followed Wilson in office, and Warren Harding.[68] Before his election, Barber also predicted that Reagan would be a passive-positive leader; Reagan's easygoing manner, his fondness for naps, his keen sense of humor, and his reluctance to rein in his advisers, who are also personal friends all seemed to point in this direction.[69] On the other hand, the passive-negative President feels out of place in the White House. He is there because it is his duty. After serving his "sentence," this type of leader simply wants out. The classic example is Calvin Coolidge, who refused renomination in 1928 by the famous disclaimer: "I do not choose to run." Eisenhower is a more controversial entry into this category.[70]

One thing should be immediately clear: All of the great Presidents listed in Table 6-3 except Wilson have been active-positives. But, of course, so were many who could not be considered such unqualified success stories, such as Kennedy and Carter. Although this approach of Barber's may help us understand the psychological make-up of potential candidates,[71] it is not without its detractors even among those who also "practice" psychohistory.[72] Let us consider some of the problems with the approach. First, psychology, much less history, is hardly a science in which the findings are beyond dispute. There is no universally agreed on method for examining childhood experiences to predict later behavior. Second, this approach seems to rule out the possibility of learning from experience. A President's character is set early in life. There is no mention of later development or even learning from experience in the White House. One can understand, perhaps, how someone's basic character does not readily change. But it appears odd that there is no allowance for alterations in world view or style that may emerge once a person occupies the most powerful position in the world. There is little that can completely prepare anyone for such responsibilities. The White House environment may indeed produce different perceptions of the way the world works. So may changes in the world situation, as occurred for Wilson, Hoover, and Johnson. Had the crises in each of their administrations not developed (particularly in foreign policy for Wilson and Johnson, two men who felt much more comfortable dealing with domestic issues), they might have been listed as active-positives and "great" Presidents. Indeed, despite Wilson's difficulties, most surveys *do* list him as a great leader. This points up a third difficulty with Barber's approach: It assumes that someone will either be a good (read "positive") or bad (read "negative") leader throughout his career. But for Wilson and Johnson, it is entirely possible— probably most useful—to divide their terms into periods of tremendous success and those of failure.

Fourth, as stunning as the Nixon prediction may have been, succeeding forecasts have been less helpful. Should we really still rate Carter as an active-positive? The evidence is mixed. There are some reasons to think that much of his attitude toward power was negative: he could never get along with Congress, he withdrew into the White House while the hostages were in Iran in a manner not dissimilar from Nixon during Watergate, and he seemed to lose the ability to laugh at himself. On the other hand, Reagan may not really be a passive-positive. His level of activity, his zeal for the job, and his success at difficult bargaining with the Congress during his first year in office suggest that he may indeed be an active-positive. But his relaxed style and his seeming disinterest in many foreign policy issues do suggest that he is passive in other respects. Classification is not an easy task, and we wonder if it is always the most appropriate thing to do. We suggested earlier in this chapter that leadership is not something that someone can or cannot do. There are always variations in degree. Perhaps such typologies may lead us into unwarranted conclusions. Finally, there will always be "revisionist" histories, even psychohistories, of our leaders that might very well effectively challenge dominant interpretations. We already have such treatments of Wilson,[73] Johnson,[74] and even an attempt to reconstruct Eisenhower as an active-positive leader.[75] Perhaps only William Henry Harrison, "Old Tippecanoe," will not similarly be reevaluated, and only because he served just four weeks of the term to which he had been elected in 1840.

There are other types of questions that "revisionist" historians can ask. One critical one is why each type of President sought the office in the first place. Why would a "passive" President agree to be considered for a nomination, much less put any effort into seeking it? How can we explain Reagan simultaneously as a "passive" chief executive and also as a man who sought the office doggedly for at least six years, during which time he did little else and even mounted a challenge to Ford's renomination in 1976 that almost succeeded.

Perhaps in earlier years, passive candidates could have been drafted, as Coolidge was in 1924, but in this more participatory atmosphere such a situation is virtually inconceivable. Even Eisenhower in 1952 had to challenge his party's Senate leader, Robert A. Taft of Ohio, in a closely contested drive for the nomination. If we are to use this device to screen potential candidates, we need to be a lot more secure in our belief that the interpretations are sound and will not be so much in need of revision. Even more critically, although we do not want to slight expertise, we do stress that the election of our public officials is one of the most important tasks of a citizenry in a democracy. If we trust citizens to judge candidates' economic programs, which are certainly no less complex than most other matters, we should also have faith that they can evaluate personalities.

Overall it is not difficult to predict, from the perspective of hindsight, great leaders. Nor is it problematic to find agreement on what failures had in common. But we have not always reached an accord on classifying Presidents as great, good, mediocre, or bad in the first place. If we are dissatisfied with our Presidents, particularly the range of choices we have had recently, we must do more than propose to turn over the selection process to a group of "experts." We must look not just at why we don't have better Presidents, but rather at why we don't have better candidates.

HOW TO GET BETTER CANDIDATES

The indictments of Bryce and Broder about the "old" and "new" nominating systems suggest that we should redirect our attention. There may not be very much that we can do to ensure great leadership, for Bryce is undoubtedly right that great men and women don't often go into politics. Probably there aren't that many potentially great leaders anyway. But this doesn't mean that we should not try to get better Presidents anyway. At the very least we should try to avoid choices that are viewed as dismal by a large share of the electorate. However, it does not seem that psychological profiles would be of great assistance, given the problems we have just listed. Perhaps the condemnation of both the old party-dominated and the new participatory nominating systems is telling us something. We suggested above that we may be using the wrong criteria for selecting our nominees.

The appropriate question is: How are we to convince any rational political party to give us leaders rather than popular politicians? And the answer is that the two are not necessarily distinct. A race between Mondale and Baker in 1980 surely would have pitted two more distinguished leaders against each other and might have been even more exciting to many citizens. But, as we indicated in Chapter 1, turning the matter over to party leaders probably wouldn't have produced desirable effects very often. Although these men and women in the Democratic party might well have chosen Mondale over Carter in 1980, it is far from clear that, given the amount of grass roots compaigning Reagan had been doing for six years, Republicans would have opted for Baker. Similarly, when we recall previous elections, the track record of party bosses is far from awe inspiring. What we need is a mechanism that would make it very likely that both sets of party leaders would nominate candidates such as Mondale and Baker, that has a track record of doing so, and that, if we could imagine a conversation between Bryce and Broder, would gain the approval of both men. Furthermore, recognizing that Greenfield is also partially correct (probably more so than Broder), we need to devise a scheme that will also minimize the probability that an outsider can get the nomination even if there is nothing immediate that we can do about restoring the public's confidence in our system and in its own efficacy.

This seems to be a virtually impossible task, but there is such a system and it is a remarkably simple one: Candidates of the two major parties should be nominated by their parties' membership in the Congress. Prior to 1824, the Congressional parties did make Presidential nominations, and it may not be surprising to note that four of the nine Presidents who served two full and consecutive four-year terms in American history were nominated by this system in the first thirty-five years of the new nation (Washington, Jefferson, Madison, and James Monroe). To be sure, as Bryce has noted, these men were also "heroes of the Revolution."[76] But the arguments in favor of this system of nomination are persuasive on other grounds, indeed, the ones that we have made regarding the criteria for Presidential leadership.

The first criterion was that a President should have the support of the mass public and the Congress. There is never a guarantee of anything in politics, but one would have every reason to expect that a President nominated by his or her Congressional party would be more likely to maintain a high level of support within the chamber than someone from the "outside" such as Carter, who ran against the "establishment" and beat it by winning primary elections. Particularly a President serving a first term would realize that Congressional support is critical, not just for a national program but also to ensure renomination. A President and a Congress at war with each other paralyze the government. If the President were selected by a Congressional party, there would be a sense of mutual obligation, perhaps even one of collective responsibility. The two bodies could not go their separate ways as they so often do today. Furthermore, it would be more likely than not that the Congressional parties would choose one of their own. This would mean that the President would know the Congress, have experience in bargaining with it, and recognize that he or she still remains committed to the institution. Part of the problem with the Ford Presidency is that he never was chosen by the Republicans in the House to be President, only Minority Leader. There is no direct evidence that he would have been chosen as a Presidential candidate had the Congressional party had the chance to do so. Certainly he had not sought the office before, and there were no serious attempts by GOP activists to push him into an active candidacy in earlier years. Indeed, Ford was chosen as Vice President not by the Congress but by Nixon. Because of the tensions of the time, there was considerable relief when someone was nominated who, most people thought, would be more of a caretaker than an activist. Even if a President did turn on the Congressional party, the legislators could refuse to renominate that chief executive, as parliamentary parties can turn out their Prime Ministers.

Furthermore, a President chosen in this manner would likely be just as popular, if not more so, with the mass public as our current leaders. First, there is the simple effect of legislative-executive harmony on the popularity of both bodies. When the two branches are getting along well, the public's esteem for both rises. The bringing together of the two branches through the nomination process would instill in the chief executive the need to maintain high levels of popularity not only with the legislature but also with the public. If there were greater cooperation between the branches, the public would have a clearer picture of the actions of a "government." There would finally be some place to point to, where one could fix responsibility (either praise *or* blame) for the actions of the government. The President would clearly be a party leader as well as an executive. The dilemma of our system of shared powers for the White House and the Congress was well stated by Wilson:[77]

> Our system is essentially astronomical. A President's usefulness is measured, not by efficiency, but by calendar months. It is reckoned that if he be good at all he will be good for four years. A Prime Minister must keep himself in favor with the majority, a President need only keep alive.

By tying the President's popularity to that of his party in the Congress, both branches have an incentive to cooperate and thus avoid the sorts of interbranch conflicts that have been so destructive in recent years. Perhaps the survival instincts of members of Congress, and particularly the House in which more than 90 percent of those seeking reelection in most recent years have succeeded,[78] will rub off on Presidents as the two branches have a common destiny. This sense of collective responsibility might unite the President and his or her party more clearly against the opposition and produce more party government. If our argument in Chapter 4 that clearer differences between the parties lead to higher turnout is correct, voting participation might increase as well.

Such a situation is likely to make Presidents more willing to formulate a program as a party program and to push for it, while at the same time inviting Congressional participation in shaping it. This is what happened during the Johnson administration.[79] It is difficult to predict that Congressional nominees would be more likely to argue for "sea changes," though it should be noted that only Presidents with strong backing in the Congress and a knowledge of how the two Houses operate have succeeded in pushing for such legislation.

Wilson and Roosevelt were not of the Congress, but they were quick learners and became strong party leaders. Johnson also was a strong partisan, and his knowledge of the Congress was of immeasurable help to his legislative package. It seems realistic to assume that a Congress would be more willing to go along with a series of great changes proposed by someone it had a hand in selecting for the White House. It also does not seem unreasonable to believe that Wilson might well have been nominated by a caucus of Congressional Democrats in 1912, and it is likely that Johnson rather than Kennedy would have been chosen by a similar body in 1960.

Roosevelt's nomination in 1932 seemed foreordained by any selection system, given the economic depression in the country, the candidate's record as Governor of New York, and his prodigious efforts to gain the top spot on the ticket. Similarly, Wilson's nomination in 1912 would probably not have been jeopardized since he had built a national base of support, both inside and outside the Congressional party, in his quest for the White House. It is therefore too simplistic to worry that *only* Congressional insiders could be nominated by such a process. On the other hand, it is highly unlikely that a Goldwater, a McGovern, or a Carter would have been selected as the nominee of a major party. Reagan is a more difficult case, since he did have a lot of support among Congressional Republicans. Pitted against Baker in 1980, the race for an endorsement probably would have been close.

The Congress is more likely than a system of primaries or a convention dominated by party leaders to select a candidate who can gain the support of the international community. That is not because the Congress has a strong interest in foreign policy; it generally does not. But the Congress is more likely to pay attention to the need for an executive who has some background or a strong interest in foreign policy issues if for no other reason than the Congress does not want to have all of the foreign policy failures of a President dumped in its lap. If the Congress does select its own more often than the present system, it would almost certainly do better than choosing former Governors with no foreign policy background such as Carter or Reagan.

Finally, the proposed nominating system might even increase the accountability of those who nominate the President to the mass public. We argued in Chapter 1 that the system of nominations by party leaders was undemocratic. Now we have to confront the question as to why members of a Congressional party should be permitted to make such an important decision. To be sure, we have advanced many arguments beyond the concern for widespread participation. But there is another argument that we can make regarding accountability. The delegates to national conventions, under either the "old" (pre-1972) rules or the newer reformed rules, are generally unknown to most voters. They are invisible decision-makers who meet only for a short time (less than a week) with several thousand other people like themselves. Thus it is rare when any of them even get television or newspaper coverage as individuals. As delegates they have no other official duties once the conventions are over. Many of them simply fade from view. If average citizens do not know who their delegates are, they cannot know whether they have ever held the post before.

On the other hand, members of Congress do continue to serve in office and they are eligible for reelection every two years for the House of Representatives and every six years for the Senate. If a member wants to maintain popularity in the district, he or she should not stray too far from constituents' wishes on policy issues or on preferred Presidential candidates. Most voters do recognize the names of their incumbent Representatives and Senators; 93 percent of voters can pick out the name of their Representative, compared with 96 percent for their Senator.[80] The greater awareness of voters for their Congressional representatives suggests that this nominating system would very seriously take public opinion into account, while at the same time placing outsiders at a severe disadvantage.

This proposal is not new,[81] but it has not been the subject of much sustained attention. To be sure, it is more realistic than the more radical solution of some serious students of American politics that we need to move all the way to a parliamentary system of government.[82] The major difficulty with that reform is that it is impractical. It would require a constitutional amendment, whereas a change in the nominating process, as Broder reminds us, would not even require a change in any state laws.[83] All that would be needed would be for the two parties to change their rules for nomination.

To be sure, one would lose a key element of public testing of our candidates through a long primary system. Some observers feel that this long testing period helps the public understand the candidates—perhaps enough time for them to act as their own psychohistorians—and also lets us see how the candidates perform under pressure.[84] Indeed, we argued in Chapter 1 that the advantage of a participatory nominating system ought not to be discarded unless we sincerely believed that another selection method would yield better nominees. The prospect of better nominees, however, is precisely what this new system offers. We should not worry that public opinion will be ignored in the nominating process because the very fact of a candidate's standing high in the polls will be noticed by Congressional representatives. Furthermore, if we are correct in our argument that members of Congress are more accountable to the public than are convention delegates at present, we would have every reason to expect poll results to bear heavily on their deliberations for their parties' choices.

What we might accomplish is the selection of people who are experienced at both campaigning and governing as nominees, as opposed to the high premium on campaign skills alone under the present selection process. The elimination of the lengthy campaign throughout the states might permit the nominators to focus on executive ability; certainly, it would eradicate the many "almost" victories such as those scored by Eugene J. McCarthy in the 1968

New Hampshire Democratic primary, George McGovern in the same race four years later, or Jimmy Carter in the 1976 Iowa caucuses, *near*-upsets that were treated by the press as actual victories (see Chapter 1). In turn these candidates gained great momentum and either forced an incumbent President not to seek another term or actually won the nominations for themselves. It seems that under the present system, outsiders have an advantage. At a minimum this advantage would be removed under Congressional party nominations.

NOTES

1   Alan Clymer, "Poll Finds Reagan Carter Choice Unsatisfactory to Half of Public," *The New York Times,* April 18, 1980, p. A1.
2   Leonard Lurie, *Party Politics: Why We Have Poor Presidents* (New York: Stein and Day, 1980).
3   James MacGregor Burns, *Presidential Government* (Boston: Houghton Mifflin, 1965), pp. 295ff.
4   Or parties, as in multiparty coalition government such as in Italy.
5   Jules Witcover, *Marathon: The Pursuit of the Presidency, 1972–1976* (New York: Viking Press, 1977), pp. 105–110.
6   David S. Broder, "Would You Prefer a Mondale-Baker Race?" *The Washington Post,* June 4, 1980, p. A19.
7   Alan Ehrenhalt (ed.), *Politics in America* (Washington: Congressional Quarterly Press, 1981), p. 1118.
8   Broder, "Would You Prefer a Mondale-Baker Race?"
9   Meg Greenfield, "The Cult of the Amateur," *The Washington Post,* June 11, 1980, p. A19.
10 Ibid.
11 David B. Hill and Norman R. Luttbeg, *Trends in American Electoral Behavior* (Itasca, Illinois: F. E. Peacock, 1980), pp. 114–115.
12 Morris P. Fiorina, "The Decline of Collective Responsibility in American Politics," *Daedalus,* 109 (Summer 1980), pp. 25–45.
13 See for example, Charles Mohr, "Carter's First 9 Months: Charges of Ineptness Rise," *The New York Times,* October 23, 1977, pp. A1, 36.
14 Martin Tolchin, "An Old Pol Takes on the New President," *The New York Times Magazine,* July 24, 1977, p. 6ff.
15 Jack Dennis, "Public Support for Congress," *Political Behavior,* 3, (1981), pp. 319–350.
16 Richard F. Fenno, Jr., "If, as Ralph Nader Says, Congress Is 'the Broken Branch', How Come We Love Our Congressmen So Much?," in Norman Ornstein (ed.), *Congress in Change* (New York: Praeger, 1975), pp. 277–287.
17 Greenfield, "The Cult of the Amateur."

18 Hedrick Smith, "Taking Charge of Congress," *The New York Times Magazine,* August 9, 1982, pp. 12–20, 47–50.

19 Greenfield, "The Cult of the Amateur."

20 Lawrence C. Dodd, "Congress, the President, and Cycles of Power," in Vincent Davis (ed.), *The Post-Imperial Presidency* (New Brunswick, New Jersey: Transaction Books, 1979), pp. 71–79.

21 See the discussion of the withering away of the American party system in Walter Dean Burnham, *Critical Elections and the Mainsprings of American Politics* (New York: W. W. Norton, 1970), and Norman H. Nie, Sidney Verba, and John R. Petrocik, *The Changing American Voter,* rev. ed. (Cambridge: Harvard University Press, 1979).

22 Woodrow Wilson, *Congressional Government* (Cleveland: Meridian, 1967; originally published in 1885).

23 Ibid., p. 170.

24 Ibid.

25 James Bryce, *The American Commonwealth,* Vol. 1, rev. ed. (New York: Macmillan, 1915), p. 77.

26 Ibid., p. 79.

27 Ibid., p. 80.

28 Ibid., pp. 79–81.

29 Ibid., p. 83.

30 Ibid., p. 79.

31 Ibid., pp. 79–80.

32 *Congressional Quarterly Weekly Report,* January 18, 1982, p. 18, *The Gallup Report* (April 1982), rept. no. 199, p. 22; *The Gallup Report* (November 1981), rept. No. 194, pp. 3, 23–31.

33 Emmet John Hughes, *The Living Presidency* (New York: Harper and Row, 1978), p. 279; James MacGregor Burns, *Leadership* (New York: Harper and Row, 1978), p. 39.

34 Burns, *Leadership,* p. 453.

35 Robert E. DiClerico, *The American President,* 2d ed. (Englewood Cliffs, N.J.: Prentice-Hall, 1983), pp. 340ff.

36 Woodrow Wilson, *Constitutional Government in the United States* (New York: Columbia University Press, 1961; originally published in 1908), p. 65.

37 DiClerico, *The American President,* pp. 340ff.

38 Burns, *Leadership,* p. 170.

39 Ibid., p. 454; see also pp. 406–407.

40 Ibid., pp. 394–395.

41 Ibid., p. 434.

42 Ibid., p. 455; see also Hughes, *The Living Presidency,* p. 278.

43 Hughes, *The Living Presidency,* p. 278.

44 Ibid., p. 478.

45   Ibid., pp. 277–278.

46   Richard Hofstadter, *The American Political Tradition and the Men Who Made It* (New York: Vintage, 1959), p. 258.

47   Ibid., pp. 255–257.

48   Hughes, *The Living Presidency*, p. 279; Burns, *Leadership*, p. 279.

49   Hughes, *The Living Presidency*, p. 279.

50   Wilson, *Constitutional Government in the United States*, p. 69.

51   John Spanier and Eric M. Uslaner, *Foreign Policy and the Democratic Dilemmas* (New York: Holt, Rinehart and Winston, 1982), pp. 151–154.

52   Wilson, *Congressional Government*, p. 171.

53   Spanier and Uslaner, *Foreign Policy and Democratic Dilemmas*, pp. 27–33.

54   Ibid., pp. 39–40.

55   See, *inter alia,* Robert G. Kaiser, "Is Ignorance the Answer?," *The Washington Post* (September 9, 1982, pp. 131–132.

56   Spanier and Uslaner, *Foreign Policy and the Democratic Dilemmas*, p. 31.

57   Hofstadter, *The American Political Tradition and the Men Who Made It*, p. 321.

58   This table is taken from DiClerico, *The American President.* p. 332–333.

59   "Historians Rate Five Presidents as Failures," *The Washington Post* (February 21, 1983), p. A6. The Presidents rated as failures were Warren G. Harding, Ulysses S. Grant, Richard M. Nixon, Andrew Johnson, and James Buchanan. Among recent Presidents, Johnson ranked tenth, Eisenhower eleventh, and Kennedy thirteenth, and Ford and Carter were simply listed as "average."

60   Alexander George and Juliette George, *Woodrow Wilson and Colonel House* (New York: Dover, 1964). See among others, Alexander George, "Assessing Presidential Character," *World Politics,* 26 (January 1974), pp. 234–282; Robert C. Tucker, "The Georges' Wilson Reexamined," *American Political Science Review,* 71 (March 1977), pp. 182–211; and Erik Erikson, *Ghandi's Truth* (New York: W. R. Norton, 1969).

61   James David Barber, *The Presidential Character* (Englewood Cliffs, New Jersey: Prentice-Hall, 1972), pp. 345–442. Later citations are to the 2d ed. (1977).

62   Barber, *The Presidential Character,* p. 12.

63   Greenfield, "The Cult of the Amateur."

64   Also, this possibly applies to Carter's long ordeal on the Iranian hostage issue.

65   Barber, *The Presidential Character,* chaps. 2 and 3.

66   Ibid.

67   Ibid.

68   Ibid.

69 See Anthony Ramirez, "Is Ronald Reagan Similar to Coolidge? Should You Care?," *The Wall Street Journal,* September 17, 1980, p. 1.

70 Barber, *The Presidential Character.*

71 DiClerico, *The American President,* pp. 305–307.

72 See George, "Assessing Presidential Character."

73 George and George, *Woodrow Wilson and Colonel House.*

74 Doris Kearns, *Lyndon Johnson and the American Dream* (New York: Harper and Row, 1976).

75 Fred I. Greenstein, *The Hidden Hand Presidency: Eisenhower as Leader* (New York: Basic, 1982).

76 Bryce, *The American Commonwealth,* p. 77.

77 Wilson, *Congressional Government,* pp. 167–168.

78 John F. Bibby, Thomas E. Mann, and Norman J. Ornstein, compilers, *Vital Statistics on Congress, 1980* (Washington, D.C.: American Enterprise Institute, 1980), p. 14.

79 David E. Price, *Who Makes the Laws?* (New York: Schenkman, 1972).

80 Thomas Mann and Raymond Wolfinger, "Candidates and Parties in Congressional Elections," *American Political Science Review,* 74 (September 1980), p. 623.

81 Lurie, *Party Politics: Why We Have Poor Presidents,* pp. 257–273.

82 See Dodd, "Congress, the President, and the Cycles of Power."

83 Broder, "Would You Prefer a Mondale-Baker Race?"

84 James MacGregor Burns, *Presidential Government,* pp. 295–303.

EPILOGUE

The rapid democratization of the Presidential nominating process since 1968 has led to a much more open political party system. To a degree unprecedented in American history, and indeed in other countries as well, the average citizen has the opportunity to participate in selecting the candidates for the highest office in the nation. Although each person may have only a minute influence, the collective impact of such widespread participation in the nominating process has been to banish from our political jargon the term "party boss" and to make the contests for Presidential nominations real fights indeed. The number of candidates seeking the nominations of the parties has skyrocketed. Even unknown candidates who use the media effectively and who can raise sufficient funds and otherwise organize can hope to overcome their lack of recognition and become major party nominees. We have not quite reached the apocryphal time when "every American boy or girl can grow up to become President." But the democratization of our nominating system has truly come a long way from the "smoke-filled rooms" of the first three decades of the twentieth century when party bosses nominated candidates for the Presidency who were largely unknown even to many convention delegates.

If the first thirty or so years of this century constituted the age of strong party domination of the Presidential selection process, the last thirty promise to be the antiparty age if no reforms are made in the existing process. Some of the excesses of Presidential power in the Watergate affair during the Nixon administration stemmed from the President's total control of his own reelection organization. The Committee to Re-elect the President was totally divorced from the traditional campaign machinery for a Presidential nominee, the national committee of the candidate's party. One of the lessons of Watergate is that the new antiparty era in American politics has shifted our attention away from the President and his legislative party to the Oval Office alone. Presidential candidates more and more run for office by campaigning against "the mess in Washington," including their own party's record in the Congress. Since each legislator focuses on his or her own constituency, there is little reason for any one to consider what might be best for the entire country, or even for the entire party. Kennedy, Johnson, Carter, and Reagan ran into difficulties with their own legislative parties; Eisenhower had more cordial relations at least on domestic policy with the Democrats in Congress than with his fellow Republicans; Nixon was content to leave decision-making on domestic issues to the Democratic majority in the Congress in return for considerable leeway on foreign policy. The era of weak parties certainly predated changes in the nominating process, but the new system of selecting Presidential candidates has further weakened the parties. The selection of nominees by a mass electorate, through the proliferation of Presidential primaries, has made the Presidential candidates less dependent on party leaders in and out of the Congress than at any time in the past 150 years.

The increased roles of the media and money certainly reflect major changes in our society. Both of these trends further weaken party unity between the legislative and executive branches. Television highlights the personalities, styles, and physical appearances of the candidates. We do not maintain that prior to television the average citizen was a much more thoughtful and rational voter. There is no evidence to support that claim. However, the media age does tend to focus on campaign messages that can be summarized in two minutes for a network news story. It is easy to form critical first impressions of candidates through such coverage and the messages that seep through tend to highlight personalities above party *or* program. Individual candidates spend vast amounts of money on their own campaign, including (perhaps especially) the media. Thus, they do not have to rely on organizational efforts by the parties to familiarize voters with the ticket. Once in office, candidates do not have to cater to the demands of their party because they were elected mostly without party assistance. The most striking example of this occurred in 1972 when Nixon's campaign for reelection was not at all coordinated with the Republican National Committee.

Even apart from its effect on media expenditures, money has worked toward the weakening of the parties. They must seek out funds from individual contributors scattered throughout the country and, of course, from political action committees (PACs). PACs are not associated with specific parties; most of them contribute money to candidates of both parties. The more open nominating system extends formally for a full year and informally for four years. Such long campaigns require large amounts of both media exposure and money to finance the operations. Thus, candidates scramble for money. As campaigns become more technologically sophisticated, they also become more expensive. Television time can be costly indeed; so can the almost daily polls that major contenders for the White House commission to check the pulse of the nation.

The need to accumulate such a large compaign treasure chest leads, of course, to some obligations on the part of the candidates who are ultimately successful. PACs, of course, claim that they are only buying "access" to the corridors of power, but the politicians whom they support are less likely to admit that the stakes are so small.[1] Representative John Breaux, a Louisiana Democrat, said that his vote in Congress could *not* be bought. "But it can be rented," he added.[2] We discussed several instances of influence-buying in Chapter 3. Even though those examples occurred during the Nixon administration, that is, before campaign finance reform was enacted, there is little reason to assume that the motives of money givers are more altruistic today than they were just a decade ago.

The combined impact of the democratization of the nominating process, the role of the media, and the increased influence of money in both Presidential and Congressional elections has been to reduce party influence. The emphasis in campaigns is on the individual candidate. Thus the President and his legislative party no longer run as a team, as they did in the past. Each candidate looks out for his or her own success and there is little concern for how others on "the ticket" are doing. What results is a set of candidates who excel in campaign techniques, in getting elected, but who have no common stakes with others after the election is over. Each member of Congress looks back to his or her own district; the winning Presidential candidate who is eligible for another term looks to shore up the constituency that selected the new chief executive. Thus, we have, as we argued in Chapter 6, a set of candidates who are better suited to electoral politics than to the sort of give-and-take that governing requires. This is, of course, a long-standing problem in American politics, and it would be wrong to blame all of our political ills on these "new" aspects of the selection process. It would be even more facile to absolve these developments from the difficulties we seem to have in selecting Presidents who can maintain the confidence of the public and the Congress.

To this end, we have suggested a new system of nomination of Presidential candidates, selection by the Congressional parties, as a means of strengthening the parties and also relations between the President and Congress. If we are correct, giving the responsibility for nominating Presidential candidates to the Congressional parties would tighten the bonds between the candidates for the White House and those for the legislature. In turn, this would give the Congressional party a stake in the President's performance; its members could not run for reelection claiming that the President of their own party was nothing more than an "outsider." In turn, this would give the public a clearer sense of exactly who is responsible for the actions of the government. If bickering between the legislature and the executive branch were reduced, the public standing of both might increase. If the Presidential candidate and his legislative party were to run as a team, it would be much more difficult for individual candidates to dissociate themselves from each other. There would be strong pressures for media advertising to focus on the entire ticket, perhaps even stressing the common bonds of party. Similarly, there might be movement toward the goal of funneling more of the money in the campaigns to the parties directly. Such prospects would augur well for more party coherence in governing the nation.

Again, it would be too simplistic to assume that such a system will constitute a panacea for all of our ills. There is no guarantee that a change in the nominating system would produce stronger parties and better relations between the White House and Congress. But the argument on behalf of this system seems sound and any steps toward reducing friction and increasing cooperation between these two key branches of government appear to be worthwhile. We should not expect a revolution in our politics, since the weakness of the American party system does not stem from our open selection process. Rather, it is the other way around: our democratized nomination system reflects our fragmented society. However, if legislative-executive relations improve and the public becomes more supportive of each branch, a strong leader might very well find a nation more ready to be led.

The reform would be *relatively* easy to implement, since it would only require assent by the national committees of the two major parties. No laws would have to be changed, and the Constitution certainly would not have to be amended; political parties are not even mentioned in the Constitution. The need for such a reform to develop strong, cohesive parties has long been recognized by students of political parties. With our present decentralized, highly democratic nominating system, there is simply little chance that a coherent program for governing can be formulated by a party.[3] There is, of course, a problem of how to enact even this simple reform. Once you open up a process in the way that we have opened up our Presidential nominating system, it is difficult to restrict participation. The problem is not unlike that of poor Humpty Dumpty. People seem pleased with the opportunity to participate in the Presidential nominating game. Indeed, there is a multimillion dollar industry that has a considerable stake in maintaining the long and expensive campaign. However, to fail to present the idea just because it will not be easy to adopt is to ensure that this rival system will never get serious consideration. Furthermore, as the evidence on the Electoral College shows, the longer a good idea is on the public agenda, the greater the public support that it will eventually receive. It is not inconceivable that this proposal may even gain popular support some day.

Our analysis in Chapters 4 and 6 suggests another advantage of the proposed reform: If people do raise their opinion of the political system when the

President and Congress function more as a party team, turnout rates should increase. It is likely that overall confidence in the political system will rise and with it the belief by an individual that he or she can make a difference in politics. It is ironic that we might be able to increase feelings of efficacy by reducing the opportunities for participation in the nominating process. But, as a noted student of American politics observed, what counts is not the number of decisions that people participate in, but rather the importance of those decisions.[4] And there are few more important choices than selecting among candidates and parties offering clear-cut alternative programs for governing the nation. Turnout has historically been higher when parties do offer clear-cut alternatives on major issues of public policy, and there is reason to believe that more coherent parties would again lead to higher voting rates.[5] Furthermore, many citizens abstain because they believe that the government is not addressing the fundamental problems of the country. Stronger relations between the President and the Congress, particularly through the party system, are likely to alleviate this problem of alienation. However, whatever increase in turnout that occurs will only last if the candidates and parties deliver on their promises.

To this end, a change in the method of electing the President might also help. We argued in Chapter 5 that under direct election of the President, campaigns would focus more on each party's core supporters than under the present Electoral College. The votes of key supporters would count equally throughout the country, so the parties would not have to moderate their appeals just to cater to the swing groups in the larger states. Blacks, for example, would become an even more important part of the Democratic coalition because their votes would count in states that are likely to go Republican otherwise. Furthermore, the parties are weakened by the very prospect that a misfire might occur. There have been few misfires in American history, but recent years have shown how close we might come. The explicit attempt by third-party candidate George C. Wallace in 1968 to secure enough electoral votes so as to hold the balance of power in the Electoral College is a threat to coherent party politics. To the extent that we can rid our system of such potential dangers, we strengthen our parties.

No reform package can guarantee great Presidents. The most that we can hope for is an electoral system that reduces the probability of failures and that increases the prospects for cooperation among the branches of government. The voters still must possess the wisdom to select the best qualified candidates, and they must also be lucky enough to make their choices from a group of candidates who are particularly well suited for public office.

NOTES

1 See Elizabeth Drew, "A Reporter at Large: Politics and Money," *The New Yorker* (December 6 and 13, 1982), pp. 54–149 and 57–111.
2 Thomas B. Edsal, "Democrats' Lesson: To the Loyal Belong the Spoils," *The Washington Post,* January 14, 1983, p. A7.
3 The classic statement of this argument is by E. E. Schattschneider, *Party Government* (New York: Holt, Rinehart and Winston, 1942), pp. 53ff., esp. pp. 58–59.
4 Schattschneider, *The Semisovereign People* (New York: Holt, Rinehart and Winston, 1960), p. 140.
5 Walter Dean Burnham, *The Current Crisis in American Politics* (New York: Oxford University Press, 1982), esp. chap. 4.

INDEX

INDEX